D0217346

RADICAL ENVIRONMENTALISM
Philosophy and Tactics

Peter C. List
Oregon State University

WADSWORTH PUBLISHING COMPANY
A Division of Wadsworth, Inc.
Belmont, California

Philosophy Editor: Kenneth King
Editorial Assistant: Gay Meixel
Production Editor: Merrill Peterson, Matrix Productions
Print Buyer: Diana Spence
Permissions Editor: Bob Kauser
Copy Editor: Nikki Herbst
Cover Designer: Stuart Paterson
Cover Painting: Winslow Homer, *The Fallen Deer,* Charles Henry Hayden
  Fund, courtesy Museum of Fine Arts, Boston
Signing Representative: Tamy Stenquist
Compositor: Kachina Typesetting
Printer: Malloy Lithographing

This book is printed on acid-free paper that meets Environmental Protection Agency standards for recycled paper.

Printed in the United States of America

2 3 4 5 6 7 8 9 10—97 96 95 94

Credits appear on page 273.

Library of Congress Cataloging-in-Publication Data

Radical environmentalism : philosophy and tactics / [edited by] Peter List.
    p.   cm.
  Includes bibliographical references and index.
  ISBN 0-534-17790-5
  1. Environmental policy—United States—Citizen participation.
2. Green movement—United States.   3. Deep ecology—United States.
I. List, Peter C.
HC110.E5R26   1992
363.7'057—dc20   92-20074
                                                       CIP

ISBN 0-534-17790-5

Contents

Preface

Environmental radicalism is not an altogether new phenomenon in Western culture, but radical environmentalism is. Seventeenth century Europe had its "levelers" and the nineteenth century its Luddites, groups devoted to the destruction of machines and the preservation and recreation of a kind of rural community. But these were not part of a larger environmental movement and did not reflect widespread public concerns about the destruction of the earth as a whole. They were instead small diversions in what has otherwise been a relentless attack on nature by Western and non-Western societies which began many centuries ago and accelerated rapidly during the industrial revolution.

Some argue that environmentalism in any form did not become part of our national life in the United States until shortly before the turn of the twentieth century, when conservation battles were fought over the national forests of the West. This first wave of environmental concern was influenced by European conservation ideas and practices and was promoted with particular fervor by scientists and public servants in government positions. Conservation was subsequently incorporated into federal policy during the Theodore Roosevelt administration, when it became an explicit, unifying idea in several federal resource agencies under the leadership of Gifford Pinchot.[1] However, this initial impetus toward resource conservation lost some of its political steam under the administration of President Taft and his secretary of the interior, Richard Ballinger, and was submerged in government bureaucracy for some twenty years.

The second wave of environmentalism in the United States began building after the dust bowl era of the early 1930s and peaked during Franklin Roosevelt's New Deal administration later in that decade. The emphasis was still on resource conservation, but the scale of federal involvement in conservation programs was unprecedented, as it was in other areas of national life. As Roderick Nash has argued, ". . . increasingly Americans recognized that managing the environment was a task requiring a degree of knowledge, power, and money that only the national government could command."[2] World War II interrupted this strong push for federal conservation, but the third and largest wave of environmentalism began building in the mid-1960s after the publication of Rachel Carson's *Silent Spring* and achieved tremendous momentum and public acknowledgement by Earth Day 1970. During this last wave, environmentalism became something of a social movement and gained strong public support. Considerable national energy was devoted to understanding the dimensions of the environmental crisis and to figuring out what to do about it, and mainstream environmental thinking was institutionalized in a series of innovative federal and state laws in the late 1960s and early 1970s. Government agencies then set about the task of implementing these laws, and some of the enthusiasm of the first Earth Day cooled off in the later 1970s as the public assumed something was being done about our environmental problems.

Popular fervor was rekindled during the 1980s because of the anti-environmentalism of the Reagan administration and because of growing scientific and political worries about the deteriorating global environment.[3] As a result, the American environmental movement has joined environmental movements in other countries to become focused on the fate and condition of the earth as a whole. Still, after some twenty years of experience with political and legal efforts to set aside wilderness areas, reduce pollution and waste, and preserve endangered species, many observers believe that ground continues to be lost in the fight to save the planet and to keep humans in balance with nature.[4] And the character of environmentalism in this country has come to reflect this belief.

Before the late 1960s, calls for militant defense of wild animals and ecosystems, as a response to the human war against nature, were nearly unheard of in the United States. However since that time, given increasing dissatisfaction with mainstream environmentalism in the environmental movement, growing commitment to deep ecophilosophies, and recognition of our intensified consumption and destruction of nature worldwide, radical environmentalism has become a regular force on the environmental front, particularly in Western societies. It has helped to define public and government discussion of the proper personal and social responses to environmental problems, and has become a subject of debate both within and outside of the environmental movement itself.

In conventional environmental literature, radical environmental activism has often been ignored and occasionally villified, though it is clear that moderate environmentalists are sometimes sympathetic to radical tactics. An illustration of the former approach can be found in the magazine *Sierra*, the house organ of the Sierra Club, perhaps the most powerful environmental group in the United States, where almost nothing has been published on radical activism during the past twenty years.

The standard academic journal in environmental ethics, *Environmental Ethics,* until very recently devoted almost no space to the discussion of radical "eco-tactics" or environmental civil disobedience, though it has published many articles on deep ecology and ecofeminism, two underlying philosophies in the radical wing of the environmental movement. The editor of this journal has criticized the methods of Earth First!ers, but academics have spent very little time writing about these tactics, so it is difficult to find out what they think about them.

Radical activists and philosophers tend to publish their ideas and describe their actions in more obscure newsletters, journals, and magazines, and to make their views known in other ephemeral locations such as environmental conferences and in talks before small groups. While some of their ideas are now readily accessible to the student of environmental philosophy, it still takes extra effort simply to find out what individuals in this movement believe. One of the purposes of this collection, then, is to help remedy this situation by introducing college students to certain key ideas and representative tactics as they have been formulated and practiced by some of the leading ecophilosophers and activists who have "gone to the wall" for nature.[5]

While I regard myself as a moderate environmentalist and believe that some of these tactics are ethically unacceptable, I have put this anthology together for several reasons. First, radical environmentalists are saying something worth saying about the destruction of nature and have become a significant factor in at least some environmental disputes in our society. So it is important to understand what their points of view are. Second, I find some of the ecophilosophical ideas behind this movement to be appealing and think it useful to ask how they are related to our environmental behavior. Does our war on nature require the countermeasures that radicals identify as necessary? Third, radicals believe in philosophies which, on the one hand, are designed to be a real alternative to the ideas that underlie moderate environmentalism yet, on the other hand, are sometimes drawn from exactly the same philosophical sources and the same data about the human devastation of nature.[6] Given the fact that radical environmentalism and ecophilosophy have gained strength in Western societies as environmental destruction has accelerated and intrusion into the earth's wilder landscapes has become common, this social fact alone makes this movement intriguing and implies that it should not be too hastily dismissed as outlandish or subversive of our normal ways of life. Clearly careful, critical evaluation of radical ideas, at a minimum, is worth doing. Finally, philosophies such as resource conservation which at one time may have seemed extreme have at a later date become more acceptable to a wider audience.[7] In fact empirical research already shows that some philosophical tenets of radical ecophilosophy are appealing to the American public.[8] Thus, in time, it is possible that more elements of the philosophical and activist sides of this movement will be accepted by moderate environmentalists and the general public in industrial societies. In effect, by studying radical environmentalism and ecophilosophy now, we could be looking at a part of our intellectual future, so to speak. At a minimum, understanding this movement can help moderates to sharpen their resolve to do more about environmental problems and to find solutions that check the relentless consumption of wild nature.

I do not pretend that all varieties of radical environmentalism are represented here or that all of the major thinkers in such areas as ecofeminism are adequately covered. Nor have I included much of the critical interchange that has taken place across the boundaries of the different ecophilosophies. This would be difficult to do in a short anthology since the radical literature has grown to immense size and the radical eco-movement is a fairly diverse collection of different "tribes" rather than a tightly organized social force. For example, within Earth First!, the largest activist group, the factions are quite varied and include the old guard founders and their sympathizers, younger anarchists, ecofeminists, vegetarians, animal liberators, and various eco-spiritualists, not to mention individuals of different radical political persuasions.[9] The term "deep ecology" has also been used to refer to a variety of philosophies, including social ecology, ecofeminism, bioregionalism, radical green political thought, Earth First! philosophy, Native American traditional philosophy, academic deep ecology, and animal liberationism.[10] Given this diversity, and the fact that this is an introductory anthology and necessarily must contain briefer selections from lengthier sources, it can still serve as one route into this literature for anyone who wants to think about the philosophical and practical issues of radical environmentalism and ecophilosophy. I have included enough selections to help students and interested readers decide where to go next in creating their own, more detailed maps of this terrain. The bibliography at the end of the book will help them explore further.

In preparing this collection, I have benefited from the kindness of several individuals and organizations. In 1990 the Center for the Humanities at Oregon State University gave me a fellowship to study the philosophical justifications of radical environmental activism and to begin organizing an anthology. I want to thank the director of the center, Peter Copek, for his support, and the secretary at the center, Patty Paulson, for her friendly assistance. I also want to extend my thanks to Anne Fox, Doris Tilles, Sarah Beasley, and Don Unger, for their help in tracking down some of the sources of radical environmental literature and to Lois Summers and Jennie Waite-Phillips, for assistance with wordprocessing and proofreading. Mike DeLane, of the Greenpeace office in Washington, D.C., was very accommodating in allowing me to rummage through the Greenpeace publications files in 1991. My thanks also go to Ken King, philosophy editor at Wadsworth Publishing Company, for approving the idea of this collection and seeing it through to final form. I would also like to thank the reviewers: Susan J. Armstrong, Humboldt State University; Dale Jamieson, University of Colorado, Boulder; Richard Sherlock, Utah State University; Gary Varner, Texas A & M University; and especially Arthur B. Millman, University of Massachusetts at Boston, who read the entire ms. critically. Finally, I thank my wife, Judy, for her encouragement and love.

Notes

1. Pinchot saw himself and W. J. McGee as the inventors and promoters of the idea of conservation. But it is clear that this idea existed and was advocated in America and Europe long before they discovered it. See Pinchot's book, *Breaking New Ground* (New York: Harcourt, Brace & World, 1947).
2. *The American Environment,* 2d ed. (Reading, Mass.: Addison-Wesley Publishing Company, 1976), p. 98.
3. Riley Dunlap has done a comprehensive review of public opinion data on environmental issues in the United States from 1965 to 1990. He argues that American public concern about environmental problems and support for environmental protection has reached unprecedented levels. See "Trends in Public Opinion Toward Environmental Issues: 1965–1990," *Society and Natural Resources* 4 (1991), pp. 285–312.
4. Dunlap and Angela Mertig conclude that U.S. environmentalism has been a resounding success as a social movement in maintaining its visibility and political power in our society but a failure with regard to protecting the quality of the environment. See "The Evolution of the U.S. Environmental Movement from 1970 to 1990: An Overview," *Society and Natural Resources* 4 (1991), pp. 209–218.
5. See Rik Scarce's concept of the "eco-wall" in his book, *Eco-Warriors, Understanding the Radical Environmental Movement* (Chicago: The Noble Press, Inc., 1990), Chapter 1.
6. One illustration of this is the extent to which the historic founders of environmental thinking in the United States, such as Henry David Thoreau, John Muir, and Aldo Leopold, have been heavily used by both moderate and radical environmentalists alike.
7. Conservation during the Pinchot era was sometimes labeled a "radical" policy, especially by westerners. See Roderick Nash's discussion of the response to Pinchotism in *The American Environment,* pp. 64–67.
8. Brent S. Steel, Peter List, and Bruce Shindler, "Oregon State University Survey of Natural Resource and Forestry Issues, Comparing the Responses of the 1991 National and Oregon Public Surveys," Sustainable Forestry Program, January 15, 1992.
9. See Rik Scarce on this point, *Eco-Warriors,* Chapter 5.
10. See Steven Chase (editor) in the introduction to *Defending the Earth, A Dialogue Between Murray Bookchin and Dave Foreman* (Boston: South End Press, 1991).

Introduction

What is Radical Environmentalism?

As a preliminary it will help to have a definition of the term "radical environmentalism" so that the reader will understand what is included in this anthology. Since general definitions can be misleading and can cover up the complexities of social practices and philosophical ideas, I will identify a few of the specific meanings which this expression has acquired both outside and especially inside the environmental movement.

Outside the environmental movement, particularly within the natural resource extraction industries, many ordinary environmentalist ideas, whether mainstream or not, are taken to be radical because they supposedly bear little relationship to business or economic reality. With this approach, conservation at best means what it did to the progressive conservationists at the turn of this century, such as Gifford Pinchot and W. J. McGee. And most forms of contemporary environmentalism would be identified as radical in character.

To give one illustration, in 1988 a vice president of Inco Limited, a Canadian nickel company, stated that a group of industrialists had decided that the idea of conservation "sounds suspiciously like a 'shutdown' and true conservation must be defined in terms of principles for development and consumption of resources for current and future generations that will improve standards of living for all."[1] This definition would restrict conservation to free-market business behavior and allow the continued extraction of natural resources on a long-term basis with no clear limits. The remaining nondesignated wilderness areas in North America could be converted to marketable commodities, for example, if they contained raw materials for human use. It would thus make radical even the relatively modest tactic of attempting to preserve additional wilderness through legislation. And while this lockup definition is obviously one way in which the idea of the radical is understood by some industry advocates, it is so broad that it makes too many ordinary conservation efforts extreme. Moreover it doesn't begin to define radical environmentalism as it is typically understood in the environmental

1

movement, where finer distinctions are usually made about these matters.

As will become clear in the readings, the term "radical environmentalism" within the radical wing of the environmental movement encompasses both a radicalism in environmental philosophy, or "ecological sensibility" to use John Rodman's terminology,[2] and a radicalism in tactics and actions, in the means by which the philosophy is to be implemented. Radical environmentalism is often contrasted with moderate or reform environmentalism and thus gets its meaning partly from its dissimilarity to other forms of environmentalism. As the radicals view the contrast, moderate environmentalism assumes that humans can resolve the environmental crisis by modifying their anthropocentric attitudes toward nature and by reforming laws, governmental policies, corporate behavior, and personal lifestyles to make them more sensitive to environmental considerations. No fundamental alterations in values or social, political and economic structures are needed to bring humans into harmony with nature or the environment. Radicals disagree, and suggest that deep and systematic changes in philosophies and tactics must be made if these goals are to be met.

Radical environmentalism is also seen to be radical relative to those mainstream ideas within our political and economic system which deny the legitimacy of environmental protest or of subversion of the machinery of industrialized society and which approve only of the generally accepted processes of democratic change and compromise. In short, the definition of radical environmentalism takes on a much more restricted meaning within the environmental movement than elsewhere, though it still refers to a great variety of ideas and behaviors.

In looking at this variety, it is possible to isolate at least the following meanings for this concept: radical environmentalism is (a) a wilderness fundamentalism which is backed up by deep ecology and biocentrism and makes wilderness and wild species the focus of no-compromise political action; (b) a strong *activist* orientation which de-emphasizes ecophilosophy in favor of unconventional direct action tactics such as environmental civil disobedience, monkeywrenching, and ecotage; it too is aimed at the preservation and restoration of wilderness and wild species; (c) a social and political philosophy which emphasizes anarchism and bioregionalism, as refined by ecological notions, and which advocates strong, nonviolent environmental tactics plus a new form of ecological living; and (d) an ecological feminism which integrates ecological and feminist thought and promotes a wide variety of practices to reform patriarchal society and to challenge our destruction of the earth. Of course the boundaries between these forms of environmentalism are not always very sharp; in fact they are sometimes purposely blurred by activists to show relationships and to assert common connections among radical groups.

The Development of Radical Environmentalism in North America

Greenpeace in the 1970s

In the environmental movement, one important historical impetus for the development of radical environmental activism occurred in the early 1970s when Greenpeace activists began using direct action and confrontation techniques to protest and publicize such things as underground nuclear testing and the killing of whales in the Pacific Ocean. The reaction to their actions in the environmental movement revealed some differences of opinion about whether these tactics were acceptable. To some reform or mainstream environmentalists, they were obviously too extreme and an unwelcome addition to environmentalism. But Greenpeace tactics drew public attention around the world to environmentally destructive practices on the oceans and coasts of North America and generated widespread sympathy for the plight of sea mammals, so much so that public attitudes about the ethical character of these actions softened and acceptance of the need for unconventional environmental tactics blossomed.

Moreover these advocates of environmental civil disobedience and nonviolent, direct confrontation with whalers and sealers made an effort to align themselves with a new planetary philosophy, which said that humans were not the center of the earth but were just one part of it, and that the earth and its many forms of life, human and nonhuman, required more respect. All forms of planetary life were seen to be vital to the continued existence of life on earth, and not only human life. Greenpeacers thus took up the cause of nonhumans and elevated nonhuman interests over at least some of the commercial interests of humans. Following Ghandian tenets, they argued for the practice of nonviolence toward all life forms and embraced a planetary morality which made harm to both humans and nonhumans ethically wrong. At a minimum, they invited people to take personal responsibility for human injustices to whales, seals, and other parts of nature.[3]

The Origins of Ecotage

The idea of using ecotage, or environmental sabotage, was not part of the Greenpeace way, but it was discussed in the late 1960s by American political radicals as they turned their attention to the environment. An example of this can be found in the writings of Barry Weisberg, then codirector of the Bay Area Institute in San Francisco and a critic of capitalism.[4] In January 1970 Weisberg argued that an authentic environmental movement had yet to develop, but it would when "something very basic and very revolutionary is done about the continued destruction of our life support system."[5] Weisberg suggested that militant actions against "corporate despoilers" would have to be part of this movement, "including sabotage," and he predicted that "radical ecological actions" would take place later that year.

The term "ecotage" itself seems to have been invented by several organizers of Earth Day 1970 who subsequently formed a group called "Environmental Action" to focus public concern on solutions to the environmental crisis. The group published a field manual in 1971 for citizens seeking to take individual and collective action for the environment.[6] The tactics they described ranged from conventional lobbying and electioneering to lawsuits, boycotts, pickets, marches and rallies, strikes, corporate harassment, and something they called "intervention." The group recognized that many citizens were already using creative ways of dramatizing the environmental problems in their communities and that these efforts could be helped along by soliciting new ideas from the public about how one could harass corporate polluters. So they organized a national contest in which citizens sent in their practical ideas and then published some of them in the book *Ecotage* in 1972.[7]

There were already several well-known examples of ecotage in the United States at that time, such as the actions of the Billboard Bandits in Michigan and "The Fox" in Illinois. The Fox was an anonymous individual who conducted a widely publicized and condoned one-person campaign against polluting corporations in the Chicago area in the early 1970s. Environmental Action decided that the term "ecotage" fit these examples perfectly and defined it as "sabotage done in the name of ecology."[8] The author of *Earth Tool Kit* argued that when all appeals for environmental change had been exhausted and the results were slow in coming, it was necessary for individuals to use civil disobedience and "direct action tactics which break laws." The book defined direct environmental action to be action undertaken "without any intermediate steps and with a specific objective in mind." It could be violent or non-violent, but it was to be carefully planned to avoid confusion and to generate the right results and sympathies among a larger group of people. The idea was to get the public to apply "social pressures to corporations and other institutions that are polluting, exploiting or otherwise acting as bad citizens."[9] Creative tactics were needed which would put pressure on those in power to change their abuses of the environment, and the public was seen as an ally in this struggle.

This definition of ecotage implied that activists were working outside the system to effect change but were implementing policies and ideas that were morally correct within the system and that were shared by many citizens. Some radicals went further, though, and argued that society would need a revolution to truly resolve its environmental problems. In fact the term "revolution" was a common part of environmental rhetoric by Earth Day 1970, even among the leaders of such mainstream environmental groups as the Sierra Club.[10] However its meaning varied rather widely from the strict sense of (a) outright overthrow of the political system, to more watered-down meanings which implied either (b) extensive changes in our legal and economic institutions, (c) wholesale alterations of our values and attitudes toward nature, or (d) significant changes in our personal life-styles. Radical environmentalists thus disagreed among themselves about what tactics and social changes were needed to resolve the environmental crisis, and the radical wing of the movement was divided between those who believed that capitalist society was the source of the crisis and must be overthrown, and others who thought that industrial society could be transformed without political revolution through the use of various direct action techniques.[11] For the most part it was this second group which dominated radical environmentalism during the 1980s.

The most publicly visible and successful radical activist environmental group of the 1970s, Greenpeace, thus embodied the moderate dimensions of radicalism. Greenpeace was not in favor of any form of violence and rejected acts that could destroy property or cause harm to humans. Greenpeace members used some ingenious and dramatic direct action techniques and a clever understanding of how to manipulate the communications media in their early campaigns to stop nuclear testing in Alaska and the South Pacific. They created international pressure for a worldwide moratorium on whaling and an end to the harp seal slaughter in Newfoundland.

The Monkey Wrench Gang

The organization's strong adherence to a nonviolent philosophy and refusal to approve of ecotage caused several of Greenpeace's more radical members to part company with it in the late 1970s. These activists believed that sabotage of the tools of industrial civilization was needed to save the environment; non-violent, direct action had its place, but new practices were required which would either thwart or destroy the machinery of nature destruction and, in the process, save wild animals and wild areas. This form of radical activism was sometimes called "monkeywrenching" and was described by Edward Abbey in his novel *The Monkey Wrench Gang,* published in 1975. The expulsion of activist Paul Watson from Greenpeace in 1977 is a significant event in the evolution of thinking about these more radical tactics and reflects the division within Greenpeace and the environmental movement over the meaning and practical directions of environmental activism.

The radical environmentalism described by Abbey was also inspired by various radical ecophilosophies which were being formulated in the 1970s, such as deep ecology, and by certain aspects of moderate environmentalism that were frustrating to some activists. Environmentalists had been warned by radicals in the early 1970s that conventional and nonviolent political action would only be a stop-gap or delaying tactic for those seeking to halt environmental destruction.[12] And in time some came to agree and concluded that mainline environmental groups, with their techniques of cooperation and thus compromise with the powers-that-be, were failing to block the destruction of de facto federal wilderness areas or to stop the continuing slaughter of wild animals. Some of these radicals may have admired the successes of Greenpeace, but its tactics were criticized as being insufficient to change the industrial exploitation of nature. The moderate radicals thus lost part of their authority in the radical environmental movement, and those committed to ecotage migrated to such groups as the Sea Shepherd Society and Earth First!. In fact by the early 1980s Earth First! became the central locus of monkeywrenching activism, and its activities were perhaps the most widely publicized of any radical group throughout the 1980s. Adherents of Earth First! described themselves as warriors in the radical land army while activists in the Sea Shepherd Society, under Watson, were called its "navy."

Earth First!

The Earth First! group acquired a kind of purist environmental flavor under the direction of its old guard founders in 1981, for radical environmentalism here came to refer to that apolitical radicalism for the earth which had been first advocated in 1970. Dave Foreman, one of the founders of Earth First!, called this form of thinking "wilderness fundamentalism," and this newly invigorated wing of radical environmentalism made the idea of no compromise in defense of mother earth the consuming focus of its actions. This also made Earth First!'s practical philosophy unique, for it implied that the core of social and political life should be reoriented towards wilderness preservation and restoration, instead of to other social issues. The human destruction of wilderness, wild lands, and wild species, especially the larger mammals, and the reduction of biodiversity were now to become central political concerns for American society. The underlying political philosophy behind this stance was deep ecology, which was identified as the philosophical basis of Earth First! by its old guard.

The idea that nature should come first in one's political agenda was recognized as important by various groups and individuals during Earth Day 1970, for example by some of the authors of *Ecotactics,* and also by members of Greenpeace later in the 1970s. But an important difference is that Earth Day thinkers put the earth first primarily because they believed that human survival was at stake, and not because of the inherent or intrinsic value of nature itself. This made their brand of thinking anthropocentric in contrast to the biocentric orientation of the deep ecologists, the Sea Shepherd Society, and the Earth First! founders. At the same time, this biocentric commitment to wilderness over other political issues, such as racism, poverty, militarism, and sexism, was thought to be a mistake by more traditional political radicals. To them it naïvely assumed that real change in our behavior toward wild nature could occur without revolutionizing capitalist economic systems and social structures. This radical political critique was submerged in Earth First! for some years because of tolerance for ideological diversity in this movement and the strength of the founders, but it has resurfaced recently and caused a falling out of the ways in this tribe.

Radical Ecophilosophy

The rise in radical environmental activism in the 1980s was accompanied by a corresponding growth in radical ecophilosophies. While the theoretical dimensions of these ecophilosophies did not always logically imply radical environmental tactics, there is no doubt that these ecophilosophies inspired and stimulated radical activists to pursue direct action tactics with more vigor and commitment. They also provided personal justifications for their behavior in the face of considerable social criticism of radical tactics. Deep ecology, ecofeminism, and social ecology are the most well known of these ecophilosophies.

Deep Ecology

Early on in its young history, Earth First! founders argued that they stood fast with the deep ecologists, such as Arne Naess, in calling for a fundamental change in human consciousness. Some Earth First!ers wanted deep changes in human attitudes toward nature. This would be expressed in a new biocentered philosophy which would emphasize the intrinsic value of all natural things, the biocentric equality of all species, the submergence of the human self in a larger, natural self, and the importance of biodiversity. Our anthropocentric or human centered philosophies in Western society would have to be jettisoned, since they arrogantly assumed that humans were more important than other parts of nature, and that wild species and natural objects derived their value from the way they served human desires and interests. This narrow point of view was not consistent with the realities of nature, they believed, because humans are not the only locus of natural values, and the members of other species have interests and lives of their own which often have very little and sometimes nothing to do with human life. The fate of all life on earth and all natural processes would have to become the dominant focus of our political system, and radical ecotactics would be the one practical expression of this new ideology.

Of course not all Earth First!ers were philosophically inclined; many of them were preoccupied with physically saving wild species and wild areas. Environmental direct action to them was the real focus of their involvement in environmentalism, and environmental philosophy was more like window dressing. In any event what was important to these environmental "purists" in Earth First! was not so much their explicit *political* philosophy as their militant commitment to saving the earth from human destruction and desecration. In their view, philosophy had to fall in line with this practical commitment, and deep ecology served this purpose well.

Deep ecology is a philosophy that was first identified by Arne Naess, a Norwegian philosopher, in 1972. Naess roughly distinguished between two kinds of ecology, the shallow and the deep. The shallow variety was characteristic of ecological thinking in the dominant worldview of Western culture and was therefore the most powerful and influential approach thus far to the environmental crisis. It emphasized the fight against pollution and resource depletion because of concerns about the health and affluence of people in the industrial countries, Naess claimed. Deep ecology on the other hand adopted a more global and biocentric approach to this crisis. It consisted of various norms and intuitions about how humans should fit into nature, how they should relate to the members of other species and to their own species, and how they should organize themselves socially and politically. Naess argued that people needed to adopt the general principles of the deep ecology platform, formulate their own individual interpretations of it, and then put these "ecosophies" to work in their own lives.

Bill Devall and George Sessions, two American academics who also worked on formulating this ecophilosophy and became well-known as deep ecologists, argued that the ecological crisis was in part a crisis of consciousness and that human society would have to develop a new form of ecological philosophy and new forms of ecological insight if significant changes in our traditional treatment of nature were to occur. The real work that had to be done, they suggested, was very personal and "interior"; it involved making deep changes in our personal consciousness, in our basic conceptions of ourselves. They also thought that changes in our philosophy and behavior could take place together; in fact changes in the self and changes in culture were two sides of the same coin. They therefore called for deep questioning of our traditional attitudes toward nature and our behavior in nature. We needed to experience new intuitions about our personhood so we could see how we fit into a larger, natural whole, and we needed to experience new intuitions about the rights of other forms of life to live and blossom within this whole. After all, they argued, nature has intrinsic value rather than merely instrumental value. Natural objects and species have value just because they exist, they asserted, and not because they serve human purposes or are important to human life and welfare.

To Devall and Sessions, this deep wisdom about ourselves and about nature could be found in the minority tradition in both Western and Eastern societies, since some cultures and philosophers had already learned what it meant to truly live in profound harmony with nature and to value natural objects for what they are in themselves. Devall and Sessions were fairly eclectic in identifying the sources of this ecophilosophy, and their platform was general enough to allow individuals to work on themselves in a wide variety of ways.

Earth First! founders enthusiastically embraced the biocentric norms of deep ecology, for deep ecologists created a philosophical approach to nature that was much more systematic than earlier environmental philosophies had been. Deep ecology also carried implications for action which Earth First!ers believed supported their use of monkeywrenching tactics. While the adoption of these tactics has not been typical of environmentalists to this day, deep ecology has now become a very influential means of interpreting the earth's environmental crisis in the environmental movement. It is clearly one of the leading contenders for philosophical belief in the radical wing of this movement and is seen to have important implications for action by many "moderate" environmentalists as well.

Alternatives to Environmental Purism

In the middle 1980s, the Earth First! brand of wilderness environmentalism came itself to be criticized by traditional political radicals, anarchists, and also by feminists who were gaining ground in the radical environmental movement. This wilderness purism was thought to be flawed by its supposed political and social naïvete. While the tactics were often admired by other radicals, they were said to be motivated by an incomplete analysis of the reasons for our destruction of the earth in industrialized, authoritarian, and patriarchal societies. And thus the philosophical side of deep ecology came in for its share of radical criticism as well. As a result, Earth First! has recently been split by internal disputes between those who want to keep it concentrated on wilderness and environmental issues and others who think it necessary to tie these issues to problems of social justice and social change. This division is a sign that radical environmentalism in the U.S. has once again become a social location for traditional political radicalism, and that the latter is a force to be reckoned with in this movement after a gap of some years. Here the destruction of the environment and the oppression of wild nature are not isolated from the oppression of women, minorities, Native Americans, and the poor, nor from the critique of our political and economic system. Questions of political and social justice thus become as important as questions about the loss of wild species.

Ecofeminism

The division within Earth First! also shows that feminism has extended its influence throughout American society during the past twenty years. Feminism turned itself partly toward ecological issues in the 1970s to produce a new synthesis of feminism and ecology called "ecofeminism." While it has had its own forms of historical development, one path into ecofeminism has been environmentalism,[13] and some now believe that ecofeminism is the overarching philosophical underpinning for saving the earth.

Ecofeminism is a diverse collection of philosophies and tactical ideas, but it is based on the notion that there are important and essential connections between the oppression of nature and the oppression of women in patriarchal societies. Ecofeminists argue that understanding these connections is crucial for understanding why humans are destroying nature and for learning how humans might live in harmony with nature in the future. Environmentalism must thus take on feminist perspectives and feminism must adopt ecological perspectives, to create a proper philosophy about humans, culture, and nature.[14]

Ecofeminism also redefines what constitutes environmental activism, for ecofeminist activism is much broader in character than the more purely conceived forms of activism that one finds in some wilderness fundamentalism. Aside from standard forms of ecological resistance and feminist resistance to oppression against women, it includes many "innovative practices—from tree-planting communities, alternative healing communities, organic food co-ops, performance art happenings, Witchcraft covens, and the retelling of ancient myths and tales to new forms of political resistance such as the *Chipko* (hugging) tree actions and women's peace camps," as two ecofeminists have reported.[15] Some ecofeminists in fact reject the idea that you can neatly separate ecological resistance into acts that focus on nature and those that focus on women's place in the social structure. To them the objectification of women takes many forms in industrial societies, and since the oppression of nature and women are part of the same phenomenon, resistance to nature oppression is in principle no different from resistance to direct attacks against women. Conversely, resistance to the oppression of women in society is no different than ecological resistance. The broader idea here is that we live in a human-nature nexus where all behavior is interconnected and thus one cannot isolate rape from wildnerness destruction. The focus on one to the exclusion of the other is misguided, and it is important to ecofeminists not to limit the forms of social activism to wilderness issues alone.

Ecofeminism has posed a critical challenge to deep ecology, for the leading deep ecologists did not analyze the intellectual causes of the ecological crisis with patriarchal male-female relationships in mind. Ecofeminists have argued that deep ecologists have thus ignored the major causes of nature oppression and have falsely assumed that the earth could be saved without undermining patriarchal structures in our society. This criticism has led to a dialogue between the deep ecologists and the ecofeminists about whether these two philosophies can be reconciled with each other and which system of ecothought is really deeper in its analysis of the causes of the earth's destruction. Because of the power of ecofeminism in the radical environmental movement, this critical dialogue has spilled over into the discussion of social ecology, an ecophiloso-phy that has also criticized practitioners of deep ecology and wilderness fundamentalism for their political and social short-sightedness.

Social Ecology

Social ecology is primarily the invention of Murray Bookchin, an an-archist philosopher who has a long list of credentials in the radical ecophilosophical tradition and some influence in the green movement in this country, a movement to introduce ecological wisdom into American politics.[16] In fact he was one of the very first thinkers in the United States to provide a radical ecological critique of our society, having done so already in the early 1960s. Since that time he has produced a large body of writings about our ecological crisis and the social and political sources of ecological destruction, and has promoted their application through his Institute of Social Ecology in Vermont.

Along with the ecofeminists, Bookchin has been a vocal critic of deep ecology, particularly of the Earth First! variety advocated by Dave Foreman.[17] Bookchin has argued that wilderness political purism is an antihumanist and "eco-brutalist" environmentalism that is hopelessly naïve about social change. As long as it focuses on the preservation of wilderness and the reduction of population to the exclusion of examining the fundamental social and political pathology in our society, Earth First! thinking is bound to fail, he believes.

Bookchin argues in his social critique that our society has created an ecological crisis because of the power of our hierarchical and au-thoritarian social, economic, and political structures, and the kinds of technologies we have used to provide for our wants. To him these structures and technologies permit some humans to dominate others and also to dominate nature. As a result, our very survival is threatened on earth. If we pay attention to the non-human world, we can find models for redefining our human relationships, for there organisms cooperate and complement each other in their diversity, creating unified communi-ties that further natural, evolutionary goals. The domination of nature through hierarchy is thus not inevitable in human society, since humans are both cultural and natural beings.

Motivated by the ideas of such anarchist philosophers as Petr Kropot-kin, Bookchin has concluded that we cannot solve the environmental crisis in free-market and bureaucratic capitalistic societies in the in-dustrial world but must decentralize our social and economic rela-tionships, and seriously alter our smothering technological approach to nature. Large-scale, centralized political and social systems and corpo-rate interests perpetuate the domination of humans by humans and nature by humans, and thus must be dissolved. Their dissolution requires that we find and create new forms of democratic community, new forms of economic production, and new forms of ecotechnology that are more modest in scale, less consumptive, and thus more consistent with the carrying capacities of local ecological regions.

Bioregionalism

Social ecology as defined by Bookchin is compatible in many respects with bioregionalism, another philosophy in the radical environmental movement. Bioregionalism is a synthesis of various philosophies within environmentalism of the 1960s and 1970s, such as back-to-the-land communalism, appropriate technology, social anarchism, and feminism, and shows some promise of bringing together different radical factions which would otherwise be separated. Neither Bookchin nor the bioregionalists like to call themselves environmentalists, however. To Bookchin environmentalism is impossibly reformist, while the bioregionalists think of bioregionalism as more than environmentalism.

Bioregionalists share a commitment to reinhabiting local places or homes in the various bioregions on our planet. They seek an ecologically sustainable, stable, and self-sufficient way of life that integrates their small and diverse social communities with local natural systems and develops a cooperative and unique politics of place. Combining decentralized social and political structures with beliefs about the biological integrity of human communities, bioregionalists aim for spiritual renewal in their deep regard for the value and significance of all life. To them, defending the land also takes on a different character than it does in other forms of environmentalism. "Showing solidarity with a region", to use Gary Snyder's expression, becomes radical both when it refuses to participate in the dominant culture or political system and thus leads to new ways of ecological living, and when it resists the destruction of natural systems and creatures by the use of the same non-violent, direct action techniques practiced by other radical environmentalists.[18]

Some feminists have found bioregionalism to be an acceptable framework within which to practice ecofeminism and have located themselves in bioregional communities as full-working equals. The notions of community and home, so central to bioregionalism, are important feminist ideas and serve to tie together feminist attitudes about social relationships with ecological attitudes about the right forms of harmonious environmental living. Ecofeminists have sometimes argued that women are more in tune with the earth's natural processes and can thus offer unique insights about adapting human life to the earth's regional ecosystems, insights that would otherwise be absent in patriarchal societies and communities. Their perspectives on personal, family, and work relationships have thus become key elements of bioregionalism. Of course ecofeminist analyses of domination and hierarchy in society are different than Bookchin's analysis, since Bookchin has largely ignored the domination of women by men in his theoretical discussions of social ecology.

Ecophilosophical differences among the various tribes of the radical environmental movement are numerous, and the members of these groups are very aware of this fact. However, many of them are united over the imperative need to work in concert to defend the earth with radical tactics and to create new forms of personal and social community that are based on the equal value of all parts of the earth and the importance of seriously adapting ourselves to nature.

The Reading Selections

In the selections that follow, I have included some key examples of the different positions and groups within radical environmentalism, using the original writings of radical activists and ecophilosophers. It is useful to see both of these kinds of writings together, since it is then clear that philosophy and practice are interrelated in this movement. Philosophy takes shape as a form of general justification and rationale for personal and political acts in defense of nature, and provides specific arguments to this effect. Personal and political activism for the earth in turn helps to shape the character of radical ecophilosophy.

The reader should remember that radical activists are not all philosophers, nor are radical ecophilosophers all activists. And the logical connections between philosophy and tactics are not always very direct or clear. Activists give different readings to ecophilosophy and thus disagree about what tactics are legitimate. Sometimes this has produced an attitude of tolerance for individually chosen actions, with activists respecting each other as individuals who must decide for themselves what must be done. At other times it has led to controversy within the radical activist community, especially about the propriety of tactics such as monkeywrenching. Given the diversity of belief about the connections between philosophy and practice, it is difficult, then, to argue that specific ecophilosophies always justify certain practical tactics or that specific tactics always reflect certain ecophilosophical ideas. As the deep ecologists affirm, there is much work to be done. The introductions to the chapters in Part II will discuss some of these connections, but the selections from individual activists and thinkers will serve as a more complete guide to the interrelationships.

Notes

1. W. R. O. Aitkin, "A View from Inco," *EPA Journal* 14 (July/August 1988), p. 21.
2. John Rodman, "Four Forms of Ecological Consciousness Reconsidered," in *Ethics and the Environment,* edited by Donald Scherer and Thomas Attig (Englewood Cliffs, N.J.: Prentice-Hall, Inc., 1983), p. 88.
3. See Robert Hunter, *Warriors of the Rainbow* (New York: Holt, Rinehart and Winston, 1979), for an amusing chronicle of the early Greenpeace movement and a statement of the Greenpeace philosophy and ethics.

4. *Beyond Repair, the Ecology of Capitalism* (Boston: Beacon Press, 1971).
5. "The Politics of Ecology," in *The Ecological Conscience,* edited by Robert Disch (Englewood Cliffs, N.J.: Prentice-Hall, Inc., 1970), p. 159.
6. Sam Love, ed., *Earth Tool Kit* (New York: Pocket Books, 1971).
7. Sam Love and David Obst, eds., *Ecotage!* (New York: Pocket Books, 1972).
8. *Ibid.,* p. 14.
9. *Earth Tool Kit,* pp. 95–96.
10. See Michael McCloskey, "Foreword," in *Ecotactics: The Sierra Club Handbook for Environment Activists,* edited by J. G. Mitchell with C. L. Stallings (New York: Pocket Books, 1970), p. 11.
11. One radical perspective located the root of the environmental crisis in "the very structure of American society" and called for "a revolutionary reconstruction of that social order." See *Eco-Catastrophe,* by the editors of *Ramparts* magazine (San Francisco: Canfield Press, 1970).
12. Weisberg, p. 157; Ecology Action East, "The Power to Destroy, the Power to Create," in Disch, *The Ecological Conscience,* p. 167.
13. Charlene Spretnak describes some of the roots of ecofeminism in her article "Ecofeminism: Our Roots and Flowering," in *Reweaving the World, The Emergence of Ecofeminism,* edited by Irene Diamond and Gloria Feman Orenstein (San Francisco: Sierra Club Books, 1990), pp. 3–8.
14. See Karen J. Warren, "Feminism and Ecology: Making Connections," *Environmental Ethics* 9 (Spring 1987), pp. 3–20.
15. Irene Diamond and Gloria Feman Orenstein, *Reweaving the World, the Emergence of Ecofeminism,* p. xi.
16. For a fuller statement of the key principles and values of green politics, see Chapters 2 and 10 of the book by Spretnak and Capra listed in the Selected Bibliography, Part I.
17. See Bookchin's "Social Ecology versus 'Deep Ecology': A Challenge for the Ecology Movement," *Green Perspectives, Newsletter of the Green Program Project, Burlington, Vt.* Nos. 4 and 5 (Summer 1987), pp. 1–23.
18. The language is from Gary Snyder, "Bioregional Perspectives," in *Home! A Bioregional Reader,* edited by Van Andruss et al. (Philadelphia: New Society Publishers, 1990), p. 19.

PART I

Radical Ecophilosophy

CHAPTER 1

Deep Ecology

Introduction to the Selections

The Norwegian philosopher Arne Naess is considered to be the founder of deep ecology, and Bill Devall and George Sessions its two important early and also contemporary American interpreters. Naess introduced some of the basic ideas of deep ecology in a now famous article published in the philosophical journal *Inquiry,* in 1973, which is the first selection in this chapter. He has continued to refine and rework those ideas for many years in an extensive series of papers, talks, articles, manuscripts, and books. A fuller statement of this ecophilosophy can be found in Naess' book *Ecology, Community and Lifestyle, Outline of an Ecosophy,* which was first published in Norwegian in 1976, then translated and revised by David Rothenberg and published in English in 1989.[1]

In the 1973 article, Naess presents his famous distinction between the shallow and deep ecology movements, a distinction which is not intended to be precise but which describes very general contrasts in environmental thinking and environmentalism. He tells us that there is a difference between a movement which is concerned with ecological problems because of their effects on people in the developed world and one which is more deeply concerned with such issues as biospherical equality and our basic relationships with nature. It is a difference in the depth of our philosophical and practical attitudes. This distinction has become one of the most influential ideas in ecophilosophy and outlines some of the central insights of the first radical ecophilosophy in this anthology. Watered-down versions of the distinction have spread to many discussions of environmentalism and environmental problems in scientific and popular literature. It is also the beginning focus for most evaluations of deep ecology, including those given by such critics as the Australian philosopher Richard Sylvan, the ecofeminist philosopher and sociologist Ariel Kay Salleh, and the Indian sociologist Ramachandra Guha.[2]

The second selection by Naess, "Identification as a Source of Deep Ecological Attitudes," is a more recent effort on his part to explain several of the major ideas in this important ecophilosophy. It discusses his concepts of the development of self-realization and the process of identification. Identification is here conceived as the opposite of alienation from nature and is the means by which one proceeds toward self-realization in a series of ever-widening steps from one's friends to one's community, tribe, race, humanity, and on to the larger Self. One expected result of this process is the widening and deepening of our connections with other parts of nature through the expansion of the self and the loss of our narrow ego. Naess also discusses the important concepts of the intrinsic value of living beings and the rights of all beings to live and flourish in their own distinctive ways, concepts which are pervasive in many ecophilosophies today.[3]

Bill Devall is a sociologist at Humboldt State University and George Sessions is a philosopher teaching at Sierra College, both in California. They are responsible for recognizing the significance of Naess' basic distinction in the 1970s and giving Naess' deep ecology ideas a forum in this country and elsewhere, through an ecophilosophy newsletter which they published at that time and other publications on aspects of this philosophy. Both of them have continued to interpret the major concepts of deep ecology for different audiences and to interest other philosophers and environmentalists in Naess' ecophilosophy, well into the present. Outside of Naess' own writings, their book, *Deep Ecology,* is the standard source available in print for understanding this philosophy.

The reading selection from Chapter 5 of *Deep Ecology* identifies the core ideas in this philosophy as originally formulated by Naess. These include the central intuition and two ultimate norms of this view. Devall and Sessions also explain in some detail the eight basic principles of deep ecology, first summarized by Naess and Sessions in 1984. Other chapters in *Deep Ecology* discuss such useful topics as the following: the deep ecology critique of reform environmentalism and of other bases for an ecology movement; the notion of the minority tradition from which deep ecology draws its inspiration; the ideas of the dominant worldview in Western cultures which deep ecology rejects; the varied sources of deep ecology in both Western and Eastern religion and philosophy; the importance of wilderness to deep ecologists; the deep ecology critique of resource conservation management; the outlines of a deep ecology "ecotopia"; and many ideas for ecological resistance and direct action.

Notes

1. Published by Cambridge University Press, 1989.
2. See the Selected Bibliography, Part I, for references to their work.
3. Warwick Fox gives excellent explanations of all of these concepts in Naess' ecophilosophy. See his book, *Toward a Transpersonal Ecology,* cited in the Selected Bibliography, Part I.

THE SHALLOW AND THE DEEP, LONG-RANGE ECOLOGY MOVEMENT: A SUMMARY
Arne Naess

Ecologically responsible policies are concerned only in part with pollution and resource depletion. There are deeper concerns which touch upon principles of diversity, complexity, autonomy, decentralization, symbiosis, egalitarianism, and classlessness.

The emergence of ecologists from their former relative obscurity marks a turning-point in our scientific communities. But their message is twisted and misused. A shallow, but presently rather powerful movement, and a deep, but less influential movement, compete for our attention. I shall make an effort to characterize the two.

1. The Shallow Ecology Movement

Fight against pollution and resource depletion. Central objective: the health and affluence of people in the developed countries.

2. The Deep Ecology Movement

(1) Rejection of the man-in-environment image in favour of the relational, total-field image.   Organisms as knots in the biospherical net or field of intrinsic relations. An intrinsic relation between two things A and B is such that the relation belongs to the definitions or basic constitutions of A and B, so that without the relation, A and B are no longer the same things. The total-field model dissolves not only the man-in-environment concept, but every compact thing-in-milieu concept—except when talking at a superficial or preliminary level of communication.

(2) Biospherical egalitarianism—in principle.   The 'in principle' clause is inserted because any realistic praxis necessitates some killing, exploitation, and suppression. The ecological field-worker acquires a deep-seated respect, or even veneration, for ways and forms of life. He reaches an understanding from within, a kind of understanding that others reserve for fellow men and for a narrow section of ways and forms of life. To the ecological field-worker, *the equal right to live and blossom* is an intuitively clear and obvious value axiom. Its restriction to humans is an anthropocentrism with detrimental effects upon the life quality of humans themselves. This quality depends in part upon the deep pleasure

and satisfaction we receive from close partnership with other forms of life. The attempt to ignore our dependence and to establish a master–slave role has contributed to the alienation of man from himself.

Ecological egalitarianism implies the reinterpretation of the future-research variable, 'level of crowding', so that *general* mammalian crowding and loss of life-equality is taken seriously, not only human crowding. (Research on the high requirements of free space of certain mammals has, incidentally, suggested that theorists of human urbanism have largely underestimated human life-space requirements. Behavioural crowding symptoms [neuroses, aggressiveness, loss of traditions . . .] are largely the same among mammals.)

(3) Principles of diversity and of symbiosis.   Diversity enhances the potentialities of survival, the chances of new modes of life, the richness of forms. And the so-called struggle of life, and survival of the fittest, should be interpreted in the sense of ability to coexist and cooperate in complex relationships, rather than ability to kill, exploit, and suppress. 'Live and let live' is a more powerful ecological principle than 'Either you or me'.

The latter tends to reduce the multiplicity of kinds of forms of life, and also to create destruction within the communities of the same species. Ecologically inspired attitudes therefore favour diversity of human ways of life, of cultures, of occupations, of economies. They support the fight against economic and cultural, as much as military, invasion and domination, and they are opposed to the annihilation of seals and whales as much as to that of human tribes or cultures.

(4) Anti-class posture.   Diversity of human ways of life is in part due to (intended or unintended) exploitation and suppression on the part of certain groups. The exploiter lives differently from the exploited, but both are adversely affected in their potentialities of self-realization. The principle of diversity does not cover differences due merely to certain attitutes or behaviours forcibly blocked or restrained. The principles of ecological egalitarianism and of symbiosis support the same anti-class posture. The ecological attitude favours the extension of all three principles to any group conflicts, including those of today between developing and developed nations. The three principles also favour extreme caution towards any over-all plans for the future, except those consistent with wide and widening classless diversity.

(5) Fight against pollution and resource depletion.   In this fight ecologists have found powerful supporters, but sometimes to the detriment of their total stand. This happens when attention is focused on pollution and resource depletion rather than on the other points, or when projects are implemented which reduce pollution but increase evils of the other kinds. Thus, if prices of life necessities increase because of the installation

of anti-pollution devices, class differences increase too. An ethics of responsibility implies that ecologists do not serve the shallow, but the deep ecological movement. That is, not only point (5), but all seven points must be considered together.

Ecologists are irreplaceable informants in any society, whatever their political colour. If well organized, they have the power to reject jobs in which they submit themselves to institutions or to planners with limited ecological perspectives. As it is now, ecologists sometimes serve masters who deliberately ignore the wider perspectives.

(6) Complexity, not complication.   The theory of ecosystems contains an important distinction between what is complicated without any Gestalt or unifying principles—we may think of finding our way through a chaotic city—and what is complex. A multiplicity of more or less lawful, interacting factors may operate together to form a unity, a system. We make a shoe or use a map or integrate a variety of activities into a workaday pattern. Organisms, ways of life, and interactions in the biosphere in general, exhibit complexity of such an astoundingly high level as to colour the general outlook of ecologists. Such complexity makes thinking in terms of vast systems inevitable. It also makes for a keen, steady perception of the profound *human ignorance* of biospherical relationships and therefore of the effect of disburbances.

Applied to humans, the complexity-not-complication principle favours division of labour, *not fragmentation of labour*. It favours integrated actions in which the whole person is active, not mere reactions. It favours complex economies, an integrated variety of means of living. (Combinations of industrial and agricultural activity, of intellectual and manual work, of specialized and non-specialized occupations, of urban and non-urban activity, of work in city and recreation in nature with recreation in city and work in nature . . .)

It favours soft technique and 'soft future-research', less prognosis, more clarification of possibilities. More sensitivity towards continuity and live traditions, and—most importantly—towards our state of ignorance.

The implementation of ecologically responsible policies requires in this century an exponential growth of technical skill and invention—but in new directions, directions which today are not consistently and liberally supported by the research policy organs of our nation-states.

(7) Local autonomy and decentralization.   The vulnerability of a form of life is roughly proportional to the weight of influences from afar, from outside the local region in which that form has obtained an ecological equilibrium. This lends support to our efforts to strengthen local self-government and material and mental self-sufficiency. But these efforts presuppose an impetus towards decentralization. Pollution problems,

including those of thermal pollution and recirculation of materials, also lead us in this direction, because increased local autonomy, if we are able to keep other factors constant, reduces energy consumption. (Compare an approximately self-sufficient locality with one requiring the importation of foodstuff, materials for house construction, fuel and skilled labour from other continents. The former may use only five per cent of the energy used by the latter.) Local autonomy is strengthened by a reduction in the number of links in the hierarchical chains of decision (For example a chain consisting of local board, municipal council, highest sub-national decision-maker, a state-wide institution in a state federation, a federal national government institution, a coalition of nations, and of institutions, e.g. E.E.C. top levels, and a global institution, can be reduced to one made up of local board, nation-wide institution, and global institution.) Even if a decision follows majority rules at each step, many local interests may be dropped along the line, if it is too long.

Summing up, then, it should, first of all, be borne in mind that the norms and tendencies of the Deep Ecology movement are not derived from ecology by logic or induction. Ecological knowledge and the lifestyle of the ecological field-worker have *suggested, inspired, and fortified* the perspectives of the Deep Ecology movement. Many of the formulations in the above seven-point survey are rather vague generalizations, only tenable if made more precise in certain directions. But all over the world the inspiration from ecology has shown remarkable convergencies. The survey does not pretend to be more than one of the possible condensed codifications of these convergencies.

Secondly, it should be fully appreciated that the significant tenets of the Deep Ecology movement are clearly and forcefully *normative*. They express a value priority system only in part based on results (or lack of results, cf. point [6]) of scientific research. Today, ecologists try to influence policy-making bodies largely through threats, through predictions concerning pollutants and resource depletion, knowing that policy-makers accept at least certain minimum *norms* concerning health and just distribution. But it is clear that there is a vast number of people in all countries, and even a considerable number of people in power, who accept as valid the wider norms and values characteristic of the Deep Ecology movement. There are political potentials in this movement which should not be overlooked and which have little to do with pollution and resource depletion. In plotting possible futures, the norms should be freely used and elaborated.

Thirdly, in so far as ecology movements deserve our attention, they are *ecophilosophical* rather then ecological. Ecology is a *limited* science which makes *use* of scientific methods. Philosophy is the most general forum of debate on fundamentals, descriptive as well as prescriptive, and political philosophy is one of its subsections. By an *ecosophy* I mean a philosophy of ecological harmony or equilibrium. A philosophy as a kind of *sofia* wisdom, is openly normative, it contains *both* norms, rules, postulates, value priority announcements *and* hypotheses concerning the state of affairs in our universe. Wisdom is policy wisdom, prescription, not only scientific description and prediction.

The details of an ecosophy will show many variations due to significant differences concerning not only 'facts' of pollution, resources, population, etc., but also value priorities. Today, however, the seven points listed provide one unified framework for ecosophical systems.

In general system theory, systems are mostly conceived in terms of causally or functionally interacting or interrelated items. An ecosophy, however, is more like a system of the kind constructed by Aristotle or Spinoza. It is expressed verbally as a set of sentences with a variety of functions, descriptive and prescriptive. The basic relation is that between subsets of premises and subsets of conclusions, that is, the relation of derivability. The relevant notions of derivability may be classed according to rigour, with logical and mathematical deductions topping the list, but also according to how much is implicitly taken for granted. An exposition of an ecosophy must necessarily be only moderately precise considering the vast scope of relevant ecological and normative (social, political, ethical) material. At the moment, ecosophy might profitably use models of systems, rough approximations of global systematizations. It is the global character, not preciseness in detail, which distinguishes an ecosophy. It articulates and integrates the efforts of an ideal ecological team, a team comprising not only scientists from an extreme variety of disciplines, but also students of politics and active policy-makers.

Under the name of *ecologism,* various deviations from the deep movement have been championed—primarily with a one-sided stress on pollution and resource depletion, but also with a neglect of the great differences between under- and over-developed countries in favour of a vague global approach. The global approach is essential, but regional differences must largely determine policies in the coming years.

Selected Literature

Commoner, B., *The Closing Circle: Nature, Man, and Technology,* Alfred A. Knopf, New York 1971.

Ehrlich, P. R. and A. H., *Population, Resources, Environment: Issues in Human Ecology,* 2nd ed., W. H. Freeman & Co., San Francisco 1972.

Ellul, J., *The Technological Society,* English ed., Alfred A. Knopf, New York 1964.

Glacken, C. J., *Traces on the Rhodian Shore. Nature and Culture in Western Thought,* University of California Press, Berkeley 1967.

Kato, H., 'The Effects of Crowding', Quality of Life Conference, Oberhausen, April 1972.

McHarg, Ian L., *Design with Nature,* 1969. Paperback 1971, Doubleday & Co., New York.

Meynaud, J., *Technocracy,* English ed., Free Press of Glencoe, Chicago 1969.

Mishan, E. J., *Technology and Growth: The Price We Pay,* Frederick A. Praeger, New York 1970.

Odum, E. P., *Fundamentals of Ecology,* 3rd ed., W. E. Saunders Co., Philadelphia 1971.

Shepard, Paul, *Man in the Landscape,* A. A. Knopf, New York 1967.

IDENTIFICATION AS A SOURCE OF DEEP ECOLOGICAL ATTITUDES
Arne Naess

The Shallow and the Deep Ecological Movement

In the 1960s two convergent trends made headway: a deep ecological concern, and a concern for saving deep cultural diversity. These may be put under the general heading "deep ecology" if we view human ecology as a genuine part of general ecology. For each species of living beings there is a corresponding ecology. In what follows I adopt this terminology which I introduced in 1973 (Naess 1973).

The term *deep* is supposed to suggest explication of fundamental presuppositions of valuation as well as of facts and hypotheses. Deep ecology, therefore, transcends the limit of any particular science of today, including systems theory and scientific ecology. *Deepness of normative and descriptive premises questioned* characterize the movement.

The difference between the shallow and deep ecological movement may perhaps be illustrated by contrasting typical slogans, formulated very roughly on the following page:[1]

SHALLOW ECOLOGY	DEEP ECOLOGY
Natural diversity is valuable as a resource for us.	Natural diversity has its own (intrinsic) value.
It is nonsense to talk about value except as value for mankind.	Equating value with value for humans reveals a racial prejudice.
Plant species should be saved because of their value as genetic reserves for human agriculture and medicine.	Plant species should be saved because of their intrinsic value.
Pollution should be decreased if it threatens economic growth.	Decrease of pollution has priority over economic growth.
Third World population growth threatens ecological equilibrium.	World population at the present level threatens ecosystems but the population and behavior of industrial states more than that of any others. Human population is today excessive.
"Resource" means resource for humans.	"Resource" means resource for living beings.
People will not tolerate a broad decrease in their standard of living.	People should not tolerate a broad decrease in the quality of life but in the standard of living in overdeveloped countries.
Nature is cruel and necessarily so.	Man is cruel but not necessarily so.

Deep ecological argumentation questions both the left-hand and the right-hand slogans. But tentative conclusions are in terms of the latter.

The shallow ecological argument carries today much heavier weight in political life than the deep. It is therefore often necessary for tactical reasons to hide our deeper attitudes and argue strictly homocentrically. This colors the indispensible publication, *World Conservation Strategy*.[2]

As an academic philosopher raised within analytic traditions it has been natural for me to pose the questions: How can departments of philosophy, our establishment of professionals, be made interested in the matter? What are the philosophical problems explicitly and implicitly raised or answered in the deep ecological movement? Can they be formulated so to be of academic interest?

My answer is that the movement is rich in philosophical implications. There has however, been only moderately eager response in philosophical institutions.

The deep ecological movement if furthered by people and groups with much in common. Roughly speaking, what they have in common concerns ways of experiencing nature and diversity of cultures. Furthermore, many share priorities of life style, such as those of "voluntary simplicity." They wish to live 'lightly' in nature. There are of course differences, but until now the conflicts of philosophically relevant opinion and of recommended policies have, to a surprisingly small degree, disturbed the growth of the movement.

In what follows I introduce some sections of a philosophy inspired by the deep ecological movement. Some people in the movement feel at home with that philosophy or at least approximately such a philosophy, others feel that they, at one or more points, clearly have different value priorities, attitudes or opinions. To avoid unfruitful polemics, I call my philosophy "Ecosophy T," using the character T just to emphasize that other people in the movement would, if motivated to formulate their world view and general value priorities, arrive at different ecosophies: Ecosophy "A," "B," . . ., "T," . . ., "Z."

By an "ecosophy" I here mean a philosophy inspired by the deep ecological movement. The ending- *sophy* stresses that what we modestly try to realize is wisdom rather than science or information. A philosophy, as articulated wisdom, has to be a synthesis of theory and practice. It must not shun concrete policy recommendations but has to base them on fundamental priorities of value and basic views concerning the development of our societies.[3]

Which societies? The movement started in the richest industrial societies, and the words used by its academic supporters inevitably reflect the cultural provinciality of those societies. The way I am going to say things perhaps reflects a bias in favor of analytic philosophy intimately related to social science, including academic psychology. It shows itself in my acceptance in Ecosophy T of the theory of thinking in terms of "gestalts." But this provinciality and narrowness of training does not imply criticism of contributions in terms of trends or traditions of wisdom with which I am not at home, and it does not imply an underestimation of the immense value of what artists in many countries have contributed to the movement.

Selected Ecosophical Topics

The themes of Ecosophy T which will be introduced are the following:

The narrow self (ego) and the comprehensive Self (written with capital S)

Self-realization as the realization of the comprehensive Self, not the cultivation of the ego

The process of identification as the basic tool of widening the self and as a natural consequence of increased maturity

Strong identification with the whole of nature in its diversity and interdependence of parts as a source of active participation in the deep ecological movement

Identification as a source of belief in intrinsic values. The question of 'objective' validity.[4]

Self-Realization, Yes, But Which Self?

When asked about *where* their self, their "I," or their ego is, some people place it in the neighborhood of the *larynx*. When thinking, we can sometimes perceive movement in that area. Others find it near their eyes. Many tend to feel that their ego, somehow, is inside their body, or identical with the whole of it, or with its functioning. Some call their ego spiritual, or immaterial and not within space. This has interesting consequences. A Bedouin in Yemen would not have an ego nearer the equator than a whale-hunting eskimo. 'Nearer' implies space.

William James (1890: Chapter 10) offers an excellent introduction to the problems concerning the constitution and the limits of the self.

> The Empirical Self of each of us is all that he is tempted to call by the name of *me*. But it is clear that between what a man calls *me* and what he simply calls *mine* the line is difficult to draw. We feel and act about certain things that are ours very much as we feel and act about ourselves. Our fame, our children, the work of our hands, may be as dear to us as our bodies are, and arouse the same feelings and the same acts of reprisal if attacked. And our bodies, themselves, are they simply ours, or are they *us*?
>
> The body is the innermost part of *the material Self* in each of us; and certain parts of the body seem more intimately ours than the rest. The clothes come next. . . . Next, our immediate family is a part of ourselves. Our father and mother, our wife and babes, are bone of our bone and flesh of our flesh. When they die, a part of our very selves is gone. If they do anything wrong, it is our shame. If they are insulted, our anger flashes forth as readily as if we stood in their place. Our *home* comes next. Its scenes are part of our life; its aspects awaken the tenderest feelings of affection.

One of his conclusions is of importance to the concepts of self-realization: "We see then that we are dealing with a fluctuating material. The same object being sometimes treated as a part of me, at other times is simply mine, and then again as if I had nothing to do with it all."

If the term *self-realization* is applied, it should be kept in mind that "I," "me," "ego," and "self" have shifting denotations. Nothing is evident and indisputable. Even *that* we are is debatable if we make the question dependent upon answering *what* we are.

One of the central terms in Indian philosophy is *ātman*. Until this century it was mostly translated with "spirit," but it is now generally recognized that "self" is more appropriate. It is a term with similar connotations and ambiguities as those of "self"—analyzed by William James and other Western philosophers and psychologists. Gandhi represented a *maha-ātman*, a *mahatma*, a great (and certainly very wide) self. As a term for a kind of metaphysical maximum self we find *ātman* in *The Bhagavadgita*.

Verse 29 of Chapter 6 is characteristic of the truly great *ātman*. The Sanskrit of this verse is not overwhelmingly difficult and deserves quotation ahead of translations.

> sarvabhūtastham ātmānam
> sarvabhutāni cā'tmani
> Itsate yogayuktātmā
> sarvatra samadarśanah

Radhakrisnan: "He whose self is harmonized by yoga seeth the Self abiding in all beings and all beings in Self; everywhere he sees the same."

Eliot Deutsch: "He whose self is disciplined by yoga sees the Self abiding in all beings and all beings in the Self; he sees the same in all beings."

Juan Mascaró: "He sees himself in the heart of all beings and he sees all beings in his heart. This is the vision of the Yogi of harmony, a vision which is ever one."

Gandhi: "The man equipped with *yoga* looks on all with an impartial eye, seeing *Atman* in all beings and all beings in *Atman.*"

Self-realization in its absolute maximum is, as I see it, the mature experience of oneness in diversity as depicted in the above verse. The minimum is the self-realization by more or less consistent egotism—by the narrowest experience of what constitutes one's self and a maximum of alienation. As empirical beings we dwell somewhere in between, but increased maturity involves increase of the wideness of the self.

The self-realization maximum should not necessarily be conceived as a mystical or meditational state. "By meditation some perceive the Self in the self by the self; others by the path of knowledge and still others by the path of works *(karma-yoga)*" [*Gita:* Chapter 13, verse 24]. Gandhi was a *karma-yogi*, realizing himself through social and political action.

The terms *mystical union* and *mysticism* are avoided here for three reasons: First, strong mystical traditions stress the dissolution of individual selves into a nondiversified supreme whole. Both from cultural and ecological point of view diversity and individuality are essential. Second, there is a strong terminological trend within scientific communities to associate mysticism with vagueness and confusion.[5] Third, mystics tend to agree that mystical consciousness is rarely sustained under normal, everyday conditions. But strong, wide identification *can* color experience under such conditions.

Gandhi was only marginally concerned with 'nature.' In his *ashram* poisonous snakes were permitted to live inside and outside human dwellings. Anti-poison medicines were frowned upon. Gandhi insisted that trust awakens trust, and that snakes have the same right to live and blossom as the humans (Naess, 1974).

The Process of Identification

How do we develop a wider self? What kind of process makes it possible? One way of answering these questions: There is a process of ever-widening identification and ever-narrowing alienation which widens the self. The self is as comprehensive as the totality of our identifications. Or, more succinctly: Our Self is that with which we identify. The question then reads: How do we widen identifications?

Identification is a spontaneous, non-rational, but not irrational, process through which *the interest or interests of another being are reacted to as our own interest or interests.* The emotional tone of gratification or frustration is a consequence carried over from the other to oneself: joy elicits joy, sorrow sorrow. Intense identification obliterates the experience of a distinction between *ego* and *alter,* between me and the sufferer. But only momentarily or intermittently: If my fellow being tries to vomit, I do not, or at least not persistently, try to vomit. I recognize that we are different individuals.

The term *identification, in the sense used here,* is rather technical, but there are today scarcely any alternatives. 'Solidarity,' and a corresponding adjective in German, 'solidarisch,' and the corresponding words in Scandinavian languages are very common and useful. But genuine and spontaneous solidarity with others already presupposes a process of identification. Without identification, no solidarity. Thus, the latter term cannot quite replace the former.

The same holds true of empathy and sympathy. It is a necessary, but not sufficient condition of empathy and sympathy that one 'sees' or experiences something similar or identical with oneself.[6]

A high level of identification does not eliminate conflicts of interest: Our vital interests, if we are not plants, imply killing at least some other living beings. A culture of hunters, where identification with hunted animals reaches a remarkably high level, does not prohibit killing for food. But a great variety of ceremonies and rituals have the function to express the gravity of the alienating incident and restore the identification.

Identification with individuals, species, ecosystems and landscapes results in difficult problems of priority. What should be the relation of ecosystem ethics to other parts of general ethics?

There are no definite limits to the broadness and intensity of identification. Mammals and birds sometimes show remarkable, often rather touching, intraspecies and cross-species identification. Konrad Lorenz tells of how one of his bird friends tried to seduce him, trying to push him into its little home. This presupposes a deep identification between bird and man (but also an alarming mistake of size). In certain forms of mysticism, there is an experience of identification with every life form, using this term in a wide sense. Within the deep ecological movement, poetical and philosophical expressions of such experiences are not uncommon. In the shallow ecological movement, intense and wide identification is described and explained psychologically. In the deep movement this philosophy is at least taken seriously: reality consists of wholes which we cut down rather than of isolated items which we put together. In other words: there is not, strictly speaking, a primordial causal process of identification, but one of largely unconscious alienation which is overcome in experiences of identity. To some "environmental" philosophers such thoughts seem to be irrational, even "rubbish."[7] This is, as far as I can judge, due to a too narrow conception of irrationality.

The opposite of *identification* is *alienation,* if we use these ambiguous terms in one of their basic meanings.[8]

The alienated son does perhaps what is required of a son toward his parents, but as performance of moral duties and as a burden, not spontaneously, out of joy. If one loves and respects oneself, identification will be positive, and, in what follows, the term covers this case. Self-hatred or dislike of certain of one's traits induces hatred and dislike of the beings with which one identifies.

Identification is not limited to beings which can reciprocate: Any animal, plant, mountain, ocean may induce such processes. In poetry this is articulated most impressively, but ordinary language testifies to its power as a universal human trait.

Through identification, higher level unity is experienced: from identifying with "one's nearest," higher unities are created through circles of friends, local communities, tribes, compatriots, races, humanity, life, and, ultimately, as articulated by religious and philosophic leaders, unity with the supreme whole, the "world" in a broader and deeper sense than the usual. I prefer a terminology such that the largest units are not said to comprise life *and* "the not living." One may broaden the sense of "living" so that any natural whole, however, large, is a living whole.

This way of thinking and feeling at its maximum corresponds to that of the enlightened, or yogi, who sees "the same," the *ātman,* and who is not alienated from anything.

The process of identification is sometimes expressed in terms of loss of self and gain of Self through "self-less" action. Each new sort of identification corresponds to a widening of the self, and strengthens the urge to further widening, furthering Self-seeking. This urge is in the system of Spinoza called *conatus in suo esse perseverare,* striving to persevere in oneself or one's being *(in se, in suo esse).* It is not a mere urge to survive, but to increase the level of *acting out* (ex) *one's own nature or essence,* and is not different from the urge toward higher levels of "freedom" *(libertas).* Under favorable circumstances, this involves wide identification.

In Western social science, self-realization is the term most often used for the competitive development of a person's talents and the pursuit of an individual's specific interests (Maslow and others). A conflict is foreseen between giving self-realization high priority and cultivation of social bonds, friends, family, nation, nature. Such unfortunate notions have narrow concepts of self as a point of departure. They go together with the egoism-altruism distinction. Altruism is, according to this, a moral quality developed through suppression of selfishness, through sacrifice of one's 'own' interests in favor of those of others. Thus, alienation is taken to be the normal state. Identification precludes sacrifice, but not devotion. The moral of self-sacrifice presupposes immaturity. Its relative importance is clear, in so far as we all are more or less immature.

Wideness and Depth of Identification as a Consequence of Increased Maturity

Against the belief in fundamental ego-alter conflict, the psychology and philosophy of the (comprehensive) Self insist that the gradual maturing of a person *inevitably* widens and deepens the self through the process of identification. There is no need for altruism toward those with whom we identify. The pursuit of self-realization conceived as actualization and development of the Self takes care of what altruism is supposed to accomplish. Thus, the distinction egoism–altruism is transcended.

The notion of maturing has to do with getting out what is latent in the nature of a being. Some learning is presupposed, but thinking of present conditions of competition in industrial, economic growth societies, specialized learning may inhibit the process of maturing. A competitive cult of talents does not favor Self-realization. As a consequence of the imperfect conditions for maturing as persons, there is much pessimism or disbelief in relation to the widening of the Self, and more stress on developing altruism and moral pressure.

The conditions under which the self is widened are experienced as positive and are basically joyful. The constant exposure to life in the poorest countries through television and other media contributes to the spread of the voluntary simplicity movement (Elgin, 1981). But people laugh: What does it help the hungry that you renounce the luxuries of your own country? But identification makes the efforts of simplicity joyful and there is not a feeling of moral compulsion. The widening of the self implies widening perspectives, deepening experiences, and reaching higher levels of activeness (in Spinoza's sense, not as just being busy). Joy and activeness make the appeal to Self-realization stronger than appeal to altruism. The state of alienation is not joyful, and is often connected with feelings of being threatened and narrowed. The "rights" of other living beings are felt to threaten our "own" interests.

The close connection between trends of alienation and putting duty and altruism as a highest value is exemplified in the philosophy of Kant.

Acting morally, we should not abstain from maltreating animals because of their sufferings, but because of its bad effect on us. Animals were to Kant, essentially, so different from human beings, that he felt we should not have any moral obligations toward them. Their unnecessary sufferings are morally indifferent and norms of altruism do not apply in our relations to them. When we decide ethically to be kind to them, it should be because of the favorable effect of kindness of us—a strange doctrine.

Suffering is perhaps the most potent source of identification. Only special social conditions are able to make people inhibit their normal spontaneous reaction toward suffering. If we alleviate suffering because of a spontaneous urge to do so, Kant would be willing to call the act "beautiful," but not moral. And his greatest admiration was, as we all know, for stars and the moral imperative, not spontaneous goodness. The history of cruelty inflected in the name of morals has convinced me that increase of identification might achieve what moralizing cannot: beautiful actions.

Relevance of the Above For Deep Ecology

This perhaps rather lengthy philosophical discourse serves as a preliminary for the understanding of two things: first, the powerful indignation of Rachel Carson and others who, with great courage and stubborn determination, challenged authorities in the early 1960s, and triggered the international ecological movement. Second, the radical shift (see Sahlins, 1972) toward more positive appreciation of nonindustrial cultures and minorities—also in the 1960s, and expressing itself in efforts to "save" such cultures and in a new social anthropology.

The second movement reflects identification with threatened cultures. Both reactions were made possible by doubt that the industrial societies are as uniquely progressive as they usually had been supposed to be. Former haughtiness gave way to humility or at least willingness to look for deep changes both socially and in relation to nature.

Ecological information about the intimate dependency of humanity upon decent behavior toward the natural environment offered a much needed rational and economic justification for processes of identification which many people already had more or less completed. Their relative high degree of identification with animals, plants, landscapes, were seen to correspond to *factual relations* between themselves and nature. "Not man apart" was transformed from a romantic norm to a statement of fact. The distinction between man and environment, as applied within the shallow ecological movement, was seen to be illusory. Your Self crosses the boundaries.

When it was made known that the penguins of the Antarctic might die out because of the effects of DDT upon the toughness of their eggs, there was a widespread, *spontaneous* reaction of indignation and sorrow.

People who never see penguins and who would never think of such animals as "useful" in any way, insisted that they had a right to live and flourish, and that it was our obligation not to interfere. But we must admit that even the mere appearance of penguins makes intense identification easy.

Thus, ecology helped many to know more *about themselves*. We are living beings. Penguins are too. We are all expressions of life. The fateful dependencies and interrelations which were brought to light, thanks to ecologists, made it easier for people to admit and even to cultivate their deep concern for nature, and to express their latent hostility toward the excesses of the economic growth societies.

Living Beings Have Intrinsic Value and a Right to Live and Flourish

How can these attitudes be talked about? What are the most helpful conceptualizations and slogans?

One important attitude might be thus expressed: 'Every living being has a *right* to live.' One way of answering the question is to insist upon the value in themselves, the autotelic value, of every living being. This opposes the notion that one may be justified in treating any living being as just a means to an end. It also generalizes the rightly famous dictum of Kant "never use a person solely as a means." Identification tells me: if *I* have a right to live, *you* have the same right.

Insofar as we consider ourselves and our family and friends to have an intrinsic value, the widening identification inevitably leads to the attribution of intrinsic value to others. The metaphysical maximum will then involve the attribution of intrinsic value to all living beings. The right to live is only a different way of expressing this evaluation.

The End of the Why's

But why has *any* living being autotelic value? Faced with the ever returning question of "why?," we have to stop somewhere. Here is a place where we well might stop. We shall admit that the value in itself is something shown in intuition. We attribute intrinsic value to ourselves and our nearest, and the validity of further identification can be contested, and *is* contested by many. The negation may, however, also be attacked through series of "whys?" Ultimately, we are in the same human predicament of having to start somewhere, at least for the moment. We must stop somewhere and treat where we then stand as a foundation.

The use of "Every living being has a value in itself" as a fundamental norm or principle does not rule out other fundamentals. On the contrary, the normal situation will be one in which several, in part conflicting, fundamental norms are relevant. And some consequences of fundamental norms *seem* compatible, but in fact are not.

The designation "fundamental" does not need to mean more than "not based on something deeper," which in practice often is indistinguishable from "not derived logically from deeper premises." It must be considered a rare case, if somebody is able to stick to one and only one fundamental norm. (I have made an attempt to work with *a model* with only one, Self-realization, in Ecosophy T.)

The Right to Live Is One and the Same, But Vital Interests of Our Nearest Have Priority of Defense

Under symbiotic conditions, there are rules which manifest two important factors operating when interests are conflicting: vitalness and nearness. The more vital interest has priority over the less vital. The nearer has priority over the more remote—in space, time, culture, species. Nearness derives its priority from our special responsibilities, obligations and insights.

The terms used in these rules are of course vague and ambiguous. But even so, the rules point toward ways of thinking and acting which do not leave us quite helpless in the many inevitable conflicts of norms. The vast increase of consequences for life in general, which industrialization and the population explosion have brought about, necessitates new guidelines.

Examples: The use of threatened species for food or clothing (fur) may be more or less vital for certain poor, nonindustrial, human communities. For the less poor, such use is clearly ecologically irresponsible. Considering the fabulous possibilities open to the richest industrial societies, it is their responsibility to assist the poor communities in such a way that undue exploitation of threatened species, populations, and ecosystems is avoided.

It may be of vital interest to a family of poisonous snakes to remain in a small area where small children play, but it is also of vital interest to children and parents that there are no accidents. The priority rule of nearness makes it justifiable for the parents to remove the snakes. But the priority of vital interest of snakes is important when deciding where to establish the playgrounds.

The importance of nearness is, to a large degree, dependent upon vital interests of communities rather than individuals. The obligations within the family keep the family together, the obligations within a nation keep it from disintegration. But if the nonvital interests of a nation, or a species, conflict with the vital interests of another nation, or of other species, the rules give priority to the "alien nation" or "alien species."

How these conflicts may be straightened out is of course much too large a subject to be treated even cursorily in this connection. What is said only points toward the existence of rules of some help. (For further discussion, see Naess [1979].)

Intrinsic Values

The term "objectivism" may have undesirable associations, but value pronouncements within the deep ecological movement imply what in philosophy is often termed "value objectivism" as opposed to value subjectivism, for instance, "the emotive theory of value." At the time of Nietzsche there was in Europe a profound movement toward separation of value as a genuine aspect of reality, on a par with scientific, "factual" descriptions. Value tended to be conceived as something projected by man into a completely value-neutral reality. The *Tractatus Philosophico-Logicus* of the early Wittgenstein expresses a well-known variant of this attitude. It represents a unique trend of *alienation of value* if we compare this attitude with those of cultures other than our technological-industrial society.

The professional philosophical debate on value objectivism, which in different senses—according to different versions, posits positive and negative values independent of value for human subjects—is of course very intricate. Here I shall only point out some kinds of statements within the deep ecological movement which imply value objectivism in the sense of intrinsic value:

Animals have value in themselves, not only as resources for humans.

Animals have a right to live even if of no use to humans.

We have no right to destroy the natural features of this planet.

Nature does not belong to man.

Nature is worth defending, whatever the fate of humans.

A wilderness area has a value independent of whether humans have access to it.

In these statements, something *A* is said to have a value independent of whether *A* has a value for something else, *B*. The value of *A* must therefore be said to have a value inherent in *A*. *A* has *intrinsic value*. This does not imply that *A* has value *for B*. Thus *A* may have, and usually does have, both intrinsic and extrinsic value.

Subjectivistic arguments tend to take for granted that a subject is somehow implied. There "must be" somebody who performs the valuation process. For this subject, something may have value.

The burden of proof lies with the subjectivists insofar as naive attitudes lack the clear-cut separation of value from reality and the conception of value as something projected by man into reality or the neutral facts by a subject.

The most promising way of defending intrinsic values today is, in my view, to take gestalt thinking seriously. "Objects" will then be defined in terms of gestalts, rather than in terms of heaps of things with external relations and dominated by forces. This undermines the subject–object dualism essential for value subjectivism.

Outlook for the Future

What is the outlook for growth of ecological, relevant identification and of policies in harmony with a high level of identification?

A major nuclear war will involve a setback of tremendous dimensions. Words need not be wasted in support of that conclusion. But continued militarization is a threat: It means further domination of technology and centralization.

Continued population growth makes benevolent policies still more difficult to pursue than they already are. Poor people in megacities do not have the opportunity to meet nature, and shortsighted policies which favor increasing the number of poor are destructive. Even a small population growth in rich nations is scarcely less destructive.

The economic policy of growth (as conceived today in the richest nations of all times) is increasingly destructive. It does not *prevent* growth of identification but makes it politically powerless. This reminds us of the possibility of significant *growth* of identification in the near future.

The increasing destruction plus increasing information about the destruction is apt to elicit strong feelings of sorrow, despair, desperate actions and tireless efforts to save what is left. With the forecast that more than a million species will die out before the year 2000 and most cultures be done away with, identification may grow rapidly among a minority.

At the present about 10% to 15% of the populace of some European countries are in favor of strong policies in harmony with the attitudes of identification. But this percentage may increase without major changes of policies. So far as I can see, the most probable course of events is continued devastation of conditions of life on this planet, combined with a powerless upsurge of sorrow and lamentation.

What actually happens is often wildly "improbable," and perhaps the strong anthropocentric arguments and wise recommendations of *World Conservation Strategy* (1980) will, after all, make a significant effect.

Notes

1. For survey of the main themes of the shallow and the deep movement, see Naess (1973); elaborated in Naess (1981). See also the essay of G. Sessions in

Schultz (1981) and Devall (1979). Some of the 15 views as formulated and listed by Devall would perhaps more adequately be described as part of "Ecosophy D" (D for Devall!) than as parts of a common deep ecology platform.
2. Commissioned by The United Nations Environmental Programme (UNEP) which worked together with the World Wildlife Fund (WWF). Published 1980. Copies available through IUCN, 1196 Gland, Switzerland. In India: Department of Environment.
3. This aim implies a synthesis of views developed in the different branches of philosophy—ontology, epistemology, logic, methodology, theory of value, ethics, philosophy of history, and politics. As a philosopher the deep ecologist is a "generalist."
4. For comprehensive treatment of Ecosophy T, see Naess (1981, Chapter 7).
5. See Passmore (1980). For a reasonable, unemotional approach to "mysticism," see Stahl (1975).
6. For deeper study more distinctions have to be taken into account. See, for instance, Scheler (1954) and Mercer (1972).
7. See, for instance, the chapter "Removing the Rubbish" in Passmore (1980).
8. The diverse uses of the term *alienation (Entfremdung)* has an interesting and complicated history from the time of Rousseau. Rousseau himself offers interesting observations of how social conditions through the process of alienation make *amour de soi* change into *amour propre*. I would say: How the process of maturing is hindered and self-love hardens into egotism instead of softening and widening into Self-realization.

References

Elgin, Duane. 1981. *Voluntary Simplicity*. New York: William Morrow.

James, William. 1890. *The Principles of Psychology*. New York. Chapter 10: The Consciousness of Self.

Mercer, Philip. 1972. *Sympathy and Ethics*. Oxford: The Clarendon Press. Discusses forms of identification.

Naess, A. 1973. "*The Shallow and the Deep, Long Range Ecology Movement,*" *Inquiry* 16: (95–100).

———. 1974. *Gandhi and Group Conflict*. Oslo: Universitetsforlaget.

———. 1981. *Ekologi, samhälle och livsstil. Utkast til en ekosofi*. Stockholm: LTs förlag.

———. 1979. "*Self-realization in Mixed Communities of Humans, Bears, Sheep and Wolves,*" *Inquiry*, Vol. 22, (pp. 231–241).

Passmore, John. 1980. *Man's Responsibility for Nature*. 2nd ed., London: Duckworth.

Sahlins, Marshall. 1972. *Stone Age Economics*. Chicago: Aldine.

Scheler, Max. 1954. *The Nature of Sympathy*. London: Routledge & Keegan, Paul.

Schultz, Robert C. and J. D. Hughes (eds.). 1981. *Ecological Consciousness*. University Press of America.

Stahl, Frits. 1975. *Exploring Mysticism*. Berkeley: University of California Press.

World Conservation Strategy 1980. Prepared by the International Union for Conservation of Nature and Natural Resources (IUCN).

DEEP ECOLOGY
Bill Devall and George Sessions

The term *deep ecology* was coined by Arne Naess in his 1973 article, "The Shallow and the Deep, Long-Range Ecology Movements."[1] Naess was attempting to describe the deeper, more spiritual approach to Nature exemplified in the writings of Aldo Leopold and Rachel Carson. He thought that this deeper approach resulted from a more sensitive openness to ourselves and nonhuman life around us. The essence of deep ecology is to keep asking more searching questions about human life, society, and Nature as in the Western philosophical tradition of Socrates. As examples of this deep questioning, Naess points out "that we ask why and how, where others do not. For instance, ecology as a science does not ask what kind of a society would be the best for maintaining a particular ecosystem—that is considered a question for value theory, for politics, for ethics." Thus deep ecology goes beyond the so-called factual scientific level to the level of self and Earth wisdom.

Deep ecology goes beyond a limited piecemeal shallow approach to environmental problems and attempts to articulate a comprehensive religious and philosophical worldview. The foundations of deep ecology are the basic intuitions and experiencing of ourselves and Nature which comprise ecological consciousness. Certain outlooks on politics and public policy flow naturally from this consciousness. And in the context of this book, we discuss the minority tradition as the type of community most conducive both to cultivating ecological consciousness and to asking the basic questions of values and ethics addressed in these pages.

Many of these questions are perennial philosophical and religious questions faced by humans in all cultures over the ages. What does it mean to be a unique human individual? How can the individual self maintain and increase its uniqueness while also being an inseparable aspect of the whole system wherein there are no sharp breaks between self and the *other?* An ecological perspective, in this deeper sense, results in what Theodore Roszak calls "an awakening of wholes greater than the sum of their parts. In spirit, the discipline is contemplative and therapeutic."[2]

Ecological consciousness and deep ecology are in sharp contrast with the dominant worldview of technocratic-industrial societies which regards humans as isolated and fundamentally separate from the rest of Nature, as superior to, and in charge of, the rest of creation. But the view of humans as separate and superior to the rest of Nature is only part of larger cultural patterns. For thousands of years, Western culture has become increasingly obsessed with the idea of *dominance:* with dominance of humans over nonhuman Nature, masculine over the feminine, wealthy and powerful over the poor, with the dominance of the West over non-Western cultures. Deep ecological consciousness allows us to see through these erroneous and dangerous illusions.

For deep ecology, the study of our place in the Earth household includes the study of ourselves as part of the organic whole. Going beyond a narrowly materialist scientific understanding of reality, the spiritual and the material aspects of reality fuse together. While the leading intellectuals of the dominant worldview have tended to view religion as "just superstition," and have looked upon ancient spiritual practice and enlightenment, such as found in Zen Buddhism, as essentially subjective, the search for deep ecological consciousness is the search for a more objective consciousness and state of being through an active deep questioning and meditative process and way of life.

Many people have asked these deeper questions and cultivated ecological consciousness within the context of different spiritual traditions— Christianity, Taoism, Buddhism, and Native American rituals, for example. While differing greatly in other regards, many in these traditions agree with the basic principles of deep ecology.

Warwick Fox, an Australian philosopher, has succinctly expressed the central intuition of deep ecology: "It is the idea that we can make no firm ontological divide in the field of existence: That there is no bifurcation in reality between the human and the non-human realms . . . to the extent that we perceive boundaries, we fall short of deep ecological consciousness."[3]

From this most basic insight or characteristic of deep ecological consciousness, Arne Naess has developed two *ultimate norms* or intuitions which are themselves not derivable from other principles or intuitions. They are arrived at by the deep questioning process and reveal the importance of moving to the philosophical and religious level of wisdom. They cannot be validated, of course, by the methodology of modern science based on its usual mechanistic assumptions and its very narrow definition of data. These ultimate norms are *self-realization* and *biocentric equality.*

I. Self-Realization

In keeping with the spiritual traditions of many of the world's religions, the deep ecology norm of self-realization goes beyond the modern Western *self* which is defined as an isolated ego striving primarily for hedonistic gratification or for a narrow sense of individual salvation in this life or the next. This socially programmed sense of the narrow self or social self dislocates us, and leaves us prey to whatever fad or fashion is prevalent in our society or social reference group. We are thus robbed of beginning the search for our unique spiritual/biological personhood. Spiritual growth, or unfolding, begins when we cease to understand or see ourselves as isolated and narrow competing egos and begin to identify with other humans from our family and friends to, eventually, our species. But the deep ecology sense of self requires a further maturity and growth, an identification which goes beyond humanity to include the nonhuman world. We must see beyond our narrow contemporary cultural assumptions and values, and the conventional wisdom of our time and place, and this is best achieved by the meditative deep questioning process. Only in this way can we hope to attain full mature personhood and uniqueness.

A nurturing nondominating society can help in the "real work" of becoming a whole person. The "real work" can be summarized symbolically as the realization of "self-in-Self" where "Self" stand for organic wholeness. This process of the full unfolding of the self can also be summarized by the phrase, "No one is saved until we are all saved," where the phrase "one" includes not only me, an individual human, but all humans, whales, grizzly bears, whole rain forest ecosystems, mountains and rivers, the tiniest microbes in the soil, and so on.

II. Biocentric Equality

The intuition of biocentric equality is that all things in the biosphere have an equal right to live and blossom and to reach their own individual forms of unfolding and self-realization within the larger Self-realization. This basic intuition is that all organisms and entities in the ecosphere, as parts of the interrelated whole, are equal in intrinsic worth. Naess suggests that biocentric equality as an intuition is true in principle, although in the process of living, all species use each other as food, shelter, etc. Mutual predation is a biological fact of life, and many of the world's religions have struggled with the spiritual implications of this. Some animal liberationists who attempt to side-step this problem by advocating vegetarianism are forced to say that the entire plant kingdom including rain forests have no right to their own existence. This evasion flies in the face of the basic intuition of equality.[4] Aldo Leopold expressed this intuition when he said humans are "plain citizens" of the biotic community, not lord and master over all other species.

Biocentric equality is intimately related to the all-inclusive Self-realization in the sense that if we harm the rest of Nature then we are harming ourselves. There are no boundaries and everything is interrelated. But insofar as we perceive things as individual organisms or entities, the insight draws us to respect all human and nonhuman individuals in their own right as parts of the whole without feeling the need to set up hierarchies of species with humans at the top.

The practical implications of this intuition or norm suggest that we should live with minimum rather than maximum impact on other species and on the Earth in general. Thus we see another aspect of our guiding principle: "simple in means, rich in ends." Further practical implications of these norms are discussed at length in chapters seven and eight.

A fuller discussion of the biocentric norm as it unfolds itself in practice begins with the realization that we, as individual humans, and as communities of humans, have vital needs which go beyond such basics as food, water, and shelter to include love, play, creative expression, intimate relationships with a particular landscape (or Nature taken in its entirety) as well as intimate relationships with other humans, and the vital need for spiritual growth, for becoming a mature human being.

Our vital material needs are probably more simple than many realize. In technocratic-industrial societies there is overwhelming propaganda and advertising which encourages false needs and destructive desires designed to foster increased production and consumption of goods. Most of this actually diverts us from facing reality in an objective way and from beginning the "real work" of spiritual growth and maturity.

Many people who do not see themselves as supporters of deep ecology nevertheless recognize an overriding vital human need for a healthy and high-quality natural environment for humans, if not for all life, with minimum intrusion of toxic waste, nuclear radiation from human enterprises, minimum acid rain and smog, and enough free flowing wilderness so humans can get in touch with their sources, the natural rhythms and the flow of time and place.

Drawing from the minority tradition and from the wisdom of many who have offered the insight of interconnectedness, we recognize that deep ecologists can offer suggestions for gaining maturity and encouraging the processes of harmony with Nature, but that there is no grand solution which is guaranteed to save us from ourselves.

The ultimate norms of deep ecology suggest a view of the nature of reality and our place as an individual (many in the one) in the larger scheme of things. They cannot be fully grasped intellectually but are ultimately experiential. We encourage readers to consider our further discussion of the psychological, social and ecological implications of these norms in later chapters.

As a brief summary of our position thus far, figure 1 summarizes the contrast between the dominant worldview and deep ecology.

Figure 1

DOMINANT WORLDVIEW	DEEP ECOLOGY
Dominance over Nature	Harmony with Nature
Natural environment as resource for humans	All nature has intrinsic worth/ biospecies equality
Material/economic growth for growing human population	Elegantly simple material needs (material goals serving the larger goal of self-realization)
Belief in ample resource reserves	Earth "supplies" limited
High technological progress and solutions	Appropriate technology; nondominating science
Consumerism	Doing with enough/recycling
National/centralized community	Minority tradition/bioregion

III. Basic Principles of Deep Ecology

In April 1984, during the advent of spring and John Muir's birthday, George Sessions and Arne Naess summarized fifteen years of thinking on the principles of deep ecology while camping in Death Valley, California. In this great and special place, they articulated these principles in a literal, somewhat neutral way, hoping that they would be understood and accepted by persons coming from different philosophical and religious positions.

Readers are encouraged to elaborate their own versions of deep ecology, clarify key concepts and think through the consequences of acting from these principles.

BASIC PRINCIPLES

1. The well-being and flourishing of human and nonhuman Life on Earth have value in themselves (synonyms: intrinsic value, inherent value). These values are independent of the usefulness of the nonhuman world for human purposes.

2. Richness and diversity of life forms contribute to the realization of these values and are also values in themselves.

3. Humans have no right to reduce this richness and diversity except to satisfy *vital* needs.

4. The flourishing of human life and cultures is compatible with a substantial decrease of the human population. The flourishing of nonhuman life requires such a decrease.

5. Present human interference with the nonhuman world is excessive, and the situation is rapidly worsening.

6. Policies must therefore be changed. These policies affect basic economic, technological, and ideological structures. The resulting state of affairs will be deeply different from the present.

7. The ideological change is mainly that of appreciating *life quality* (dwelling in situations of inherent value) rather than adhering to an increasingly higher standard of living. There will be a profound awareness of the difference between big and great.

8. Those who subscribe to the foregoing points have an obligation directly or indirectly to try to implement the necessary changes.

NAESS AND SESSIONS PROVIDE COMMENTS ON THE BASIC PRINCIPLES

RE (1). This formulation refers to the biosphere, or more accurately, to the ecosphere as a whole. This includes individuals, species, populations, habitat, as well as human and nonhuman cultures. From our current knowledge of all-pervasive intimate relationships, this implies a fundamental deep concern and respect. Ecological processes of the planet should, on the whole, remain intact. "The world environment should remain 'natural' " (Gary Snyder).

The term "life" is used here in a more comprehensive nontechnical way to refer also to what biologists classify as "nonliving"; rivers (watersheds), landscapes, ecosystems. For supporters of deep ecology, slogans such as "Let the river live" illustrate this broader usage so common in most cultures.

Inherent value as used in (1) is common in deep ecology literature ("The presence of inherent value in a natural object is independent of any awareness, interest, or appreciation of it by a conscious being.")[5]

RE (2). More technically, this is a formulation concerning diversity and complexity. From an ecological standpoint, complexity and symbiosis are conditions for maximizing diversity. So-called simple, lower, or primitive species of plants and animals contribute essentially to the richness and diversity of life. They have value in themselves and are not merely steps toward the so-called higher or rational life forms. The second principle presupposes that life itself, as a process over evolutionary time, implies an increase of diversity and richness. The refusal to acknowledge that some life forms have greater or lesser intrinsic value than others (see points 1 and 2) runs counter to the formulations of some ecological philosophers and New Age writers.

Complexity, as referred to here, is different from complication. Urban life may be more complicated than life in a natural setting without being more complex in the sense of multifaceted quality.

RE (3). The term "vital need" is left deliberately vague to allow for considerable latitude in judgment. Differences in climate and related factors, together with differences in the structures of societies as they now exist, need to be considered (for some Eskimos, snowmobiles are necessary today to satisfy vital needs).

People in the materially richest countries cannot be expected to reduce their excessive interference with the nonhuman world to a moderate level overnight. The stabilization and reduction of the human population will take time. Interim strategies need to be developed. But this in no way excuses the present complacency—the extreme seriousness of our current situation must first be realized. But the longer we wait the more drastic will be the measures needed. Until deep changes are made, substantial decreases in richness and diversity are liable to occur: the rate of extinction of species will be ten to one hundred times greater than any other period of earth history.

RE (4). The United Nations Fund for Population Activities in their State of World Population Report (1984) said that high human population growth rates (over 2.0 percent annum) in many developing countries "were diminishing the quality of life for many millions of people." During the decade 1974–1984, the world population grew by nearly 800 million—more than the size of India. "And we will be adding about one Bangladesh (population 93 million) per annum between now and the year 2000."

The report noted that "The growth rate of the human population has declined for the first time in human history. But at the same time, the number of people being added to the human population is bigger than at any time in history because the population base is larger."

Most of the nations in the developing world (including India and China) have as their official government policy the goal of reducing the rate of human population increase, but there are debates over the types of measures to take (contraception, abortion, etc.) consistent with human rights and feasibility.

The report concludes that if all governments set specific population targets as public policy to help alleviate poverty and advance the quality of life, the current situation could be improved.

As many ecologists have pointed out, it is also absolutely crucial to curb population growth in the so-called developed (i.e., overdeveloped) industrial societies. Given the tremendous rate of consumption and waste production of individuals in these societies, they represent a much greater threat and impact on the biosphere per capita than individuals in Second and Third World countries.

RE (5). This formulation is mild. For a realistic assessment of the situation, see the unabbreviated version of the I.U.C.N.'s *World Conservation Strategy*. There are other works to be highly recommended, such as Gerald Barney's *Global 2000 Report to the President of the United States*.

The slogan of "noninterference" does not imply that humans should not modify some ecosystems as do other species. Humans have modified the earth and will probably continue to do so. At issue is the nature and extent of such interference.

The fight to preserve and extend areas of wilderness or near-wilderness should continue and should focus on the general ecological functions of these areas (one such function: large wilderness areas are required in the biosphere to allow for continued evolutionary speciation of animals and plants). Most present designated wilderness areas and game preserves are not large enough to allow for such speciation.

RE (6). Economic growth as conceived and implemented today by the industrial states is incompatible with (1)–(5). There is only a faint resemblance between ideal sustainable forms of economic growth and present policies of the industrial societies. And "sustainable" still means "sustainable in relation to humans."

Present ideology tends to value things because they are scarce and because they have a commodity value. There is prestige in vast consumption and waste (to mention only several relevant factors).

Whereas "self-determination," "local community," and "think globally, act locally," will remain key terms in the ecology of human societies, nevertheless the implementation of deep changes requires increasingly global action—action across borders.

Governments in Third World countries (with the exception of Costa Rica and a few others) are uninterested in deep ecological issues. When the governments of industrial societies try to promote ecological measures through Third World governments, practically nothing is accomplished (e.g., with problems of desertification). Given this situation, support for global action through nongovernmental international organizations becomes increasingly important. Many of these organizations are able to act globally "from grassroots to grassroots," thus avoiding negative governmental interference.

Cultural diversity today requires advanced technology, that is, techniques that advance the basic goals of each culture. So-called soft, intermediate, and alternative technologies are steps in this direction.

RE (7). Some economists criticize the term "quality of life" because it is supposed to be vague. But on closer inspection, what they consider to be vague is actually the nonquantitative nature of the term. One cannot quantify adequately what is important for the quality of life as discussed here, and there is no need to do so.

RE (8). There is ample room for different opinions about priorities: what should be done first, what next? What is most urgent? What is clearly necessary as opposed to what is highly desirable but not absolutely pressing?

Notes

1. Arne Naess, "The Shallow and The Deep, Long-Range Ecology Movements: A Summary," *Inquiry* 16 (Oslo, 1973), pp. 95–100.
2. Theodore Roszak, *Where the Wasteland Ends* (New York: Anchor, 1972).
3. Warwick Fox, "Deep Ecology: A New Philosophy of Our Time?" *The Ecologist,* v. 14, 5–6, 1984, 194–200. Arnie Naess replies, "Intuition, Intrinsic Value and Deep Ecology," *The Ecologist,* v. 14, 5–6, 1984, pp. 201–204.
4. Tom Regan, *The Case for Animal Rights* (New York: Random House, 1983). For excellent critiques of the animal rights movement, see John Rodman, "The Liberation of Nature?" *Inquiry* 20 (Oslo, 1977). J. Baird Callicott, "Animal Liberation," *Environmental Ethics* 2, 4 (1980); see also John Rodman, "Four Forms of Ecological Consciousness Reconsidered" in T. Attig and D. Scherer, ed., *Ethics and the Environment* (Englewood Cliffs, N.J.: Prentice-Hall, 1983).
5. Tom Regan, "The Nature and Possibility of an Environmental Ethic," *Environmental Ethics* 3 (1981), pp. 19–34.

CHAPTER *2*

Ecofeminism

Introduction to the Selections

Ecofeminism is the English version of a term that was first used by a French feminist, Françoise d'Eaubonne, in 1974. One of the leading lights in the American green politics movement, Charlene Spretnak, has traced the roots of ecofeminism in the United States back to radical or cultural feminism in the mid-1970s.[1] According to Spretnak, the radical/cultural feminists, as compared to the liberal feminists and socialist feminists, were the first to develop a feminist theory about the domination of women. This theory explained why the oppression of women by men in patriarchal society was so important to understand, and it became a supporting pillar of ecofeminism. Spretnak identifies several routes into ecofeminism at that time, including the feminist study of political theory and history which critiqued Marxist ideas of class domination, the exposure to nature-based religion or "the Goddess" which honored the female and took nature as the book to study, and the participation by women in environmentalism through careers in environmental groups, universities, and government. She states that the ecofeminist movement developed from diverse beginnings and was aided by the writings and ideas of many thinkers, including Carolyn Merchant and Ynestra King, both included in this chapter.

Carolyn Merchant is one of those thinkers and historians whose important book *The Death of Nature,* first published in 1980, was widely read by feminists and later identified as an ecofeminist classic. The book reexamined the scientific revolution of the sixteenth and seventeenth centuries in Europe and showed how the worldview of early modern science replaced an earlier, prescientific view of the cosmos as an organism with the idea of it as a machine. In so doing, she argued, it "sanctioned the domination of both nature and women." She also suggested in the book that the ecology movement and the women's movement had certain critical concerns in common, for they both were rejecting values from this modern scientific picture of the world.[2] On a different note, the Merchant selection in this chapter discusses four types of feminism with their corresponding views about environmental-

47

ism, and argues for the priority of socialist feminism over the others. Her article provides some useful definitional preliminaries for understanding the different ecological directions which feminism can take.

The selection by Elizabeth Dodson Gray from her book *Green Paradise Lost* presents a version of spiritual ecofeminism which has been important in defining the dimensions of an ecofeminist ethic. Gray's book has been widely read by feminists and environmentalists alike, since it ties together many ethical themes from feminist critiques of Western philosophy, religion, and psychology with new ecological ideas in the environmental movement. She calls for a new religious covenant which will reject our alienation from each other and the earth, and a new vision or myth of a refashioned Garden of Eden in which there is justice for all and an emphasis on harmony, wholeness, diversity, and interconnection.

The selections by Ynestra King and Karen J. Warren represent two versions of less explicitly spiritual ecofeminist thought. King has long been one of the leading voices of ecofeminism and explains some its theses about the connections between ecology and feminism and the nature of domination. In the process she makes clear why the social ecology approach of Murray Bookchin, is incomplete, and she also discusses how ecofeminist theory requires an ecofeminist praxis, stressing the importance of feminist antimilitarism. Karen J. Warren is a newly emerging and important philosophical ecofeminist who outlines the essential features of an ecofeminist ethic and explains why it is necessary for any responsible environmental ethic to embrace feminism. This is a crucial point for current and future discussions of environmental ethics; can anyone formulate the dimensions of such an ethic without indicating its feminist roots? Can our society have a revolution in its environmental values without basing it on an understanding of the "interconnected dominations of nature and women," to use Warren's language?

Notes

1. See Spretnak in Diamond and Orenstein, *Reweaving the World,* mentioned in the Selected Bibliography, Part I.
2. See the introduction to Merchant's book *The Death of Nature, Women, Ecology and the Scientific Revolution* (New York: Harper & Row, Publishers, Inc., 1980).

ECOFEMINISM AND FEMINIST THEORY
Carolyn Merchant

T HE TERM *ecofeminisme* was coined by the French writer Françoise d'Eaubonne in 1974 to represent women's potential for bringing about an ecological revolution to ensure human survival on the planet.[1] Such an ecological revolution would entail new gender relations between women and men and between humans and nature. Liberal, radical, and socialist feminism have all been concerned with improving the human/nature relationship, and each has contributed to an ecofeminist perspective in different ways.[2] Liberal feminism is consistent with the objectives of reform environmentalism to alter human relations with nature through the passage of new laws and regulations. Radical ecofeminism analyzes environmental problems from within its critique of patriarchy and offers alternatives that could liberate both women and nature. Socialist ecofeminism grounds its analysis in capitalist patriarchy and would totally restructure, through a socialist revolution, the domination of women and nature inherent in the market economy's use of both as resources. While radical feminism has delved more deeply into the woman/nature connection, I believe that socialist feminism has the potential for a more thorough critique of the domination issue.

Liberal feminism characterized the history of feminism from its beginnings in the seventeenth century until the 1960s. Its roots are liberalism, the political theory that incorporates the scientific analysis that nature is composed of atoms moved by external forces with a theory of human nature that views humans as individual rational agents who maximize their own self-interest and capitalism as the optimal economic structure for human progress. Historically, liberal feminists have argued that women do not differ from men as rational agents and that exclusion from educational and economic opportunities have prevented them from realizing their own potential for creativity in all spheres of human life.[3]

For liberal feminists (as for liberalism generally), environmental problems result from the overly rapid development of natural resources and the failure to regulate environmental pollutants. Better science, conservation, and laws are the proper approaches to resolving resource problems. Given equal educational opportunities to become scientists, natural resource managers, regulators, lawyers, and legislators, women like men can contribute to the improvement of the environment, the conservation of natural resources, and the higher quality of human life. Women, therefore, can transcend the social stigma of their biology and join men in the cultural project of environmental conservation.

Radical feminism developed in the late 1960s and 1970s with the second wave of feminism. The radical form of ecofeminism is a response to the perception that women and nature have been mutually associated and devalued in Western culture and that both can be elevated and liberated through direct political action. In prehistory an emerging patriarchal culture dethroned the mother Goddesses and replaced them with male gods to whom the female deities became subservient.[4] The scientific revolution of the seventeenth century further degraded nature by replacing Renaissance organicism and a nurturing earth with the metaphor of a machine to be controlled and repaired from the outside. The Earth is to be dominated by male-developed and -controlled technology, science, and industry.

Radical feminism instead celebrates the relationship between women and nature through the revival of ancient rituals centered on Goddess worship, the moon, animals, and the female reproductive system. A vision in which nature is held in esteem as mother and Goddess is a source of inspiration and empowerment for many ecofeminists. Spirituality is seen as a source of both personal and social change. Goddess worship and rituals centered around the lunar and female menstrual cycles, lectures, concerts, art exhibitions, street and theater productions, and direct political action (web weaving in antinuclear protests) are all examples of the re-visioning of nature and women as powerful forces. Radical ecofeminist philosophy embraces intuition, an ethic of caring, and weblike human/nature relationships.

For radical feminists, human nature is grounded in human biology. Humans are biologically sexed and socially gendered. Sex/gender relations give men and women different power bases. Hence the personal is political. Radical feminists object to the dominant society's perception that women are limited by being closer to nature because of their ability to bear children. The dominant view is that menstruation, pregnancy, nursing, and nurturing of infants and young children should tie women to the home, decreasing their mobility and inhibiting their ability to remain in the work force. Radical feminists argue that the perception that women are totally oriented toward biological reproduction degrades them by association with a nature that is itself devalued in Western culture. Women's biology and nature should instead be celebrated as sources of female power.

Turning the perceived connection between women and biological reproduction upside down becomes the source of women's empowerment and ecological activism. Women argue that male-designed and -produced technologies neglect the effects of nuclear radiation, pesticides, hazardous wastes, and household chemicals on women's reproductive organs and on the ecosystem. They argue that radioactivity from nuclear wastes, power plants, and bombs is a potential cause of birth defects, cancers, and the elimination of life on Earth.[5] They expose hazardous waste sites near schools and homes as permeating soil and drinking water and contributing to miscarriage, birth defects, and leukemia. They object to pesticides and herbicides being sprayed on crops and forests as potentially affecting children and the childbearing women living near them. Women frequently spearhead local actions against spraying and power plant siting and organize others to demand toxic cleanups. When coupled with an environmental ethic that values rather than degrades nature, such actions have the potential both for raising women's consciousness of their own oppression and for the liberation of nature from the polluting effects of industrialization. For example, many lower-middle-class women who became politicized through protests over toxic chemical wastes at Love Canal in New York simultaneously became feminists when their activism spilled over into their home lives.[6]

Yet in emphasizing the female, body, and nature components of the dualities male/female, mind/body, and culture/nature, radical ecofeminism runs the risk of perpetuating the very hierarchies it seeks to overthrow. Critics point to the problem of women's own reinforcement of their identification with a nature that Western culture degrades.[7] If "female is to male as nature is to culture," as anthropologist Sherry Ortner argues,[8] then women's hopes for liberation are set back by association with nature. Any analysis that makes women's essence and qualities special ties them to a biological destiny that thwarts the possibility of liberation. A politics grounded in women's culture, experience, and values can be seen as reactionary.

To date, socialist feminists have had little to say about the problem of the domination of nature. To them, the source of male domination of women is the complex of social patterns called capitalist patriarchy, in which men bear the responsibility for labor in the marketplace and women for labor in the home. Yet the potential exists for a socialist ecofeminism that would push for an ecological, economic, and social revolution that would simultaneously liberate women, working-class people, and nature.

For socialist ecofeminism, environmental problems are rooted in the rise of capitalist patriarchy and the ideology that the Earth and nature can be exploited for human progress through technology. Historically, the rise of capitalism eroded the subsistence-based farm and city workshop in which production was oriented toward use values and men and women were economic partners. The result was a capitalist economy dominated by men and a domestic sphere in which women's labor in the home was unpaid and subordinate to men's labor in the marketplace. Both women and nature are exploited by men as part of the progressive liberation of humans from the constraints imposed by nature. The consequence is the alienation of women and men from each other and both from nature.

Socialist feminism incorporates many of the insights of radical feminism, but views both nature and human nature as historically and socially constructed. Human nature is seen as the product of historically

Feminism and the Environment

	Nature	Human Nature	Feminist Critique of Environmentalism	Image of a Feminist Environmentalism
Liberal Feminism	Atoms Mind/body dualism Domination of nature	Rational agents Individualism Maximization of self-interest	"Man and his environment" leaves out women	Women participate in natural resources and environmental sciences
Marxist Feminism	Transformation of nature by science and technology for human use Domination of nature as a means to human freedom Nature is material basis of life: food, clothing, shelter, energy	Creation of human nature through mode of production, praxis Historically specific—not fixed Species nature of humans	Critique of capitalist control of resources and accumulation of goods and profits	Socialist/communist society will use resources for good of all men and women Resources will be controlled by workers Environmental pollution will be minimal since no surpluses will be produced Environmental research by men and women

Radical Feminism	Nature is spiritual and personal Conventional science and technology problematic because of their emphasis on domination	Biology is basic Humans are sexually reproducing bodies Sexed by biology/ Gendered by society	Unaware of interconnectedness of male domination of nature and women Male environmentalism retains hierarchies Insufficient attention to environmental threats to women's reproduction (chemicals, nuclear war)	Woman/nature both valued and celebrated Reproductive freedom Against pornographic depictions of both women and nature Radical ecofeminism
Socialist Feminism	Nature is material basis of life: food, clothing, shelter, energy Nature is socially and historically constructed Transformation of nature by production	Human nature created through biology and praxis (sex, race, class, age) Historically specific and socially constructed	Leaves out nature as active and responsive Leaves out women's role in reproduction and reproduction as a category Systems approach is mechanistic not dialectical	Both nature and human production are active Centrality of biological and social reproduction Dialectic between production and reproduction Multileveled structural analysis Dialectical (not mechanical) systems Socialist ecofeminism

changing interactions between humans and nature, men and women, classes, and races. Any meaningful analysis must be grounded in an understanding of power not only in the personal but also in the political sphere. Like radical feminism, socialist feminism is critical of mechanistic science's treatment of nature as passive and of its male-dominated power structures. Similarly, it deplores the lack of a gender analysis in history and the omission of any treatment of women's reproductive and nurturing roles. But rather than grounding its analysis in biological reproduction alone, it also incorporates social reproduction. Biological reproduction includes the reproduction of the species and the reproduction of daily life through food, clothing, and shelter; social reproduction includes socialization and the legal/political reproduction of the social order.[9]

Like Marxist feminists, socialist feminists see nonhuman nature as the material basis of human life, supplying the necessities of food, clothing, shelter, and energy. Materialism, not spiritualism, is the driving force of social change. Nature is transformed by human science and technology for use by all humans for survival. Socialist feminism views change as dynamic, interactive, and dialectical, rather than as mechanistic, linear, and incremental. Nonhuman nature is dynamic and alive. As a historical actor, nature interacts with human beings through mutual ecological relations. Socialist feminist environmental theory gives both reproduction and production central places. A socialist feminist environmental ethic involves developing sustainable, nondominating relations with nature and supplying all peoples with a high quality of life.

In politics, socialist feminists participate in many of the same environmental actions as radical feminists. The goals, however, are to direct change toward some form of an egalitarian socialist state, in addition to resocializing men and women into nonsexist, nonracist, nonviolent, antiimperialist forms of life. Socialist ecofeminism deals explicitly with environmental issues that affect working-class women, Third World women, and women of color. Examples include support for the women's *Chipco* (tree-hugging) movement in India that protects fuel resources from lumber interests, for the women's Green Belt movement in Kenya that has planted more than 2 million trees in 10 years, and for Native American women and children exposed to radioactivity from uranium mining.[10]

Although the ultimate goals of liberal, radical, and socialist feminists may differ as to whether capitalism, women's culture, or socialism should be the ultimate objective of political action, shorter-term objectives overlap. In this sense there is perhaps more unity than diversity in women's common goal of restoring the natural environment and quality of life for people and other living and nonliving inhabitants of the planet.

Notes

1. Françoise d'Eaubonne, "Feminism or Death," in Elaine Marks and Isabelle de Courtivron (eds.), *New French Feminisms: An Anthology* (Amherst: University of Massachusetts Press, 1980).
2. See Karen Warren, "Feminism and Ecology: Making Connections," *Environmental Ethics* 9 (no. 1: 1981): 3–20.
3. See Alison M. Jaggar, *Feminist Politics and Human Nature* (Totowa, NJ: Rowman and Allanheld, 1983).
4. Merlin Stone, *When God Was a Woman* (New York: Harcourt Brace Jovanovich, 1976).
5. See Dorothy Nelkin, "Nuclear Power as a Feminist Issue," *Environment* 23 (no. 1: 1981): 14–20, 38–39.
6. Carolyn Merchant, "Earthcare: Women and the Environmental Movement," *Environment* 22 (June 1970): 7–13, 38–40.
7. Donna Haraway, "A Manifesto for Cyborgs," *Socialist Review* 15 (no. 80: 1985): 65–107.
8. Sherry Ortner, "Is Female to Male as Nature Is to Culture?" in Michelle Rosaldo and Louise Lamphere (eds.), *Woman, Culture, and Society* (Stanford, CA: Stanford University Press, 1974), pp. 67–87.
9. Carolyn Merchant, "The Theoretical Structure of Ecological Revolutions," *Environmental Review* 11 (no. 4: Winter 1987): 265–74.
10. See Jeanne Henn, "Female Farmers—The Doubly Ignored," *Development Forum* 14 (nos. 7 and 8: 1986); and Gillian Goslinga, "Kenya's Women of the Trees," *Development Forum* 14 (no. 8: 1986): 15.

WE MUST RE-MYTH GENESIS
Elizabeth Dodson Gray

This hour of the day is so incredibly beautiful that I am filled with wonder. The late afternoon sun, still vigorous with warmth but mellow with diminishing, is flooding our deck and beach and small cove with lustrous sidelighting. Like a Vermeer painting, it catches the white sides of the moored boats, making them gleam like translucent ivory. The sun goes in for a moment. I look up and see sheaths of lighted vapor shooting up out of the cloud like streaks of ethereal power. The sun comes back, and the sea is lit to an incredible aqua blue which shines back at me with a liquid sheen.

I have always wanted to paint this hour and the evening time which follows it—to attempt to capture, as the French impressionists did, the wondrous glories of light in nature. When my children were small and constantly demanding and interrupting at this hour, it seemed to me the very first thing I would do with post-motherhood leisure would be to try to paint this. But I never have, perhaps because I fear the failure to capture such an elusive essence. Instead I find I want simply to experience it deeply, over and over.

And so I sit on my deck and look out. And I feel and see and notice everything—the small white butterflies playing in twos and threesomes over the beach roses, the gulls flying in lazy swoops over their island, the different way each evening takes shape as the pale blue sky gradually deepens until it almost matches the deepening blue-purple of the water, striated now with a thousand ripple lines which catch the sun and cast their own tiny shadows. Each evening is different, unique, special. The sun and the earth, the wind and the water and the birds—each is a glorious gift of life to me . . . if I participate, . . . if I am still, . . . if I can listen and receive and wonder and worship.

The Covenant in Creation

We have never understood that there is a covenant in creation itself. God reaches out to us in creation, births us into being, surrounds us with the splendors of sensual life in a sensuous universe, and pledges faithfulness to us in the steadiness of the seasons and in the bounty of food for eyes, mind, ears and stomachs. God's gift to us *is* this life, this world, this creation. God's pledge to us is the constancy of the pulse of life in creation itself.

The poet laureate of South Carolina, Archibald Rutledge, has this sense of the creation as the foundational communication from God.

> The more I thought about this, the more it appeared that Creation supplies us with only two kinds of things: necessities and extras. Sunlight, air, water, food, shelter—these are among the bare necessities. With them we can exist. But moonlight and starlight are distinctly extras; so are music, the perfumes, flowers. The wind is perhaps a necessity; but the song that it croons through the morning pines is a different thing.

> I stood recently on the shores of a mountain lake at sundown after a heavy rain, and watched for an hour the magnificence of the west; the huge clouds smoldering, the long lanes of emerald light between them, then isolated clouds like red roses climbing up some oriel window of the sky, the deep refulgence behind it all. Superb as it was, momently it changed, so that I saw in reality a score of sunsets. I looked across the lonely, limpid lake, past the dark forest, far into the heart of the flaming, fading skies. . . .
> Neither a day-dawning nor a sunset (with all its attendant beauty) is really a necessity. It is one of life's extras. It is a visit to an incomparable art gallery; and no one has to pay any admission fee.

Almost the whole complex and wonderful matter of color in the world seems an extra. The color of the sky might have been a dingy gray, or a painful yellow, or a plum-colored purple. But it is sapphire. And my philosophy makes me believe that such a color for the sky is by no means the result of mere chance. Granted that it is the result of the operation of certain laws, forces, and conditions; yet behind it all, back of the realized dream, is the mighty intelligence of the Creator, the vast amplitude of the dreamer's comprehension. . . .

. . . I went one day into the forest to try to escape from a grief that had come to me. . . . All about me were the rejoicing looks of the flowers, and the shining hush and loveliness of dew-hung ferns and bushes, and the gentle, pure passion of the sunlight. And music there was from myriads of sources; gossamer lyrics from bees; the laughter of a little stream jesting with the roots of a mighty pine. . . . God seemed very near to me in that wood. . . . I saw there both life and death—in the green leaves and the brown, in the standing trees and the fallen.[1]

Rutledge tells here of the renewal of his sense of the constancy of the pulse of life in creation: "Passing from a state of keenest grief I came to one of quiet reconcilement—to the profound conviction that, living or dying, God will take care of us."[2]

The Covenant Set Apart from Creation

The covenant in creation has never been properly understood. Instead, the covenant has always been construed as something apart from creation. Even though the Genesis myth pronounced the goodness of all of creation, Judeo-Christian religion never saw that in the creation of the world there had been a covenant given. Instead the ancient Hebrew made another covenant with God and made circumcision its sign and seal (Gen. 17:1–14). It was that covenant-pledge (circumcision) that constituted them as God's people.

This covenant religion, with its relation to a transcendent moral God, was sharply distinguished by all of Abraham's heirs from the Baal worship of the female fertility cults that flourished in neighboring regions of Canaan in the first millenium of their existence as a people. Yet in a strange way the ancient Hebrews had produced their own version, a male fertility cult, in which the central cultic act defining membership in the religion and tracing the descent of the bloodline focused upon the circumcised male phallus!

Within the dimensions of the biblical convenant, nature became a backdrop. It was a carpet and a stage-setting upon which the drama of salvation was being played out between sinful man and the transcendent God. Nature became in that perception of things a non-category. When nature was not completely ignored in theological discussion, it became a foil against which to display the human and honor that part of creation which was inward, spiritual, and "supernatural."

What had been completely overlooked was that God long ago had made a fundamental, initial and sustaining covenant with all of creation. Through the millenia God has been continually loyal to this covenant with an ongoing renewal of the seasons, the generations, and of creation itself. Because we missed seeing all that, we have not seen "honoring creation" as our side of the covenant.

Honoring the Diversity God Has Created

What God created was and is diverse. And complex. So the covenant is not just between us and God. Nor is it just between a few of the parts of what God has created and their Creator. The covenant, like the creation, goes in many directions. It is a covenant connecting, supporting and shaping all that in the intricate creation web sustains what has been made and recycles what is being reused and renewed.

To honor the covenant means to honor not only the Creator but to honor all those sustaining and renewing relationships. The poet Phyllis McGinley pointed to this in her poem on the occasion of a Phi Beta Kappa dinner. Such occasions usually honor excellence, but "In Praise of Diversity" directs praise and honor toward the entire covenant—toward all that the fantastically inventive mind of God has birthed into being.

> Since this ingenious earth began
>   To shape itself from fire and rubble;
> Since God invented man, and man
>   At once fell to, inventing trouble,
> One virtue, one subversive grace
> Has chiefly vexed the human race.
>
> One whimsical beatitude,
>   Concocted for his gain and glory,
> Has man most stoutly misconstrued
>   Of all the primal category—
> Counting no blessing, but a flaw,
> That Difference is the mortal law.
>
> Adam, perhaps, while toiling late,
>   With life a book still strange to read in,
> Saw his new world, how variegate,
>   And mourned, "It was not so in Eden,"
> Confusing thus from the beginning
> Unlikeness with original sinning.

And still the sons of Adam's clay
   Labor in person or by proxy
At altering to a common way
   The planet's holy heterodoxy.
Till now, so dogged is the breed,
Almost it seems that they succeed

         . . . Yet who would dare
   Deny that nature planned it other,
When every freckled thrush can wear
   A dapple various from his brother,
When each pale snowflake in the storm
Is false to some imagined norm?

Recalling then what surely was
   The earliest bounty of Creation:
That not a blade among the grass
   But flaunts its difference with elation,
Let us devoutly take no blame
If similar does not mean the same.

And grateful for the wit to see
   Prospects through doors we cannot enter,
Ah! let us praise Diversity
   Which holds the world upon its center.[3]

Value has already been given to everything in creation by God's birthing it into being. Its value is its given function within a niche in the interconnecting webs of ecosystems, species, organs, tissues, cells, molecules and subatomic particles. Our present ethical and legal systems, which only give value to humans and to what humans value, are so hopelessly anthropocentric that they deserve a place in Garrett Hardin's suggested Museum of Obsolescence along with the notion of "an away you can throw things to."

Christopher Stone's proposal of rights for natural objects is a first step in an appropriate correction of such systems. If we truly honored the diversity in creation, we would move our culture to *a creation-based valuing of all the parts of nature*. We would not place the value of any one species always above the others. All species would be validated by their basic imprimatur of worth given to them in creation itself.

But some say to me: How could we possibly make decisions outside in the real world without valuing humans more than mosquitoes? How could we decide what to do, if all were of equal worth? My answer comes out of my experience with a similar situation in family life. Do parents consider all of their children to be of equal worth because they brought each of them into life? Then, if their children are of equal worth, how do parents make decisions about or between children? If the eldest is not superior because older or bigger, does the whole process of parental decision-making grind to a halt? Hardly! The point is that we parents continually find some grounds for making our decisions, grounds other than ranking our children in some hierarchy of their worth. What we perceive instead is that our children have differing needs, differing strengths, differing weaknesses. And occasions differ too. It is upon the basis of some convergence of all these factors that we make our decisions. And our decisions are always made within the overriding imperative that we seek to preserve the welfare of each of them as well as the welfare of the entire family!

It will be a new experience for humans to make decisions within creation's family *without* our confident assumption that "we are of course always the most loved and most valued child in creation's family." We will need to learn and gain practice in a different sort of decision-making. It will be, I think, a decision-making akin to the decision-making of parents. Such decision-making will appreciate diversity and reward it—without ranking it. Such decision-making finds value in each part as well as in the welfare of the whole. To say that such decision-making cannot be done outside the family in the "real world" is simply to prefer the thought-ways of the present because they are more familiar and therefore seem easier.

Consider these reflections upon the value of some other parts of creation:

> If you are in the mood to be enchanted, stop, look, and notice fireflies. If these tiny insects came but once a decade, we would be arranging festivals for them, writing articles, and having private viewing parties to appreciate properly their nightly dance. Yet here they are for weeks absolutely free, transforming meadows, fields, backyards and lawns. These mysterious little creatures that baffle scientists with their ability to produce cold light are one of nature's most enchanting productions. Sit on your terrace some clear, moonless evening with all electric lights out and watch the night around you come alive with the weaving of a thousand pricks of light. This tiny light is their guide to each other.[4]

> For several weeks our light blue delphinium in the perennial bed near the roses has been in full bloom. . . . It had been the center of interest for the local hummingbirds who come several times a day to sip nectar. Now today one little creature appeared, darting and hovering first here and then there. . . . The tiny bird rose in the air, perhaps ten feet high and a little to one side of the perennial bed. Flying so fast I could hardly follow him with my eye, he described an arc whose central low point was the delphinium itself. Here he swung back and forth like a pendulum in a great semi-circle. He did this about ten times and then took off.
>
> I was fascinated by his performance, and by the brief glimpse into one of

the many other worlds that interpenetrate ours. When it was over I rushed to the bird book and found that this is what hummingbirds do. The lady is always somewhere near the lowest part of the arc—next time I must look for her. It's a kind of courting dance although it seems a little late for courting now.[5]

The rainbow as a symbol in our time seems to be dawning, suggesting the spectrum of diversity we now are beginning to acknowledge and honor in our culture. A ray of light broken open by a prism into the whole spread of primary colors seems an apt metaphor or parable pointing to a creation which likewise breaks forth into all the variegate beauty of interdependent diversity. The rainbow is like a banner or flag, waving as a symbol of diversity over the movements of ethnicity and difference, celebrating the dissolution of the norm and of monochromatic uniformity. Let's hear it for the chocolate brown of the good earth and dark skins! Hurrah for roseate tones of sunsets and Indian skins. Cheers for the yellows of sunlight and oriental skins. Here's to the blue-purple of skies and butterflies. Let's celebrate the green of trees and all of nature's creatures and let's storm the law courts till we acknowledge the intrinsic value of *all* in creation's rainbow.

Human Identity Was Born a Twin

We have most especially misunderstood the covenant in creation which has come to us in human sexuality. As I write this I am in my daughter's bedroom enjoying a breeze from the land side of the house on a very hot day, and I am looking at a poster of hers which has intrigued me. It shows two strikingly striped black-and-white zebras and has the enigmatic inscription: "Happiness was born a twin."

Just so, human identity was born a twin. But not an identical twin, a different twin—a pair, one male and one female. But somehow the male-born could not handle this fact of "difference." Apparently the inner need has been irresistible to perceive this difference in hierarchical terms of who's above whom, so that men as mythmakers and portrayers of their worlds have in millenia past never understood and mythed the true dimensions of this human twinship and difference.

Always Woman Has Been Mythed Upon

Never has woman spoken for herself or mythed the world out of her own psyche. "Out of the relics of thirty thousand years," writes Elizabeth Janeway, "there is no image of woman that we can point to and say: This was made by women alone, apart from the eyes or direction of men." She then goes on to consider the earliest evidence:

Take the earliest images of all, the little "Venuses" of the Old Stone Age which have been found across Europe and Asia from the Atlantic littoral to Siberia. To name them Venuses is to imply that they are goddesses; and so they have been called by many an archeologist. But look at them with a human eye: they are not goddesses, they are fetishes, lucky pieces for a desperate man, hunter or hunted, starving or wounded, to thumb in time of need; a memory of Mum and Mum's protection and thus not a portrait of woman, but of man's need for her. . . .

Even when the Goddess appears, her image is that of the woman seen by man from outside. She is the Great Mother, feared and adored, both mediator with and representative of necessity. This is not a picture drawn by woman. No girl child would form such an identify for himself, for there is nothing of her inner personal experience in it. . . . The Mother Goddess is an image shaped by emotions projected onto women, reflecting the desires and needs of others. In that pattern of making, a woman cannot be allowed to feel or express her own emotions, nor to originate any act, for her purpose is not to create her own life, but to validate the experience of others. *Her* experience isn't and can't be part of the reckoning, for it would confuse it hopelessly. It simply doesn't count and so she is absent from history.[6]

Simone de Beauvoir has written powerfully of how women have been mythed or imaged as "other"—that which is not-male. Elizabeth Janeway writes equally powerfully about what having woman as "other" has meant both to women and men.

Woman-as-other provides a focus for many needs and yearnings: for tenderness, given and asked for; for maternal protection; for divine assurance; for support against forces of depersonalization; for evidence of the existence of self-sacrifice and loving-kindness. Women are thought of by men (and thus they are instructed to be) upholders and transmitters of high virtues and values. They are validators of emotions and interpreters of experience. To men, this seems a role of great dignity and nobility, an elevation. Why do women refuse the pedestal?

How very hard it is for women to make clear that to the extent that one's life is spent as only a terribly necessary aspect of someone else's life, one ceases to be a person in oneself. To accept that one is "other" rather than human is to deny one's identity *as* a human and feel one's own personality as obtrusive, clouding the mirror one is supposed to be.[7]

One Twin's Curious Psychic Blindness

Mything the world always from the male viewpoint has resulted in a curious psychic blindness. This can be discerned in phrases such as Freud's "the fact of female castration." As Elizabeth Janeway sardonically observes, "What kind of fact can that be? So far as I know, no woman in Western society has suffered even the trauma of circumcision."[8] Only from the male point of view is the female castrated. From her point of view he has outside equipment he may seem obsessively and neurotically preoccupied with! Freud's remark is in the same category with "the body is the hero" and "flesh-colored Band-Aids" (which match only Caucasian flesh). When you think about these phrases, the blindness they reveal staggers the mind.

The ultimate problem with this dominance of male mything and imaging of the world is not its oppression of women *or* its effects upon men in any given generation. The most fundamental problem is that it has allowed the psyche of male culture to become a worldwide monoculture, with all the vulnerability ecologists are familiar with in biological monocultures. Only what male culture perceives is perceived. What male culture does not perceive does not exist for that male culture. The boardrooms and the seats of power are occupied by males and occasional token females carefully preselected from among those trained to perceive just like men. So there is no one to cry out, "Look! The emperor has no clothes on!"

The Other Twin Is Awakening

What is now happening to that other human twin? What of woman, who through the ages has been mythed upon? She stands, as Elizabeth Janeway so aptly put it, "between myth and morning."

> It is consciousness, it is presence, it is woman wakened from a millenial slumber and looking around at a world in which, astonishingly, one might be at home; Galatea without Pygmalion, dreaming herself out of the stone by her own force of creation.[9]

"It will be a long time yet," writes Janeway, "before we understand all that means, for first we have a great deal to unlearn."[10] We must unlearn all the male generic language and linear styles of thought we were so carefully taught in masculine culture. But more subtle, we must unlearn all the projections of female otherness—passivity, sexual seductiveness, the need to please, the expectation that women will find her fulfillment in living vicariously for others. It becomes like starting again as a person, being born anew.

I still remember vividly a morning in a theological library some years ago when I read for the first time Valerie Saiving Goldstein's essay, "The Human Situation: A Feminine View."[11] I suddenly realized with her help that all of the theologians whose views I had so assiduously studied and assimilated in theological school were *male!* Valerie Saiving Goldstein was suggesting the possibility that their naming (or description) of the basic human condition as "anxiety" was a naming done from their male point of view. Perhaps women, she was suggesting, would name it differently. It was as if I had been engaged in a long, long game of intellectual Monopoly and suddenly I had been told: "Go back to Go. Do not collect $200. You must begin all over again." This was not good news. "You must try to 'undo' all that centuries of male thinking has done to you. And then you must see from your own flesh and your own intuition and your own experience how you yourself would name the human condition." This book has been my pilgrimage to do just that.

The woman really *is* between myth and morning. The consciousness of the woman-twin is just awakening. What lies ahead is a new interplay of male and female perspectives which goes beyond old stereotypes, a mutuality and symbiosis in which both are truly autonomous. I do not think masculine and feminine will then be understood in terms of androgyny and Jungian categories—which seem to me to accept that "masculine" is innately rational and active, while "feminine" is innately intuitive and passive. I doubt also that masculine and feminine will be cast in Yin/Yang terms—which again confine the one to activity and the other to passivity. And talk of "complementarity" in these matters usually means using the female to add what the male feels he is lacking. All of these ways of thinking still confine woman, define her territory for her, locate her in a psychic space defined and named from the male perspective and experience. Who but woman knows what woman is, how she perceives herself and world—until she awakes, and out of her own experience of herself and her own autonomy she myths for herself her world awake? Who knows yet what can be for the world and for creation's human twins—until they see and myth the world together, and each is "subject" mutually and none is "other"?

Yearning to Be "at Home" in the Earth

I have been saying in this chapter, first, that there is a covenant in creation itself which we have never understood and so have not been faithful to; second, that we have most especially misunderstood the covenant in creation which has come to us in human sexuality—in human identity being born a twin. Now all of this misunderstanding and misappropriation of creation has resulted in our alienation from each other and from the earth, our home. This alienation has been expressed in how we have thought and mythed God, ourselves, our world.

"If you put God outside," Gregory Bateson warns, "and set him vis-a-vis his creation and if you have the idea that you are created in his image, you will logically and naturally see yourself as outside and against the things around you. And as you arrogate all mind to yourself, you will see the world around you as mindless and therefore not entitled to moral or ethical consideration. The environment will seem to be yours to exploit. Your survival unit will be you and your folks or conspecifics against the environment of other social units, other races, and the brutes and vegetables."[12]

To myth ourselves apart is to myth ourselves alienated. Yet we yearn to be "at home"—at home with ourselves, at home with one another, at home with our world and our shared destinies that lead us through joys and pains and finally to our dying. In her quiet yet translucent description of her life in her home in New Hampshire May Sarton gives us a glimpse of an "at-homeness" in which the house, the woods, the meadows, the furniture from her past, the presences of friends and relatives mediated by flowers, habits, memories, and finally the silence, are all appropriate and interwoven into a wholeness of space and time.

> Silence was the food I was after, silence and the country itself—trees, meadows, hills, the open sky. I had wanted air, light, and space, and now I saw that they were exactly what the house had to give. The light here is magic. Even after all these years, it still takes me by surprise, for it changes with every hour of the day and with every season. In those first days it was a perpetual revelation, as sunlight touched a bunch of flowers or a piece of furniture and then moved on. Early in the morning I watched it bring alive the bronzed-gray of the bird's-eye maple of mother's desk in my study and make the flowers in the wreaths suddenly glow. In the afternoon, when I lay down for an hour in the cozy room, I saw it dapple the white mantlepiece and flow in waves across the wall there. And when I went into the kitchen to make tea, there it was again, lying in long dazzling rectangles on the yellow floor. This flowing, changing light plays a constant silent fugue, but in those first days I had still to learn how different the music is as the seasons come and go.
>
> Winter is the season when both animals and humans get stripped down to the marrow, but many animals hibernate, take the winter easy as it were; we humans are exposed naked to the currents of elation and depression. Here at Nelson it is the time of the most extraordinary light and the most perfect silence. When the first snow floats down on the rock-hard earth, first a flake at a time, then finally in soft white curtains, an entirely new silence falls. It feels as if one were being wound up into a cocoon, sealed in. There will be no escape, the primitive person senses, always with the same shiver of apprehension. At the same time, there is elation. One is lifted up in a cloud, a little above the earth, for soon there is no earth to be seen, only whiteness—whiteness without a shadow, while the snow falls. Is it dawn or dusk? Who can tell? And this goes on all night and occasionally all the next day, until there is no way out of the house. I am sealed in tight. Many times during the night I wake to listen, listen, but there is no sound at all. The silence is as thick and soft as wool. Will the snow ever stop falling?
>
> But when at last the sun comes out again, we are born into a pristine world, into the snow light. The house has become a ship riding long white slopes of waves. The light! It is like living in a diamond in this house where the white walls reflect the snow outside. There are shadows again, but now they are the most brilliant blue, lavender, even purple at dusk. And sooner or later I must push hard to open the front door against the drifts and get myself out with seed for the bird feeders. Then, when I come to sit at my desk, I look out on an air full of wings as they come to dart, swoop, and

settle—jays, nuthatches, chickadees, evening grosbeaks, woodpeckers, making a flurry of brilliant color across the white. The plows go roaring down the road, and I am safe inside with a fire burning in the study, lifted up on such excitement at my changed world that I can hardly sit still.[13]

The house itself, well-formed and graceful in design, spare and white, ordered and quiet. It seems a part of the woods and encroaching rough fields as birds and visiting animals and neighbors counterpoint May Sarton's solitude.

I found out very soon that the house demanded certain things of me. Because the very shape of the windows has such good proportions, because the builder cared about form, because of all I brought with me, the house demands that everywhere the eye falls it fall on order and beauty. So, for instance, I discovered in the first days that it would be necessary to keep the kitchen counter free of dirty dishes, and that means washing up after each meal; that the big room is so glorious, and anyone in the house is so apt to go to the kitchen windows to look out at the garden or into the sunset, that it would be a shame to leave it cluttered up. The white walls are a marvelous background for flowers, and from the beginning I have considered flowers a necessity, quite as necessary as food.

Choosing, defining, creating harmony, bringing that clarity and shape that is rest and light out of disorder and confusion—the work that I do at my desk is not unlike arranging flowers. Only it is much harder to get started on writing something! . . . Here again the house itself helps. From where I sit at my desk I look through the front hall, with just a glimpse of staircase and white newel post, and through the warm colors of an Oriental rug on the floor of the cozy room, to the long window at the end that frames distant trees and sky from under the porch roof where I have hung a feeder for woodpeckers and nuthatches. This sequence pleases my eye and draws it out in a kind of geometric progression to open space. Indeed, it is just the way rooms open into each other that is one of the charms of the house, a seduction that can only be delt when one is alone here. People often imagine that I must be lonely. How can I explain? I want to say, "Oh no! You see the house is with me." And it is with me in this particular way, as both a demand and a support, only when I am alone here.[14]

This is a portrait by one woman of her establishment of "at-homeness" within and around her. I don't think it is a making and mything of one's world and home you would expect of a man, even a man who was a writer. There is here a sturdy concreteness of attention to the form of living as well as a delicate sensitivity to the nuance of presence and to the past of memory. There is a pulling together of things cerebral and things physical, an interplay of the bounty of nature with the best subtleties of civilization. There is an openness to all that light and color, sound and texture, can bring—to all that human and animal, living and dead, surround one with.

Here the dead are not so much presences as part of the very fabric of my life; they are a living part of the whole. This way of absorbing death is not mourning. It does not look back romantically on the past; it builds the past into the present. So in a way I do not so much think about my father and mother as find myself in a hundred ways doing things as they would do. My mother tasted color as if it were food, and when I get that shiver of delight at a band of sun on the yellow floor in the big room, or put an olive-green pillow onto a dark-emerald corduroy couch, I am not so much thinking of her as being as she was.[15]

The Perverse Power of Negating Symbols

May Sarton indicates in her title "Plant Dreaming Deep" the role of dreaming, the role of mything, the role and power of *positive* symbolization. "I had first to dream the house alive inside myself," she writes.[16] But as we ourselves reach to create such at-homeness, the Genesis myth of the Fall intrudes upon the consciousness even of those who do not normally think of themselves as in any sense believers.

The powerful mythic tradition of which we are the involuntary inheritors has it that the harmonious life of the Garden of Eden existed only in some never-never land. We remain somehow deeply convinced that the lion will never lie down with the lamb, at least until some distant and unexpected Messiah comes. In short, to aspire to "being at home" with one's world, one's neighbors, one's self, is to evoke (from oneself as well as from others) the quashing epithet of Utopian or Romantic or hopelessly idealistic.

Through the centuries the doctrine of the Fall and its concommitant, the doctrine of Original Sin, have functioned to pronounce the very worst side of the human self as eternal and inescapable, at least in this life. It is not just that Adam and Eve in the myth were banished from the Garden. The doctrine of Original Sin (based upon that biblical myth) has come to have sufficient mythic power and universality to overwhelm and seem to negate our faltering human outreach toward any world of greater peace, justice and wholeness with the earth. The perverse power of this negating symbol has been to take all those goals which would otherwise be socially catalyzing and banish them to an Eden so irrelevant to our present lives and aspirations that it might just as well never have been. Eden has been portrayed as an unachievable Utopia we spoiled long ago and that we cannot now dream of or hope for or work toward, let alone live in—all because of the Fall.

The Genesis myth of the expulsion from the garden of Eden has been interpreted in the Christian tradition as "the Fall," even though the word "down" is not in the biblical account and there exists in Hebrew no word for "original sin." Jewish biblical scholars see no textual basis for what the Christian tradition has done with that bit of biblical material. Biblical theologian Bruce Birch has commented to me in private conversation that

"Never have we hung such a large doctrine on such a slender strand of biblical material." Nonetheless, the Genesis account of the expulsion of Adam and Eve from the garden of Eden has been construed by the Christian tradition as the basis for the doctrine of the Fall and the sinfulness of Man. Both have functioned to legitimate as inevitable our worst side, to justify as normal "man's inhumanity to man," and to declare every non-oppressive social vision to be an impossible and sentimental dream.

A Vision of the Garden Revisited

We must re-myth our world! Lewis Mumford has observed that humanity dreams itself into existence.[17] Our old dream has become a nightmare; we must dream a better dream. Perhaps like the old woman I wrote of in chapter 6, we will see a new vision, a vision of the Garden revisited, without the old oppressive patriarchal stories. It is a vision of justice among groups, races, sexes, species. It is a vision of harmony, of wholeness. It is a vision of diversity and interconnection. It is a vision of human life—from the cell to the household to the whole human society—caught up in a symbiotic dance of cosmic energy and sensual beauty, throbbed by a rhythm that is greater than our own, which births us into being and decays us into dying, yet whose gifts of life are incredibly good though mortal and fleeting.

Perhaps what we need to do is to turn the Genesis myth upon its head. Perhaps this finite planet and the here-and-now *is* our Eden. Perhaps our forebears erred in thinking that we were expelled from Eden long ago in some pre-history we never knew. What if the Fall was not down into sin and our worst self but more ironically a Fall *up*—a Fall *up* in which we fail to accept or "claim" our full humanness, and the finitude of our bodies, and our mortality, and our trajectory toward dying? What if our Fall was *up* into the illusion that we were above dying, above mortality, above and apart from Creation?

Perhaps the limits of our finite planet are like the biblical angel with the flaming sword, ready to cast into outer darkness those unable to perceive and live within the mixed blessings of the creation that God has prepared equally for all species, all sexes, all races, all classes. Perhaps our appropriate aspiration is not "dominion" but "praise"!

> *This is the day which the Lord hath made,*
>   Shining like Eden absolved of sin,
> Three parts glitter to one part shade:
>   *Let us be glad and rejoice therein.*
>
> Everything's scoured brighter than metal.
>   Everything sparkles as pure as glass—

The leaf on the poplar, the zinnia's petal,
    The wing of the bird, and the blade of the grass.

All, all is luster. The glossy harbor
    Dazzles the gulls that, gleaming, fly.
Glimmers the wasp on the grape in the arbor.
    Glisten the clouds in the polished sky.

Tonight—tomorrow—the leaf will fade,
    The waters tarnish, the dark begin.
But *this is the day which the Lord hath made:*
    Let us be glad and rejoice therein.[18]

Notes

1. Archibald Rutledge, *Peace in the Heart* (Garden City, N.Y.: Doubleday & Co., 1927). Cited in *These Times* (April 1977), p. 8; p. 9; p. 11.
2. Rutledge, cited in *These Times,* p. 11.
3. Phyllis McGinley, "In Praise of Diversity," in *The Love Letters of Phyllis McGinley* (New York: Viking Press, Compass Books, 1954), pp. 12–14, selections.
4. Jean Hersey, *A Sense of Seasons* (New York: Dodd, Mead & Co., 1964), p. 170.
5. Jean Hersey, *The Shape of a Year* (New York: Charles Scribner's Sons, 1967), pp. 135–136.
6. Elizabeth Janeway, *Between Myth and Morning: Women Awakening* (New York: William Morrow & Co., 1975), pp. 3–4.
7. Janeway, pp. 206–207.
8. Janeway, p. 150.
9. Janeway, pp. 2–3.
10. Janeway, p. 7.
11. Valerie Saiving Goldstein, "The Human Situation: A Feminine Viewpoint," in *The Nature of Man,* ed. Simon Doniger (New York: Harper and Bros., 1962).
12. Gregory Bateson, *Steps to an Ecology of Mind* (New York: Ballentine Books, 1972), p. 462.
13. May Sarton, *Plant Dreaming Deep* (New York: W. W. Norton & Co., 1968), p. 55; pp. 85–86.
14. Sarton, p. 57; pp. 57–59.
15. Sarton, p. 184.
16. Sarton, p. 31.
17. Lewis Mumford, "Reflections," *New Yorker,* 1975. Cited by Dorothy Dinnerstein, *The Mermaid and the Minotaur: Sexual Arrangements and Human Malaise* (New York: Harper & Row, 1976), p. 251.
18. Phyllis McGinley, "Sunday Psalm," in *Love Letters,* p. 32. Emphasis added.

TOWARD AN ECOLOGICAL FEMINISM AND A FEMINIST ECOLOGY
Ynestra King

> [Woman] became the embodiment of the biological function, the image of nature, the subjugation of which constituted that civilization's title to fame. For millennia men dreamed of acquiring absolute mastery over nature, of converting the cosmos into one immense hunting ground. It was to this that the idea of man was geared in a male-dominated society. This was the significance of reason, his proudest boast.
> —Horkheimer and Adorno 1972, p. 248.

All human beings are natural beings. That may seem like an obvious statement, yet we live in a culture which is founded on repudiation and domination of nature. This has a special significance for women because, in patriarchal thought, women are believed to be closer to nature than men. That gives women a particular stake in ending the domination of nature—in healing the alienation between human and nonhuman nature. That is the ultimate goal of the ecology movement, but the ecology movement is not necessarily feminist. For the most part, ecologists, with their concern for nonhuman nature, have yet to understand that they have a particular stake in ending the domination of women because a central reason for woman's oppression is her association with the despised nature they are so concerned about. The hatred of women and the hatred of nature are intimately connected and mutually reinforcing. Starting with this premise, this chapter explores why feminism and ecology need each other and suggests the very beginnings of a theory of ecological feminism—ecofeminism.

What is ecology? Ecological science concerns itself with the interrelationships of all forms of life. It aims to harmonize nature, human and nonhuman. It is an integrative science in an age of fragmentation and specialization of knowledge. It is also a critical science, which grounds and necessitates a critique of our existing society. It is a reconstructive science in that it suggests directions for reconstructing human society in harmony with the natural environment.

Ecologists are asking the pressing questions of how we might survive on the planet and develop systems of food and energy production, architecture, and ways of life which will allow human beings to fulfill our material needs and live in harmony with nonhuman nature. This work has led to a social critique by biologists and an exploration of biology and ecology by social thinkers. The perspective that self-consciously attempts to integrate both biological and social aspects of the relationship between human beings and their environment is known as "social ecology." This perspective, developed primarily by Murray Bookchin (1982), has embodied the anarchist critique which links domination and hierarchy in human society to the despoliation of nonhuman nature.[1] While this analysis is useful, social ecology without feminism is incomplete.

Feminism grounds this critique of domination by identifying the prototype of other forms of domination, that of man over woman. Potentially, feminism creates a concrete global community of interests among particularly life-oriented peoples of the world: women. Feminist analysis supplies theory, program, and process without which the radical potential of social ecology remains blunted. The theory and movement known as ecofeminism pushes social ecology to understand the necessary connections between ecology and feminism so that social ecology can reach its own avowed goal of creating a free and ecological way of life.

What are these connections? Social ecology challenges the dualistic belief that nature and culture are separate and opposed. Ecofeminism finds misogyny at the root of that opposition. Ecofeminist principles are based on the following beliefs:

1. The building of Western industrial civilization in opposition to nature interacts dialectically with and reinforces the subjugation of women because women are believed to be closer to nature in this culture against nature.

2. Life on earth is an interconnected web, not a hierarchy. There is not a natural hierarchy, but a multitiered human hierarchy projected onto nature and then used to justify social domination. Therefore ecofeminist movement politics and culture must show the connections between all forms of domination, including the domination of nonhuman nature, and be itself antihierarchical.

3. A healthy, balanced ecosystem, including human and nonhuman inhabitants, must maintain diversity. Ecologically, environmental simplification is as significant a problem, as environmental pollution. Biological simplification, i.e., wiping out of whole species, corresponds to reducing human diversity into faceless workers, or to the homogenization of taste and culture through mass consumer markets. Social life and natural life are literally simplified to the inorganic for the convenience of market society. Therefore, we need a decentralized global movement founded on common interests but celebrating diversity and opposing all forms of domination and violence. Potentially, ecofeminism is such a movement.

4. The survival of the species necessitates a renewed understanding of our relationship to nature, of our own bodily nature and nonhu-

man nature around us; it necessitates a challenging of the nature-culture dualism and a corresponding radical restructuring of human society according to feminist and ecological principles.

> When we speak of transformation we speak more accurately out of the vision of a process which will leave neither surfaces nor depths unchanged, which enters society at the most essential level of the subjugation of women and nature by men. . . . (Rich 1979, p. 248).

The ecology movement, in theory and practice, attempts to speak for nature, the "other" which has no voice and is not conceived of subjectively in our civilization. Feminism represents the refusal of the original "other" in patriarchal human society to remain silent or to be the "other" any longer. Its challenge of social domination extends beyond sex to social domination of all kinds because the domination of sex, race, class, and nature are mutually reinforcing. Women are the "others" in human society who have been silent in public, and who now speak through the feminist movement.

Women, Nature, and Culture: The Ecofeminist Position

In the process of building Western industrial civilization, nature became something to be dominated, overcome, made to serve the needs of men. She was stripped of her magical powers and properties as these beliefs were relegated to the trashbin of superstition. Nature was reduced to "natural resources" to be exploited by human beings to fulfill human needs and purposes which were defined in opposition to nature (see Merchant 1980).[2] A dualistic Christianity had become ascendant with the earlier demise of old Goddess religions, paganism, and animistic belief systems (Reuther 1975). With the disenchantment of nature came the conditions for unchecked scientific exploration and technological exploitation (Merchant 1980). We bear the consequences today of beliefs in unlimited control over nature and in science's ability to solve any problem, as nuclear power plants are built without provisions for waste disposal, or satellites sent into space without provision for retrieval.

In this way, nature became "other," something essentially different from the dominant to be objectified and thus subordinated. Women, who are identified with nature, have been similarly objectified and subordinated in patriarchal society. Women and nature, in this sense, are the original "others." Simone de Beauvoir (1968) has clarified this connection. For de Beauvoir, "transcendence" is the work of culture, it is the work of men. It is the process of overcoming immanence, a process of culture-building which is opposed to nature and which is based on the increasing domination of nature. It is enterprise. Immanence, symbolized by woman, is that which calls man back, that which reminds man of what he wants to forget. It is his own links to nature that he must forget and overcome to achieve manhood and transcendence:

> Man seeks in woman the Other as Nature and as his fellow being. But we know what ambivalent feelings Nature inspires in man. He exploits her, but she crushes him, he is born of her and dies in her; she is the source of his being and the realm that he subjugates to his will; Nature is a vein of gross material in which the soul is imprisoned, and she is the supreme reality; she is contingence and Idea, the finite and the whole; she is what opposes the Spirit, and the Spirit itself. Now ally, now enemy, she appears as the dark chaos from whence life wells up, as this life itself, and as the over-yonder toward which life tends. Woman sums up Nature as Mother, Wife, and Idea; these forms now mingle and now conflict, and each of them wears a double visage (de Beauvoir 1968. p. 144).

For de Beauvoir, patriarchal civilization is almost the denial of men's mortality—of which women and nature are incessant reminders. Women's powers of procreation are distinguished from the powers of creation, the accomplishments through the vehicles of culture by which men achieve immortality. And yet, this transcendence over women and nature can never be total. Hence, the ambivalence, the lack of self without other, the dependence of the self on the other both materially and emotionally. Thus develops a love-hate fetishization of women's bodies, which finds its ultimate manifestation in the sadomasochistic, pornographic displays of women as objects to be subdued, humiliated, and raped—the visual enactment of these fears and desires.[3]

An important contribution of de Beauvoir's work is to show that men seek to dominate women and nature for reasons which are not simply economic. They do so as well for psychological reasons which involve a denial of a part of themselves, as do other male culture-making activities. The process begins with beating the tenderness and empathy out of small boys and directing their natural human curiosity and joy in affecting the world around them into arrogant attitudes and destructive paths.

For men raised in woman-hating cultures, the fact that they are born of women and dependent upon nonhuman nature for existence is frightening. The process of objectification, of the making of women and nature into "others" to be appropriated and dominated, is based on a profound forgetting by men. They forget that they are born of women, dependent on women in their early helpless years, and dependent on nonhuman nature all their lives, which allows first for objectification and then for domination. "The loss of memory is a transcendental condition for science. All objectification is a forgetting" (Horkheimer & Adorno 1972, p. 230).

But the denied part of men is never fully obliterated. The memory remains in the knowledge of mortality and the fear of women's power. A basic fragility of gender identity therefore exists that surfaces when received truths about women and men are challenged and the sexes depart from the "natural" roles. Opposition to the not-very-radical U.S. Equal Rights Amendment can be partially explained on these grounds. More threatening are homosexuality and the gay liberation movement because they name a more radical truth—that sexual orientation is not indelible, nor is it naturally heterosexual. Lesbianism, particularly, which suggests that women, who possess this bottled up, repudiated primordial power, can be self-sufficient, reminds men that they may not be needed. Men are forced into remembering their own need for women to enable them to support and mediate the construction of their private reality and their public civilization. Again, there is the need to repress memory and suppress women.

The recognition of the connections between woman and nature or of women's bridge-like position poses three possible directions for feminism. One direction is the integration of women into the world of culture and production by severing the woman/nature connection. Writes anthropologist Sherry Ortner, "Ultimately both men and women can and must be equally involved in projects of creativity and transcendence. Only then will women be seen as aligned with culture, in culture's ongoing dialectic with nature" (1974, p. 87). This position does not necessarily question nature/culture dualism itself, and it is the position taken by most socialist-feminists (see King 1981) and by de Beauvoir and Ortner despite their insights into the connections between women and nature. They seek the severance of the woman/nature connection as a condition of women's liberation. Other feminists have built on the woman/nature connection by reinforcing this connection: woman and nature, the spiritual and intuitive versus men and the culture of patriarchal rationality.[4] This position also does not neccessarily question nature/culture dualism itself or recognize that women's ecological sensitivity and life orientation is a socialized perspective which could be socialized right out of us depending on our day-to-day lives. There is no reason to believe that women placed in positions of patriarchal power will act any differently from men or that we can bring about feminist revolution without a conscious understanding of history and a challenge to economic and political power structures.

Ecofeminism suggests a third direction: that feminism recognize that although the nature/culture opposition is a product of culture, we can, nonetheless, *consciously choose* not to sever the woman nature connections by joining male culture. Rather, we can use it as a vantage point for creating a different kind of culture and politics that would integrate intuitive/spiritual and rational forms of knowledge, embracing both science and magic insofar as they enable us to transform the nature/culture distinction itself and to envision and create a free, ecological society.

Ecofeminism and the Intersections of Feminism and Ecology

The implications of a culture based on the devaluation of life-giving (both biological and social) and the celebration of life-taking are profound for ecology and for women. This fact about our culture links the theories and the politics of the ecology and the feminist movements. Adrienne Rich has written,

> We have been perceived for too many centuries as pure Nature, exploited and raped like the earth and the solar system; small wonder if we now long to become Culture; pure spirit, mind. Yet is is precisely this culture and its political institutions which have split us off from itself. In so doing it has also split itself off from life, becoming the death culture of quantification, abstraction, and the will to power which has reached its most refined destructiveness in this century. It is this culture and politics of abstraction which women are talking of changing, of bringing into accountability in human terms (1976, p. 285).

The way to ground a feminist critique of "this culture and politics of abstraction" is with a self-conscious ecological perspective that we apply to all theories and strategies, in the way that we are learning to apply race and class factors to every phase of feminist analysis.

Similarly, ecology requires a feminist perspective. Without a thorough feminist analysis of social domination that reveals the interconnected roots of misogyny and a hatred of nature, ecology remains an abstraction: it is incomplete. If male ecological scientists and social ecologists fail to deal with misogyny, the deepest manifestation of nature-hating in their own lives, they are not living the ecological lives or creating the ecological society they claim.

The goals of harmonizing humanity and nonhuman nature, at both the experiential and theoretical levels, cannot be attained without the radical vision and understanding available from feminism. The ecofeminist perspective thus affects our technology. Including everything from the digging stick to nuclear bombs, technology signifies the tools that human beings use to interact with nature. The twin concerns of ecofeminism with human liberation and with our relationship to nonhuman nature open the way to developing a set of technological ethics required for decision making about technology.

Ecofeminism also contributes an understanding of the connections between the domination of persons and the domination of nonhuman nature. Ecological science tells us that there is no hierarchy in nature itself, but rather a hierarchy in human society. Building on this unmasking of the ideology of natural hierarchy of persons, ecofeminism uses its ecological perspective to develop the position that there is no hierarchy in nature: among persons, between persons and the rest of the natural world, or among the many forms of nonhuman nature. We live on the earth with millions of species, only one of which is the human species. Yet, the human species, in its patriarchal form, is the only species which holds a conscious belief that it is entitled to dominion over the other species, and the planet. Paradoxically, the human species is utterly dependent on nonhuman nature. We could not live without the rest of nature: it could live without us.

Ecofeminism draws on another basic principle of ecological science, unity in diversity, and develops it politically. Diversity in nature is necessary, and enriching. One of the major effects of industrial technology—capitalist or socialist—is environmental simplification. Many species are being simply wiped out, never to be seen on the earth again. In human society, commodity capitalism is intentionally simplifying human community and culture so that the same products can be marketed anywhere to anyone. The prospect is for all of us to be alike, with identical needs and desires, around the globe: Coca Cola in China, blue jeans in Russia, and American rock music virtually everywhere. Few peoples of the earth have not had their lives touched and changed to some degree by the technology of industrialization. Ecofeminism as a social movement resists this social simplification through supporting the rich diversity of women the world over, and finding a oneness in that diversity. Politically, ecofeminism opposes the ways that differences can separate women from each other through the oppressions of class, privilege, sexuality, race, and nationality.

The special message of ecofeminism is that, when women suffer through both social domination and the domination of nature, most of life on this planet suffers and is threatened as well. For the brutalization and oppression of women is connected with the hatred of nature and with other forms of domination, and with threatened ecological catastrophe. It is significant that feminism and ecology as social movements have emerged now, as nature's revolt against domination plays itself out in human history and nonhuman nature at the same time. As we face slow environmental poisoning and the resulting environmental simplification, or the possible unleashing of our nuclear arsenals, we can hope that the prospect of the extinction of life on the planet will provide a universal impetus to social change. Ecofeminism supports utopian visions of harmonious, diverse, decentralized communities, using only those technologies based on ecological principles, as the only practical solution for the continuation of life on earth.

Visions and politics are joined as an ecofeminist culture and politic begin to emerge. Central to this development is ecofeminist praxis: taking direct action to effect changes that are immediate and personal as well as long term and structural. Direct actions include learning holistic health and alternate ecological technologies, living in communities which explore old and new forms of spirituality that celebrate all life as diverse expressions of nature, considering the ecological consequences of our lifestyles and personal habits, and participating in creative public forms of resistance. This sometimes involves engaging in nonviolent civil disobedience to physically stop the machines which are arrayed against life.

Toward an Ecofeminist Praxis: Feminist Antimilitarism

Theory never converts simply or easily into practice; in fact, theory often lags behind practice, attempting to articulate the understanding behind things people are already doing. Praxis is the unity of thought and action, or theory and practice. Many of the women who founded the feminist antimilitarist movement in Europe and the United States share the ecofeminist perspective I have articulated. I believe that the movement as I will briefly describe it here grows out of such an understanding. For the last three years, I have been personally involved in the feminist antimilitarist movement, so the following is a firsthand account of this example of ecofeminist praxis.

The connections between violence against women, a militarized culture, and the development and deployment of nuclear weapons have long been evident to pacifist feminists (Deming 1974). Ecofeminists like myself, whose concerns with all of life stem from an understanding of the connections between misogyny and the destruction of nature, began to see militarism and the death-courting weapons industry as the most immediate threat to continued life on the planet, while the ecological effects of other modern technologies pose a more long term threat. In this manner, militarism has become a central issue for most ecofeminists. Along with this development, many of us accepted the analysis of violence made by pacifist feminists and, therefore, began to see nonviolent direct action and resistance as the basis of our political practice.

The ecofeminist analysis of militarism is concerned with the militarization of culture and the economic priorities reflected by our enormous "defense" budgets and dwindling social services budgets. Together, these pose threats to our freedom and threaten our lives, even if there is no war and none of the nuclear weapons are ever used. We have tried to make clear the particular ways that women suffer from war-making—as spoils to victorious armies, as refugees, as disabled and older women and single mothers who are dependent on dwindling social services. We connect the fear of nuclear annihilation with women's fear of male violence in our everyday lives. The level of weaponry as well as the militaristic economic priorities are products of patriarchal culture that speaks violence at every level. For ecofeminists, military technology reflects a pervasive cultural political situation. It is connected with rape, genocide, and imperialism; with starvation and homelessness; the poisoning of the environment; and the fearful lives of the world's peoples—especially those of women.

Military and state power hierarchies join and reinforce each other through military technology.

Particularly as shaped by ecofeminism, the feminist antimilitarist movement in the United States and Europe is a movement against a monstrously destructive technology and set of power relationships embodied in militarism.

Actions have been organized at the Pentagon in the United States and at military installations in Europe. The Women's Pentagon Action was conceived at an ecofeminist conference I initiated and organized with several other women in spring 1980.[5] It has taken place at the Pentagon twice so far, on November 16 and 17, 1980, and November 15 and 16, 1981. It included about 2,000 women the first year, and more than twice that the second. We took care to make the actions reflect all of our politics. Intentionally, there were no speakers, no leaders; the action sought to emphasize the connections between the military issue and other ecofeminist issues. The action was planned in four stages, reflecting the depth and range of the emotions felt and the interconnection of issues, and culminating in direct resistance. A Unity Statement, describing the group's origins and concerns was drafted collectively. In the first stage, "mourning," we walked among the graves at Arlington National Cemetery and placed tombstones symbolically for all the victims of war and other forms of violence against women, beginning with a marker for "the unknown woman." The second stage was "rage," a venting of our anger. Next, the group circled the Pentagon, reaching all the way around, and singing for the stage of "empowerment." The final stage, "defiance," included a civil disobedience action in which women blocked entrances and were arrested in an act of nonviolent direct resistance. The choice to commit civil disobedience was made individually, without pressure from the group.[6]

The themes of the Women's Pentagon Action have carried over into other actions our group has participated in, including those organized by others. At the June 12–14, 1982, disarmament demonstrations in New York City, the group's march contingent proclaimed the theme: "A feminist world is a nuclear free zone," the slogan hanging beneath a huge globe held aloft. Other banners told of visions for a feminist future and members wore bibs that read "War is manmade," "Stop the violence in our lives," and "Disarm the patriarchy." There have been similar actions, drawing inspiration from the original Women's Pentagon Actions elsewhere in the United States and in Europe. In California, the Bohemian Club—a male-only playground for corporate, government, and military elite—was the site of a demonstration by women who surrounded the club in protest (Starhawk 1982, p. 168). In England, on December 12, 1982, 30,000 women surrounded a U.S. military installation, weaving into the fence baby clothes, scarves, and other objects which meant something to them. At one point, spontaneously, the word "FREE-

DOM" rose from the lips of the women and was heard round and round the base. Three thousand women nonviolently blocked the entrances to the base on December 13 (see Fisher 1983).

The politics being created by these actions draw on women's culture: embodying what is best in women's life-oriented socialization, building on women's differences, organizing antihierarchically in small groups in visually and emotionally imaginative ways, and seeking an integration of issues. These actions exemplify ecofeminism. While technocratic experts (including feminists) argue the merits and demerits of weapons systems, ecofeminism approaches the disarmament issue on an intimate and moral level. Ecofeminism holds that a personalized, decentralized, life-affirming culture and politics of direct action are crucially needed to stop the arms race and transform the world's priorities. Because such weaponary does not exist apart from a contempt for women and all of life, the issue of disarmament and threat of nuclear war is a feminist issue. It is the ultimate human issue and the ultimate ecological issue. And so ecology, feminism, and liberation for all of nature, including ourselves, are joined.

Notes

1. I am indebted to Bookchin for my own theoretical understanding of social ecology which is basic to this chapter.
2. Merchant interprets the Scientific Revolution as the death of nature, and argues that it had a particularly detrimental effect on women.
3. See Susan Griffin (1981) for a full development of the relationship between nature-hating, woman-hating, and pornography.
4. Many such feminists call themselves ecofeminists. Some of them cite Susan Griffin's *Woman and Nature* (1978) as the source of their understanding of the deep connections between women and nature, and their politics. *Woman and Nature* is an inspirational poetic work with political implications. It explores the terrain of our deepest naturalness, but I do not read it as a delineation of a set of politics. To use Griffin's work in this way is to make it into something it was not intended to be. In personal conversation and in her more politically explicit works such as *Pornography and Silence* (1981), Griffin is antidualistic, struggling to bridge the false oppositions of nature and culture, passion and reason. Both science and poetry are deeply intuitive processes. Another work often cited by ecofeminists is Mary Daly's *Gyn/ecology* (1978). Daly, a theologian/philosopher, is also an inspirational thinker, but she is a genuinely dualistic thinker, reversing the "truths" of patriarchal theology. While I have learned a great deal from Daly, my perspective differs from hers in that I believe that any truly ecological politics including ecological feminism must be ultimately antidualistic.
5. "Women and Life on Earth: Ecofeminism in the 80s," Amherst, Mass., March 21–23, 1980. Each of my sister founders of Women and Life on Earth contributed to the theory of ecofeminism I have articulated here, and gave me faith in the political potential of an ecofeminist movement. All of them would probably disagree with parts of this chapter. Nonetheless, I thank Christine Di

Stefano, Deborah Gaventa, Anna Gyorgy, Amy Hines, Sue Hoffman, Carol Iverson, Grace Paley, Christina Rawley, Nancy Jack Todd, and Celeste Wesson.
6. See Ynestra King (1983) for my personal account and evaluation of the action.

References

Bookchin, Murray. 1982. *The ecology of freedom: The emergence and dissolution of hierarchy*. Palo Alto: Cheshire Books.

Daly, Mary. 1978. *Gyn/ecology: The metaethics of radical feminism*. Boston: Beacon Press.

de Beauvoir, Simone. 1968. *The second sex*. New York: Modern Library, Random House.

Deming, Barbara. 1974. *We cannot live without our lives*. New York: Grossman.

Fisher, Berenice. 1983. Woman ignite English movement. *Womanews* (February).

Griffin, Susan. 1978. *Woman and nature: The roaring inside her*. New York: Harper & Row.

Griffin, Susan. 1981. *Pornography and silence: Culture's revenge against nature*. New York: Harper & Row.

Horkheimer, Max; and Adorno, Theodor W. 1972. *Dialectic of enlightenment*. New York: Seabury Press.

King, Ynestra. 1981. Feminism and the revolt of nature. *Heresies* 13 (Fall):12–16.

King, Ynestra. 1983. All is connectedness: Scenes from the Women's Pentagon Action USA. *Keeping the peace: A women's peace handbook 1*. ed. Lynne Johnes. London: The Women's Press.

Merchant, Carolyn. 1980. *The death of nature: Women, ecology, and the scientific revolution*. New York: Harper & Row.

Ortner, Sherry B. 1974. Is female to male as nature is to culture? *Woman, culture and society*. eds. Michelle Zimbalist Rosaldo and Louise Lamphere. Stanford, Calif.: Stanford University Press: 67–87.

Reuther, Rosemary. 1975. *New woman/new earth: Sexist ideologies and human liberation*. New York: Seabury Press.

Rich, Adrienne. 1976. *Of woman born*. New York: W. W. Norton.

Rich, Adrienne. 1979. *On lies, secrets, and silence: Selected prose*. New York: W. W. Norton.

Starhawk, 1982. *Dreaming the dark: Magic, sex and politics*. Boston: Beacon Press.

THE POWER AND THE PROMISE
OF ECOLOGICAL FEMINISM
Karen J. Warren

Introduction

Ecological feminism (ecofeminism) has begun to receive a fair amount of attention lately as an alternative feminism and environmental ethic.[1] Since Françoise d'Eaubonne introduced the term *ecofeminisme* in 1974 to bring attention to women's potential for bringing about an ecological revolution,[2] the term has been used in a variety of ways. As I use the term in this paper, ecological feminism is the position that there are important connections—historical, experiential, symbolic, theoretical—between the domination of women and the domination of nature, an understanding of which is crucial to both feminism and environmental ethics. Here I discuss the nature of a feminist ethic and the ways in which ecofeminism provides a feminist and environmental ethic. I conclude that any feminist theory *and* any environmental ethic which fails to take seriously the twin and interconnected dominations of women and nature is at best incomplete and at worst simply inadequate. . . .

Ecofeminism as a Feminist and Environmental Ethic

A feminist ethic involves a twofold commitment to critique male bias in ethics wherever it occurs, and to develop ethics which are not male-biased. Sometimes this involves articulation of values (e.g., values of care, appropriate trust, kinship, friendship) often lost or underplayed in mainstream ethics.[3] Sometimes it involves engaging in theory building by pioneering in new directions or by revamping old theories in gender sensitive ways. What makes the critiques of old theories or conceptualizations of new ones "feminist" is that they emerge out of sex-gender analyses and reflect whatever those analyses reveal about gendered experience and gendered social reality.

As I conceive feminist ethics in the pre-feminist present, it rejects attempts to conceive of ethical theory in terms of necessary and sufficient conditions, because it assumes that there is no essence (in the sense of some transhistorical, universal, absolute abstraction) of feminist ethics. While attempts to formulate joint necessary and sufficient conditions of a feminist ethic are unfruitful, nonetheless, there are some necessary conditions, what I prefer to call "boundary conditions" of a feminist ethic. These boundary conditions clarify some of the minimal conditions of a feminist ethic without suggesting that feminist ethics has some ahistorical essence. They are like the boundaries of a quilt or collage. They delimit the territory of the piece without dictating what the interior, the design, the actual pattern of the piece looks like. Because the actual design of the quilt emerges from the multiplicity of voices of women in a cross-cultural context, the design will change over time. It is not something static.

What are some of the boundary conditions of a feminist ethic? First, nothing can become part of a feminist ethic—can be part of the quilt— that promotes sexism, racism, classism, or any other "isms" of social domination. Of course, people may disagree about what counts as a sexist act, racist attitude, classist behavior. What counts as sexism, racism, or classism may vary cross-culturally. Still, because a feminist ethic aims at eliminating sexism and sexist bias, and sexism is intimately connected in conceptualization and in practice to racism, classism, and naturism, a feminist ethic must be anti-sexist, anti-racist, anti-classist, anti-naturist and opposed to any "ism" which presupposes or advances a logic of domination.

Second, a feminist ethic is a *contextualist* ethic. A contextualist ethic is one which sees ethical discourse and practice as emerging from the voices of people located in different historical circumstances. A contextualist ethic is properly viewed as a *collage* or *mosaic,* a *tapestry* of voices that emerges out of felt experiences. Like any collage or mosaic, the point is not to have *one picture* based on a unity of voices, but a *pattern* which emerges out of the very different voices of people located in different circumstances. When a contextualist ethic is *feminist,* it gives central place to the voices of women.

Third, since a feminist ethic gives central significance to the diversity of women's voices, a feminist ethic must be structurally pluralistic rather than unitary or reductionistic. It rejects the assumption that there is "one voice" in terms of which ethical values, beliefs, attitudes, and conduct can be assessed.

Fourth, a feminist ethic reconceives ethical theory as theory in process which will change over time. Like all theory, a feminist ethic is based on some generalizations.[4] Nevertheless, the generalizations associated with it are themselves a pattern of voices within which the different voices emerging out of concrete and alternative descriptions of ethical situations have meaning. The coherence of a feminist theory so conceived is given within a historical and conceptual context, i.e., within a set of historical, socioeconomic circumstances (including circumstances of race, class, age, and affectional orientation) and within a set of basic beliefs, values, attitudes, and assumptions about the world.

Fifth, because a feminist ethic is contextualist, structurally pluralistic, and "in-process," one way to evaluate the claims of a feminist ethic is in terms of their *inclusiveness:* those claims (voices, patterns of voices) are morally and epistemologically favored (preferred, better, less partial, less biased) which are more inclusive of the felt experiences and perspectives of oppressed persons. The condition of inclusiveness requires and ensures that the diverse voices of women (as oppressed persons) will be given legitimacy in ethical theory building. It thereby helps to minimize empirical bias, e.g., bias rising from faulty or false generalizations based on stereotyping, too small a sample size, or a skewed sample. It does so by ensuring that any generalizations which are made about ethics and ethical decision making include—indeed cohere with—the patterned voices of women.[5]

Sixth, a feminist ethic makes no attempt to provide an "objective" point of view, since it assumes that in contemporary culture there really is no such point of view. As such, it does not claim to be "unbiased" in the sense of "value-neutral" or "objective." However, it does assume that whatever bias it has as an ethic centralizing the voices of oppressed persons is a *better bias*—"better" because it is more inclusive and therefore less partial—than those which exclude those voices.[6]

Seventh, a feminist ethic provides a central place for values typically unnoticed, underplayed, or misrepresented in traditional ethics, e.g., values of care, love, friendship, and appropriate trust.[7] Again, it need not do this at the exclusion of considerations of rights, rules, or utility. There may be many contexts in which talk of rights or of utility is useful or appropriate. For instance, in contracts or property relationships, talk of rights may be useful and appropriate. In deciding what is cost-effective or advantageous to the most people, talk of utility may be useful and appropriate. In a feminist *quo* contextualist ethic, whether or not such talk is useful or appropriate depends on the context; *other values* (e.g., values of care, trust, friendship) are *not* viewed as reducible to or captured solely in terms of such talk.[8]

Eighth, a feminist ethic also involves a reconception of what it is to be human and what it is for humans to engage in ethical decision making, since it rejects as either meaningless or currently untenable any gender-free or gender-neutral description of humans, ethics, and ethical decision-making. It thereby rejects what Alison Jaggar calls "abstract individualism," i.e., the position that it is possible to identify a human essence or human nature that exists independently of any particular historical context.[9] Humans and human moral conduct are properly understood essentially (and not merely accidentally) in terms of networks or webs of historical and concrete relationships.

All the props are now in place for seeing how ecofeminism provides the framework for a distinctively feminist and environmental ethic. It is a feminism that critiques male bias wherever it occurs in ethics (including environmental ethics) and aims at providing an ethic (including an environmental ethic) which is not male biased—and it does so in a way that satisfies the preliminary boundary conditions of a feminist ethic.

First, ecofeminism is quintessentially anti-naturist. Its anti-naturism consists in the rejection of any way of thinking about or acting toward nonhuman nature that reflects a logic, values, or attitude of domination. Its anti-naturist, anti-sexist, anti-racist, anti-classist (and so forth, for all other "isms" of social domination) stance forms the outer boundary of the quilt: nothing gets on the quilt which is naturist, sexist, racist, classist, and so forth.

Second, ecofeminism is a contextualist ethic. It involves a shift *from* a conception of ethics as primarily a matter of rights, rules, or principles predetermined and applied in specific cases to entities viewed as competitors in the contest of moral standing, *to* a conception of ethics as growing out of what Jim Cheney calls "defining relationships," i.e., relationships conceived in some sense as defining who one is.[10] As a contextualist ethic, it is not that rights, or rules, or principles are *not* relevant or important. Clearly they are in certain contexts and for certain purposes.[11] It is just that what *makes* them relevant or important is that those to whom they apply are entities *in relationship with* others.

Ecofeminism also involves an ethical shift *from* granting moral consideration to nonhumans *exclusively* on the grounds of some similarity they share with humans (e.g., rationality, interests, moral agency, sentiency, right-holder status) *to* "a highly contextual account to see clearly what a human being is and what the nonhuman world might be, morally speaking, *for* human beings."[12] For an ecofeminist, *how* a moral agent is in relationship to another becomes of central significance, not simply *that* a moral agent is a moral agent or is bound by rights, duties, virtue, or utility to act in a certain way.

Third, ecofeminism is structurally pluralistic in that it presupposes and maintains difference—difference among humans as well as between humans and at least some elements of nonhuman nature. Thus, while ecofeminism denies the "nature/culture" split, it affirms that humans are both members of an ecological community (in some respects) and different from it (in other respects). Ecofeminism's attention to relationships and community is not, therefore, an erasure of difference but a respectful acknowledgment of it.

Fourth, ecofeminism reconceives theory as theory in process. It focuses on patterns of meaning which emerge, for instance, from the storytelling and first-person narratives of women (and others) who deplore the twin dominations of women and nature. The use of narrative is one way to ensure that the content of the ethic—the pattern of the quilt—may/will change over time, as the historical and material realities of women's lives change and as more is learned about women-nature connections and the destruction of the nonhuman world.[13]

Fifth, ecofeminism is inclusivist. It emerges from the voices of women who experience the harmful domination of nature and the way that domination is tied to their domination as women. It emerges from listening to the voices of indigenous peoples such as Native Americans who have been dislocated from their land and have witnessed the attendant undermining of such values as appropriate reciprocity, sharing, and kinship that characterize traditional Indian culture. It emerges from listening to voices of those who, like Nathan Hare, critique traditional approaches to environmental ethics as white and bourgeois, and as failing to address issues of "black ecology" and the "ecology" of the inner city and urban spaces.[14] It also emerges out of the voices of Chipko women who see the destruction of "earth, soil, and water" as intimately connected with their own inability to survive economically.[15] With its emphasis on inclusivity and difference, ecofeminism provides a framework for recognizing that what counts as ecology and what counts as appropriate conduct toward both human and nonhuman environments is largely a matter of context.

Sixth, as a feminism, ecofeminism makes no attempt to provide an "objective" point of view. It is a social ecology. It recognizes the twin dominations of women and nature as social problems rooted both in very concrete, historical, socioeconomic circumstances and in oppressive patriarchal conceptual frameworks which maintain and sanction these circumstances.

Seventh, ecofeminism makes a central place for values of care, love, friendship, trust, and appropriate reciprocity—values that presuppose that our relationships to others are central to our understanding of who we are.[16] It thereby gives voice to the sensitivity that in climbing a mountain, one is doing something in relationship with an "other," an "other" whom one can come to care about and treat respectfully.

Lastly, an ecofeminist ethic involves a reconception of what it means to be human, and in what human ethical behavior consists. Ecofeminism denies abstract individualism. Humans are who we are in large part by virtue of the historical and social contexts and the relationships we are in, including our relationships with nonhuman nature. Relationships are not something extrinsic to who we are, not an "add on" feature of human nature; they play an essential role in shaping what it is to be human. Relationships of humans to the nonhuman environment are, in part, constitutive of what it is to be a human.

By making visible the interconnections among the dominations of women and nature, ecofeminism shows that both are feminist issues and that explicit acknowledgment of both is vital to any responsible environmental ethic. Feminism *must* embrace ecological feminism if it is to end the domination of women because the domination of women is tied conceptually and historically to the domination of nature.

A responsible environmental ethic also must embrace feminism. Otherwise, even the seemingly most revolutionary, liberational, and holistic ecological ethic will fail to take seriously the interconnected dominations of nature and women that are so much a part of the historical legacy and conceptual framework that sanctions the exploitation of nonhuman nature. Failure to make visible these interconnected, twin dominations results in an inaccurate account of how it is that nature has been and continues to be dominated and exploited and produces an environmental ethic that lacks the depth necessary to be truly *inclusive* of the realities of persons who at least in dominant Western culture have been intimately tied with that exploitation, viz., women. Whatever else can be said in favor of such holistic ethics, a failure to make visible ecofeminist insights into the common denominators of the twin oppressions of women and nature is to perpetuate, rather than overcome, the source of that oppression.

This last point deserves further attention. It may be objected that as long as the end result is "the same"—the development of an environmental ethic which does not emerge out of or reinforce an oppressive conceptual framework—it does not matter whether that ethic (or the ethic endorsed in getting there) is feminist or not. Hence, it simply is *not* the case that any adequate environmental ethic must be feminist. My argument, in contrast, has been that it *does* matter, and for three important reasons. First, there is the scholarly issue of accurately representing historical reality, and that, ecofeminists claim, requires acknowledging the historical feminization of nature and naturalization of women as part of the exploitation of nature. Second, I have shown that the conceptual connections between the domination of women and the domination of nature are located in an oppressive and, at least in Western societies, patriarchal conceptual framework characterized by a logic of domination. Thus, I have shown that failure to notice the nature of this connection leaves at best an incomplete, inaccurate, and partial account of what is required of a conceptually adequate environmental ethic. An ethic which *does* not acknowledge this is simply *not* the same as one that does, whatever else the similarities between them. Third, the claim that, in contemporary culture, one can have an adequate environmental ethic which is *not* feminist assumes that, in contemporary culture, the label *feminist* does not add anything crucial to the nature or description of environmental ethics. I have shown that at least in contemporary culture this is false, for the word *feminist* currently helps to clarify just *how* the domination of nature is conceptually linked to patriarchy and, hence, how the liberation of nature is conceptually linked to the termination of patriarchy. Thus, because it has critical bite in contemporary culture, it serves as an important reminder that in contemporary sex-gendered, raced, classed, and naturist culture, an unlabeled position functions as a privileged and "unmarked" position. That is, without the addition of the word *feminist*, one presents environmental ethics as if it has no bias, including male-gender bias, which is just what ecofeminists deny: failure to notice the connections between the twin oppressions of women and nature *is* male-gender bias.

One of the goals of feminism is the eradication of all oppressive sex-gender (and related race, class, age, affectional preference) categories and the creation of a world in which *difference does not breed domination*—say, the world of 4001. If in 4001 an "adequate environmental ethic" is a "feminist environmental ethic," the word *feminist* may then be redundant and unnecessary. However, this is *not* 4001, and in terms of the current historical and conceptual reality the dominations of nature and of women are intimately connected. Failure to notice or make visible that connection in 1990 perpetuates the mistaken (and privileged) view that "environmental ethics" is *not* a feminist issue, and that *feminist* adds nothing to environmental ethics. . . .[17]

Notes

1. Explicit ecological feminist literature includes works from a variety of scholarly perspectives and sources. Some of these works are Leonie Caldecott and Stephanie Leland, eds., *Reclaim the Earth: Women Speak Out for Life on Earth* (London: The Women's Press, 1983); Jim Cheney, "Eco-Feminism and Deep Ecology," *Environmental Ethics* 9 (1987): 115–45; Andrée Collard with Joyce Contrucci, *Rape of the Wild: Man's Violence against Animals and the Earth* (Bloomington: Indiana University Press, 1988); Katherine Davies, "Historical Associations: Women and the Natural World," *Women & Environments* 9, no. 2 (Spring 1987): 4–6; Sharon Doubiago, "Deeper than Deep Ecology: Men Must Become Feminists," in *The New Catalyst Quarterly*, no. 10 (Winter 1987/88): 10–11; Brian Easlea, *Science and Sexual Oppression: Patriarchy's Confrontation with Women and Nature* (London: Weidenfeld & Nicholson, 1981); Elizabeth Dodson Gray, *Green Paradise Lost* (Wellesley, Mass.: Roundtable Press, 1979); Susan Griffin, *Women and Nature: The Roaring Inside Her* (San Francisco: Harper and Row, 1978); Joan L. Griscom, "On Healing the Nature/History Split in Feminist Thought," in *Heresies #13: Feminism and Ecology* 4, no. 1 (1981): 4–9; Ynestra King, "The Ecology of Feminism and the Feminism of Ecology," in *Healing Our Wounds: The Power of Ecological Feminism*, ed. Judith Plant (Boston: New Society Publishers, 1989), pp. 18–28; "The Eco-feminist Imperative," in *Reclaim the Earth*, ed. Caldecott and Leland (London: The Women's Press, 1983), pp. 12–16. "Feminism and the Revolt of Nature," in *Heresies #13: Feminism and Ecology* 4, no. 1 (1981): 12–16, and "What is Ecofeminism?" *The Nation*, 12 December 1987; Marti Kheel, "Animal Liberation Is A Feminist Issue," *The New Catalyst Quarterly*, no. 10 (Winter 1987–88): 8–9; Carolyn Merchant, *The Death of Nature: Women, Ecology and the Scientific Revolution* (San Francisco, Harper and Row, 1980); Patrick Murphy, ed., "Feminism, Ecology, and the Future of the Humanities," special issue of *Studies in the Humanities* 15, no. 2 (December 1988); Abby Peterson and Carolyn Merchant, "Peace with the Earth: Women and

the Environmental Movement in Sweden," *Women's Studies International Forum* 9, no. 5–6. (1986): 465–79; Judith Plant, "Searching for Common Ground: Ecofeminism and Bioregionalism," in *The New Catalyst Quarterly,* no. 10 (Winter 1987/88): 6–7; Judith Plant, ed., *Healing Our Wounds: The Power of Ecological Feminism* (Boston: New Society Publishers, 1989); Val Plumwood, "Ecofeminism: An Overview and Discussion of Positions and Arguments," *Australasian Journal of Philosophy,* Supplement to vol. 64 (June 1986): 120–37; Rosemary Radford Ruether, *New Woman/New Earth: Sexist Ideologies & Human Liberation* (New York: Seabury Press, 1975); Kirkpatrick Sale. "Ecofeminism—A New Perspective," *The Nation,* 26 September 1987): 302–05; Ariel Kay Salleh, "Deeper than Deep Ecology: The Eco-Feminist Connection," *Environmental Ethics* 6 (1984): 339–45, and "Epistemology and the Metaphors of Production: An Eco-Feminist Reading of Critical Theory," in *Studies in the Humanities* 15 (1988): 130–39; Vandana Shiva, *Staying Alive: Women, Ecology and Development* (London: Zed Books, 1988): Charlene Spretnak, "Ecofeminism: Our Roots and Flowering," *The Elmswood Newsletter,* Winter Solstice 1988; Karen J. Warren, "Feminism and Ecology: Making Connections," *Environmental Ethics* 9 (1987): 3–21; "Toward an Ecofeminist Ethic," *Studies in the Humanities* 15 (1988): 140–156; Miriam Wyman, "Explorations of Ecofeminism," *Women & Environments* (Spring 1987): 6–7; Iris Young, " 'Feminism and Ecology' and 'Women and Life on Earth: Eco-Feminism in the 80's'," *Environmental Ethics* 5 (1983): 173–80; Michael Zimmerman, "Feminism, Deep Ecology, and Environmental Ethics," *Environmental Ethics* 9 (1987): 21–44.

2. Francoise d'Eaubonne, *Le Feminisme ou la Mort* (Paris: Pierre Horay, 1974), pp. 213–52.

3. This account of a feminist ethic draws on my paper "Toward an Ecofeminist Ethic."

4. Marilyn Frye makes this point in her illuminating paper, "The Possibility of Feminist Theory," read at the American Philosophical Association Central Division Meetings in Chicago, 29 April–1 May 1986. My discussion of feminist theory is inspired largely by that paper and by Kathryn Addelson's paper "Moral Revolution," in *Women and Values: Reading in Recent Feminist Philosophy,* ed. Marilyn Pearsall (Belmont, Calif.: Wadsworth Publishing Co., 1986) pp. 291–309.

5. Notice that the standard of inclusiveness does not exclude the voices of men. It is just that those voices must cohere with the voices of women.

6. For a more in-depth discussion of the notions of impartiality and bias, see my paper, "Critical Thinking and Feminism," *Informal Logic* 10, no. 1 (Winter 1988): 31–44.

7. The burgeoning literature on these values is noteworthy. See, e.g., Carol Gilligan, *In a Different Voice: Psychological Theories and Women's Development* (Cambridge: Harvard University Press, 1982); *Mapping the Moral Domain: A Contribution of Women's Thinking to Psychological Theory and Education,* ed. Carol Gilligan, Janie Victoria Ward, and Jill McLean Taylor, with Betty Bardige (Cambridge: Harvard University Press, 1988); Nel Noddings, *Caring: A Feminine Approach to Ethics and Moral Education* (Berkely: University of California Press, 1984); Maria Lugones and

Elizabeth V. Spelman, "Have We Got a Theory for You! Feminist Theory, Cultural Imperialism, and the Women's Voice," *Women's Studies International Forum* 6 (1983): 573–81; Maria Lugones, "Playfulness"; Annette C. Baier, "What Do Women Want In A Moral Theory?" *Noûs* 19 (1985); 53–63.

8. Jim Cheney would claim that our fundamental relationships to one another as moral agents are not as moral agents to rights holders, and that whatever rights a person properly may be said to have are relationally defined rights, not rights possessed by atomistic individuals conceived as Robinson Crusoes who do not exist essentially in relation to others. On this view, even rights talk itself is properly conceived as growing out of a relational ethic, not vice versa.

9. Alison Jaggar, *Feminist Politics and Human Nature* (Totowa, N.J.: Rowman and Allanheld, 1980), pp. 42–44.

10. Henry West has pointed out that the expression "defining relations" is ambiguous. According to West, "the 'defining' as Cheney uses it is an adjective, not a principle—it is not that ethics defines relationships: it is that ethics grows out of conceiving of the relationships that one is in as defining what the individual is."

11. For example, in relationships involving contracts or promises, those relationships might be correctly described as that of moral agent to rights holders. In relationships involving mere property, those relationships might be correctly described as that of moral agent to objects having only instrumental value, "relationships of instrumentality." In comments on an earlier draft of this paper, West suggested that possessive individualism, for instance, might be recast in such a way that an individual is defined by his or her property relationships.

12. Cheney, "Eco-Feminism and Deep Ecology," p. 144.

13. One might object that such permission for change opens the door for environmental exploitation. This is not the case. An ecofeminist ethic is anti-naturist. Hence, the unjust domination and exploitation of nature is a "boundary condition" of the ethic; no such actions are sanctioned or justified on ecofeminist grounds. What it *does* leave open is some leeway about what counts as domination and exploitation. This, I think, is a strength of the ethic, not a weakness, since it acknowledges that *that* issue cannot be resolved in any practical way in the abstract, independent of a historical and social context.

14. Nathan Hare, "Black Ecology," in *Environmental Ethics*, ed. K. S. Shrader-Frechette (Pacific Grove, Calif.: Boxwood Press, 1981), pp. 229–36.

15. For an ecofeminist discussion of the Chipko movement, see my "Toward an Ecofeminist Ethic," and Shiva's *Staying Alive*.

16. See Cheney, "Eco-Feminism and Deep Ecology," p. 122.

17. I offer the same sort of reply to critics of ecofeminism such as Warwick Fox who suggest that for the sort of ecofeminism I defend, the word *feminist* does not add anything significant to environmental ethics and, consequently, that an ecofeminist like myself might as well call herself a deep ecologist. He asks: "Why doesn't she just call it [i.e., Warren's vision of a transformative feminism] deep ecology? Why specifically attach the label *feminist* to it . . .?" (Warwick Fox, "The Deep Ecology-Ecofeminism Debate and Its Parallels,"

Environmental Ethics 11, no. 1 [1989]: 14, n. 22). Whatever the important similarities between deep ecology and ecofeminism (or, specifically, my version of ecofeminism)—and, indeed, there are many—it is precisely my point here that the word *feminist* does add something significant to the conception of environmental ethics, and that any environmental ethic (including deep ecology) that fails to make explicit the different kinds of interconnections among the domination of nature and the domination of women will be, from a feminist (and ecofeminist) perspective such as mine, inadequate.

Social Ecology and Bioregionalism

Introduction to the Selections

The selections in Chapter 3 complete the part of this anthology on radical ecophilosophy by introducing the reader to Murray Bookchin's social ecology and the related movement called "bioregionalism." Bookchin has written many lengthy articles and books on social ecology over a very long period of time, and so there is some danger in looking at only one shorter account of this ecophilosophy. But the selection "What is Social Ecology?" is a recent (1984) overview by him which can well serve new explorers of this philosophical territory.

Bookchin begins the selection by repeating an important theme in social ecology, the idea that humans have for centuries been setting themselves over nature by conceiving of it as hostile and arguing that their progress requires that it be tamed and dominated. This image of nature has done considerable mischief to our thought processes, he says, and has led to the creation of social hierarchies, institutions, marketplace economies, and governments that have threatened the very survival of humans on earth, not to mention the earth itself. Social ecology provides an antidote to this mentality by drawing on ecology to help us understand the complexities and principles in nature which are analogous to structures in social communities. Bookchin argues that nature and society form a shared continuum which teaches us something about the proper arrangement of a nonhierarchical society. He proposes a new, ecological vision of society which is "decentralized, stateless, artistic, collective, and sweepingly emancipatory." It is a society which rejects free-market competitiveness and consists of small-scale communities that are compatible with local ecosystems and utilize democratic self-management. For a more complete treatment of Bookchin's ideas, the reader should consult such books as *The Ecology of Freedom* and *The Philosophy of Social Ecology,* both listed in the Selected Bibliography, Part I.

The selections by Jim Dodge, Judith Plant, and Kirkpatrick Sale, prominent leaders of bioregionalism, show how some elements of Bookchin's social vision can be implemented through this philosophy. Dodge makes an effort to define bioregionalism as a theory and show how it leads to certain practical ideas about living. And this connection distinguishes it from some of the other forms of radical ecophilosophy in this anthology: it goes beyond general philosophizing about nature and human society to spell out how one might build human social communities that are compatible with ecological systems. To Dodge the key elements of bioregionalism are the importance it gives to bioregions, its emphasis on responsible anarchism in running bioregional communities, and its spiritual regard for all life. Dodge separates bioregional practice into two categories: bioregional resistance against the continuing destruction of natural systems and renewal of those natural systems through ecosystem rehabilitation, restoration, and enhancement. Kirkpatrick Sale, a founding member of the North American Bioregional Congress and well-known popularizer of bioregionalism, also gives us a sense of some of the processes most central to the bioregional idea. He outlines how bioregionalism compares with the dominant paradigm of industrial and scientific thought in our society, referring us to "four basic determinants of any organized civilization: scale, economy, polity, and society." His book *Dwellers in the Land, the Bioregional Vision* explains in more detail how the bioregional paradigm approaches these determinants and fills out the bioregional vision of an ecologically sound society.

The selection by Judith Plant, a well known bioregionalist and ecofeminist, rounds out Chapter 3 by considering why bioregionalism is incomplete without feminism. Since bioregionalism places so much importance on the idea of home, the values and activities of women become central for understanding how bioregional communities must be structured, she suggests. Feminism emphasizes such things as the value of personal relations and the rejection of oppression; it thereby supplies important perspectives on how domestic life should be revalued in local places. Social ecology is thus integrated with bioregionalism and feminism to produce a new synthesis of ideas about ecological living.

For other useful ideas about the character of bioregionalism, the reader should consult some of the writings of the California bioregionalist Peter Berg mentioned in the Selected Bibliography, Part I.

WHAT IS SOCIAL ECOLOGY?
Murray Bookchin

We are clearly beleaguered by an ecological crisis of monumental proportions—a crisis that visibly stems from the ruthless exploitation and pollution of the planet. We rightly attribute the social sources of this crisis to a competitive marketplace spirit that reduces the entire world of life, including humanity, to merchandisable objects, to mere commodities with price tags that are to be sold for profit and economic expansion. The ideology of this spirit is expressed in the notorious marketplace maxim: "Grow or die!"—a maxim that identifies limitless growth with "progress" and the "mastery of nature" with "civilization." The results of this tide of exploitation and pollution have been grim enough to yield serious forecasts of complete planetary breakdown, a degree of devastation of soil, forests, waterways, and atmosphere that has no precedent in the history of our species.

In this respect, our market-oriented society is unique in contrast with other societies in that it places no limits on growth and egotism. The antisocial principles that "rugged individualism" is the primary motive for social improvement and competition the engine for social progress stand sharply at odds with all past eras that valued selflessness as the authentic trait of human nobility and cooperation as the authentic evidence of social virtue, however much these prized attributes were honored in the breach. Our marketplace society has, in effect, made the worst features of earlier times into its more honored values and exhibited a degree of brutality in the global wars of this century that makes the cruelties of history seem mild by comparison.

In our discussions of modern ecological and social crises, we tend to ignore a more underlying mentality of domination that humans have used for centuries to justify the domination of each other and, by extension, of nature. I refer to an image of the natural world that sees nature itself as "blind," "mute," "cruel," "competitive," and "stingy," a seemingly demonic "realm of necessity" that opposes "man's" striving for freedom and self-realization. Here, "man" seems to confront a hostile "otherness" against which he must oppose his own powers of toil and guile. History is thus presented to us as a Promethean drama in which "man" heroically defies and willfully asserts himself against a brutally hostile and unyielding natural world. Progress is seen as the extrication of humanity from the muck of a mindless, unthinking, and brutish domain or what Jean Paul Sartre so contemptuously called the "slime of history," into the presumably clear light of reason and civilization.

This image of a demonic and hostile nature goes back to the Greek world and even earlier, to the Gilgamesh Epic of Sumerian society. But it reached its high point during the past two centuries, particularly in the Victorian Age, and persists in our thinking today. Ironically, the idea of a "blind," "mute," "cruel," "competitive," and "stingy" nature forms the basis for the very social sciences and humanities that profess to provide us with a civilized alternative to nature's "brutishness" and "law of claw and fang." Even as these disciplines stress the "unbridgeable gulf" between nature and society in the classical tradition of a dualism between the physical and the mental, economics literally defines itself as the study of "scarce resources" (read: "stingy nature") and "unlimited needs," essentially rearing itself on the interconnection between nature and humanity. By the same token, sociology sees itself as the analysis of "man's" ascent from "animality." Psychology, in turn, particularly in its Freudian form, is focused on the control of humanity's unruly "internal nature" through rationality and the imperatives imposed on it by "civilization"—with the hidden agenda of sublimating human powers in the project of controlling "external nature."

Many class theories of social development, particularly Marxian socialism, have been rooted in the belief that the "domination of man by man" emerges from the need to "dominate nature," presumably with the result that once nature is subjugated, humanity will be cleansed of the "slime of history" and enter into a new era of freedom. However warped these self-definitions of our major social and humanistic disciplines may be, they are still embedded in nature and humanity's relationships with the natural world, even as they try to bifurcate the two and impart a unique autonomy to cultural development and social evolution.

Taken as a whole, however, it is difficult to convey the enormous amount of mischief this image of nature has done to our ways of thinking, not to speak of the ideological rationale it has provided for human domination. More so than any single notion in the history of religion and philosophy, the image of a "blind," "mute," "cruel," "competitive, and "stingy" nature has opened a wide, often unbridgeable chasm between the social world and the natural world, and in its more exotic ramifications, between mind and body, subject and object, reason and physicality, technology and "raw materials," indeed, the whole gamut of dualisms that have fragmented not only the world of nature and society but the human psyche and its biological matrix.

From Plato's view of the body as a mere burden encasing an ethereal soul, to René Descartes' harsh split between the God-given rational and the purely mechanistic physical, we are the heirs of a historic dualism: between, firstly, a misconceived nature as the opponent of every human endeavor, whose "domination" must be lifted from the shoulders of humanity (even if human beings themselves are reduced to mere instruments of production to be ruthlessly exploited with a view toward their eventual liberation), and, secondly, a domineering humanity whose goal is to subjugate the natural world, including human nature itself.

Nature, in effect, emerges as an affliction that must be removed by the technology and methods of domination that excuse human domination in the name of "human freedom."

This all-encompassing image of an intractable nature that must be tamed by a rational humanity has given us a domineering form of reason, science, and technology—a fragmentation of humanity into hierarchies, classes, state institutions, gender, and ethnic divisions. It has fostered nationalistic hatreds, imperialistic adventures, and a global philosophy of rule that identifies order with dominance and submission. In slowly corroding every familial, economic, aesthetic, ideological, and cultural tie that provided a sense of place and meaning for the individual in a vital human community, this antinaturalistic mentality has filled the awesome vacuum created by an utterly nihilistic and antisocial development with massive urban entities that are neither cities nor villages, with ubiquitous bureaucracies that impersonally manipulate the lives of faceless masses of atomized human beings, with giant corporate enterprises that spill beyond the boundaries of the world's richest nations to conglomerate on a global scale and determine the material life of the most remote hamlets on the planet, and finally, with highly centralized State institutions and military forces of unbridled power that threaten not only the freedom of the individual but the survival of the species.

The split that clerics and philosophers projected centuries ago in their visions of a soulless nature and a denatured soul has been realized in the form of a disastrous fragmentation of humanity and nature, indeed, in our time, of the human psyche itself. A direct line or logic of events flows almost unrelentingly from a warped image of the natural world to the warped contours of the social world, threatening to bury society in a "slime of history" that is not of nature's making but of man's— specifically, the early hierarchies from which economic classes emerged; the systems of domination, initially of woman by man, that have yielded highly rationalized systems of exploitation; and the vast armies of warriors, priests, monarchs, and bureaucrats who emerged from the simple status groups of tribal society to become the institutionalized tyrants of a market society.

That this authentic jungle of "claw and fang" we call the "free market" is an extension of human competition into nature—an ideological, self-serving fiction that parades under such labels as social Darwinism and sociobiology—hardly requires emphasis any longer. Lions are turned into "Kings of the Beasts" only by human kings, be they imperial monarchs or corporate ones; ants belong to the "lowly" in nature only by virtue of ideologies spawned in temples, palaces, manors, and, in our own time, by subservient apologists of the powers that be. The reality, as we shall see, is different, but a nature conceived as "hierarchical," not to speak of the other "brutish" and very bourgeois traits imputed to it, merely reflects a human condition in which dominance and submission are ends in themselves, which has brought the very existence of our biosphere into question.

Far from being the mere "object" of culture (technology, science, and reason), nature is always with us: as the parody of our self-image, as the cornerstone of the very disciplines which deny it a place in our social and self-formation, even in the protracted infancy of our young which renders the mind open to cultural development and creates those extended parental and sibling ties from which an organized society emerged.

And nature is always with us as the conscience of the transgressions we have visited on the planet—and the terrifying revenge that awaits us for our violation of the ecological balance.

What distinguishes social ecology is that it negates the harsh image we have traditionally created of the natural world and its evolution. And it does so not by dissolving the social into the natural, like sociobiology, or by imparting mystical properties to nature that place it beyond the reach of human comprehension and rational insight. Indeed, as we shall see, social ecology places the human mind, like humanity itself, within a natural context and explores it in terms of its own natural history, so that the sharp cleavages between thought and nature, subject and object, mind and body, and the social and natural are overcome, and the traditional dualisms of Western culture are transcended by an evolutionary interpretation of consciousness with its rich wealth of gradations over the course of natural history.

Social ecology "radicalizes" nature, or more precisely, our understanding of natural phenomena, by questioning the prevailing marketplace image of nature from an ecological standpoint: nature as a constellation of communities that are neither "blind" nor "mute," "cruel" nor "competitive," "stingy" nor "necessitarian" but, freed of all anthropocentric moral trappings, a *participatory* realm of interactive lifeforms whose most outstanding attributes are fecundity, creativity, and directiveness, marked by complementarity that renders the natural world the *grounding* for an ethics of freedom rather than domination.

Seen from an ecological standpoint, life-forms are related in an ecosystem not by the "rivalries" and "competitive" attributes imputed to them by Darwinian orthodoxy, but by the mutualistic attributes emphasized by a growing number of contemporary ecologists—an image pioneered by Peter Kropotkin. Indeed, social ecology challenges the very premises of "fitness" that enter into the Darwinian drama of evolutionary development with its fixation on "survival" rather than differentiation and fecundity. As William Trager has emphasized in his insightful work on symbiosis:

> The conflict in nature between different kinds of organisms has been popularly expressed in phrases like the "struggle for existence" and the

"survival of the fittest." Yet few people realized that mutual cooperation between organisms—symbiosis—is just as important, and that the "fittest" may be the one that helps another to survive.[1]

It is tempting to go beyond this pithy and highly illuminating judgement to explore an ecological notion of natural evolution based on the development of *ecosystems,* not merely individual species. This is a concept of evolution as the dialectical development of ever-variegated, complex, and increasingly fecund *contexts* of plant-animal communities as distinguished from the traditional notion of biological evolution based on the atomistic development of single life-forms, a characteristically entrepreneurial concept of the isolated "individual," be it animal, plant, or bourgeois—a creature which fends for itself and either "survives" or "perishes" in a marketplace "jungle." As ecosystems become more complex and open a greater variety of evolutionary pathways, due to their own richness of diversity and increasingly flexible forms of organic life, it is not only the environment that "chooses" what "species" are "fit" to survive but species themselves, in mutualistic complexes as well as singly, that introduce a dim element of "choice"—by no means "intersubjective" or "willful" in the *human* meaning of these terms.

Concomitantly, these ensembles of species alter the environment of which they are part and exercise an increasingly *active* role in their own evolution. Life, in this *ecological* conception of evolution, ceases to be the passive *tabula rasa* on which eternal forces which we loosely call "the environment" inscribe the destiny of "a species," an atomistic term that is meaningless outside the context of an ecosystem within which a life-form is truly definable with respect to other species.[2]

Life is active, interactive, procreative, relational, and contextual. It is not a passive lump of "stuff," a form of metabolic "matter" that awaits the action of "forces" external to it and is mechanically "shaped" by them. Ever striving and always producing new life-forms, there is a sense in which life is self-directive in its own evolutionary development, not passively reactive to an inorganic or organic world that impinges upon it from outside and "determines" its destiny in isolation from the ecosystems which it constitutes and of which it is a part.

And this much is clear in social ecology: our studies of "food webs" (a not quite satisfactory term for describing the interactivity that occurs in an ecosystem or, more properly, an ecological *community*) demonstrate that the complexity of biotic interrelationships, their diversity and intricacy, is a crucial factor in assessing an ecosystem's stability. In contrast to biotically complex temperate zones, relatively simple desert and arctic ecosystems are very fragile and break down easily with the loss or numerical decline of only a few species. The thrust of biotic evolution over great eras of organic evolution has been toward the increasing diversification of species and their interlocking into highly complex, basically mutualistic relationships, without which the widespread colonization of the planet by life would have been impossible.

Unity in diversity (a concept deeply rooted in the Western philosophical tradition) is not only the determinant of an ecosystem's stability; it is the source of an ecosystem's fecundity, of its innovativeness, of its evolutionary potential to create newer, still more complex life-forms and biotic interrelationships, even in the most inhospitable areas of the planet. Ecologists have not sufficiently stressed the fact that a multiplicity of life-forms and organic interrelationships in a biotic community opens new evolutionary pathways of development, a greater variety of evolutionary interactions, variations, and degrees of flexibility in the capacity to evolve, and is hence crucial not only in the community's stability but also in its innovativeness in the natural history of life.

The ecological principle of unity in diversity grades into a richly mediated social principle, hence my use of the term *social* ecology.[3] Society, in turn, attains its "truth," its self-actualization, in the form of richly articulated, mutualistic networks of people based on community, roundedness of personality, diversity of stimuli and activities, an increasing wealth of experience, and a variety of tasks. Is this grading of ecosystem diversity into social diversity, based on humanly scaled, decentralized communities, merely analogic reasoning?

My answer would be that it is not a superficial analogy but a deep-seated continuity between nature and society that social ecology recovers from traditional nature philosophy without its archaic dross of cosmic hierarchies, static absolutes, and cycles. In the case of social ecology, it is not in the *particulars* of differentiation that plant-animal communities are ecologically united with human communities; rather, it is the *logic* of differentiation that makes it possible to relate the mediations of nature and society into a continuum.

What makes unity in diversity in nature more than a suggestive ecological metaphor for unity in diversity in society is the underlying fact of wholeness. By wholeness I do not mean any finality of closure in a development, any "totality" that leads to a terminal "reconciliation" of all "Being" in a complete identity of subject and object or a reality in which no further development is possible or meaningful. Rather, I mean varying degrees of the actualization of potentialities, the organic unfolding of the wealth of particularities that are latent in the as-yet-undeveloped potentiality. This potentiality can be a newly planted seed, a newly born infant, a newly formed community, a newly emerging society—yet, given their radically different specificity, they are all united by a processual reality, a shared "metabolism" of development, a unified catalysis of growth as distinguished from mere "change" that provides us with the most insightful way of *understanding* them we can possibly achieve. Wholeness is literally the unity that finally gives order to the particularity of each of these phenomena; it is what has emerged from the process, what integrates the particularities into a unified form, what renders the unity an operable reality and a "being" in the literal sense of the term—an order as the actualized *unity* of its diversity from the flowing and emergent process that yields its self-realization, the fixing of its directiveness into a clearly contoured form, and the creation in a dim sense of a "self" that is identifiable with respect to the "others" with which it interacts. Wholeness is the *relative* completion of a phenomenon's potentiality, the fulfillment of latent possibility as such, all its concrete manifestations aside, to become more than the realm of *mere* possibility and attain the "truth" or fulfilled reality of possibility. To think this way—in terms of potentiality, process, mediation, and wholeness—is to reach into the most underlying nature of things, just as to know the biography of a human being and the history of a society is to know them in their authentic reality and depth.

The natural world is no less encompassed by this processual dialectic and developmental ecology than the social, although in ways that do not involve will, degrees of choice, values, ethical goals, and the like. Life itself, as distinguished from the nonliving, however, emerges from the inorganic latent with all the potentialities and particularities it has immanently produced from the logic of its own nascent forms of self-organization. Obviously, so does society as distinguished from biology, humanity as distinguished from animality, and individuality as distinguished from humanity in the generic sense of the word. But these distinctions are not absolutes. They are the unique and closely interrelated phases of a shared continuum, of a process that is united precisely by its own differentiations just as the phases through which an embryo develops are both distinct from and incorporated into its complete gestation and its organic specificity.

This continuum is not simply a philosophical construct. It is an earthy anthropological fact which lives with us daily as surely as it explains the emergence of humanity out of mere animality. Individual socialization is the highly nuanced "biography" of that development in everyday life and in everyone as surely as the anthropological socialization of our species is part of its history. I refer to the biological basis of all human socialization: the protracted infancy of the human child that renders its cultural development possible, in contrast to the rapid growth of nonhuman animals, a rate of growth that quickly forecloses their ability to form a culture and develop sibling affinities of a lasting nature; the instinctual maternal drives that extend feelings of care, sharing, intimate consociation, and finally love and a sense of responsibility for one's own kin into the institutional forms we call "society"; and the sexual division of labor, age-ranking, and kin-relationships which, however culturally conditioned and even mythic in some cases, formed and still inform so much of social institutionalization today. These formative elements of society rest on biological facts and, placed in the contextual analysis I have argued for, require ecological analysis.

In emphasizing the nature-society continuum with all its gradations and "mediations," I do not wish to leave the impression that the known ways and forms in which society emerged from nature and still embodies the natural world in a shared process of cumulative growth follow a logic that is "inexorable" or "preordained" by a telos that mystically guides the unfolding by a supranatural and suprasocial process. Potentiality is not necessity; the logic of a process is not a form of inexorable "law"; the truth of a development is what is *implicit* in any unfolding and defined by the extent to which it achieves stability, variety, fecundity, and enlarges the "realm of freedom," however dimly freedom is conceived.

No specific "stage" of a process necessarily yields a still later one or is "presupposed" by it—but certain obvious conditions, however varied, blurred, or even idiosyncratic, form the determining ground for still other conditions that can be expected to emerge. Freedom and, ultimately, a degree of subjectivity that make choice and will possible along rational lines may be desiderata that the natural world renders possible and in a "self"-directive way plays an active role in achieving. But in no sense are these desiderata predetermined certainties that must unfold, nor is any such unfolding spared the very real possibility that it will become entirely regressive or remain unfulfilled and incomplete. That the *potentiality* for freedom and consciousness exists in nature and society; that nature and society are not merely "passive" in a development toward freedom and consciousness, a passivity that would make the very notion of potentiality mystical just as the notion of "necessity" would make it meaningless by definition; that natural and social history bear existential witness to the potentiality and processes that form subjectivity and bring consciousness more visibly on the horizon in the very natural history of mind—all constitute no guarantee that these latent desiderata are certainties or lend themselves to systematic elucidation and teleological explanations in any traditional philosophical sense.

Our survey of organic and social experience may stir us to interpret a development we know to have occurred as reason to presuppose that potentiality, wholeness, and *graded* evolution are realities after all, no less real than our own existence and personal histories, but presuppositions they remain. Indeed, no outlook in philosophy can ever exist that is free of presuppositions, any more than speculation can exist that is free of some stimulus by the objective world. The only truth about "first philosophy," from Greek times onward, is that what is "first" in any philosophical outlook are the presuppositions it adopts, the background of unformulated experience from which these presuppositions emerge, and the intuition of a coherence that must be validated by reality as well as speculative reason.

One of the most provocative of the graded continuities between nature and society is the nonhierarchical relationships that exist in an ecosystem, and the extent to which they provide a grounding for a nonhierarchical society.[4] It is meaningless to speak of hierarchy in an ecosystem and in the succession of ecosystems which, in contrast to a monadic species-oriented development, form the true story of natural evolution. There is no "king of the beasts" and no "lowly serf"—presumably, the lion and the ant—in ecosystem relationships. Such terms, including words like "cruel nature," "fallen nature," "domineering nature," and even "mutualistic nature" (I prefer to use the word "complementary" here) are projections of our own social relationships into the natural world. Ants are as important as lions and eagles in ecosystems; indeed, their recycling of organic materials gives them a considerable "eminence" in the maintenance of the stability and integrity of an area.

As to accounts of "dominance-submission" relationships between individuals such as "alpha" and "beta" males, utterly asymmetrical relationships tend to be grouped under words like "hierarchy" that are more analogic, often more metaphoric, than real. It becomes absurd, I think, to say that the "dominance" of a "queen bee," who in no way knows that she is a "queen" and whose sole function in a beehive is reproductive, is in any way equatable with an "alpha" male baboon, whose "status" tends to suffer grave diminution when the baboon troop moves from the plains to the forest. By the same token, it is absurd to equate "patriarchal harems" among red deer with "matriarchal" elephant herds, which simply expel bulls when they reach puberty and in no sense "dominate" them. One could go through a whole range of asymmetrical relationships to show that, even among our closest primate relatives, which include the utterly "pacific" orangutans as well as the seemingly "aggressive" chimpanzees, words like "dominance" and "submission" mean very different relationships depending upon the species one singles out and the circumstances under which they live.

I cannot emphasize too strongly that hierarchy in society is an *institutional* phenomenon, not a biological one. It is a product of organized, carefully crafted power relationships, not a product of the "morality of the gene," to use E. O. Wilson's particularly obtuse phrase in his *Sociobiology*. Only institutions, formed by long periods of human history and sustained by well-organized bureaucracies and military forces, could have placed absolute rule in the hands of mental defects like Nicholas II of Russia and Louis XVI of France. We can find nothing even remotely comparable to such institutionalized systems of command and obedience in other species, much less in ecosystems. It verges on the absurd to draw fast-and-loose comparisons between the "division of labor" (another anthropocentric phrase when placed in an ecological context) in a beehive, whose main function is reproducing bees, not making honey for breakfast tables, and human society, with its highly contrived State forms and organized bureaucracies.

What renders social ecology so important in comparing ecosystems to societies is that it decisively challenges the very function of hierarchy as a way of *ordering* reality, of dealing with differentiation and variation—with "otherness" as such. Social ecology ruptures the association of order with hierarchy. It poses the question of whether we can experience the "other," not hierarchically on a "scale of one to ten" with a continual emphasis on "inferior" and "superior," but ecologically, as variety that enhances the unity of phenomena, enriches wholeness, and more closely resembles a food-web than a pyramid. That hierarchy exists today as an even more fundamental problem than social classes, that domination exists today as an even more fundamental problem than economic exploitation, can be attested to by every conscious feminist, who can justly claim that long before man began to exploit man through the formation of social classes, he began to dominate woman in patriarchal and hierarchical relationships.

We would do well to remember that the abolition of classes, exploitation, and even the State is no guarantee whatever that people will cease to be ranked hierarchically and dominated according to age, gender, race, physical qualities, and often quite frivolous and irrational categories, unless liberation focuses as much on hierarchy and domination as it does on classes and exploitation. This is the point where socialism, in my view, must extend itself into a broader libertarian tradition that reaches back into the tribal or band-type communities ancestral to what we so smugly call "civilization," a tradition, indeed an abiding human impulse, that has surged to the surface of society in every revolutionary period, only to be brutally contained by those purely societal forms called "hierarchies."

Social ecology raises all of these issues in a fundamentally new light, and establishes entirely new ways of resolving them. I have tried to show that nature is always present in the human condition, and in the very ideological constructions that deny its presence in societal relationships. The notion of dominating nature literally *defines* all our social disciplines, including socialism and psychoanalysis. It is the apologia *par excellence* for the domination of human by human. Until that apologia is removed from our sensibilities in the rearing of the young, the first step in socialization as such, and replaced by an ecological sensibility that sees "otherness" in terms of complementarity rather than rivalry, we will never achieve human emancipation. Nature lives in us ontogenetically as different layers of experience which analytic rationalism often conceals from us: in the sensitivity of our cells, the remarkable autonomy of our organ systems, our so-called layered brain which experiences the world in different ways and attests to different worlds, which analytic reason, left to its own imperialistic claims, tends to close to us—indeed, in the *natural history* of the nervous system and mind, which bypasses the chasm between mind and body, or subjectivity and objectivity, with an organic continuum in which body grades into mind and objectivity into subjectivity. Herein lies the most compelling refutation of the traditional dualism in religion, philosophy, and sensibility that gave ideological credence to the myth of a "dominating" nature, borne by the suffering and brutalization of a dominated humanity.

Moreover, this natural history of the nervous system and mind is a cumulative one, not merely a successive one—a history whose past lies in our everyday present. It is not for nothing that one of America's greatest physiologists, Walter B Cannon, titled his great work on homeostasis *The Widsom of the Body*. Running through our entire experiential apparatus and organizing experience for us are not only the categories of Kant's first *Critique* and Hegel's *Logic,* but also the *natural history of sensibility* as it exists in us hormonally, from our undifferentiated nerve networks to the hemispheres of our brains. We metabolize with nature in production in such a way that the materials with which we work and the tools we use to work on them enter reciprocally into the technological imagination we form and the social matrix in which our technologies exist. Nor can we ever permit ourselves to forget, all our overriding ideologies of class, economic interest, and the like notwithstanding, that we socialize with each other not only as producers and property owners, but also as children and parents, young and old, female and male, with out bodies as well as our minds, and according to graded and varied impulses that are as archaic as they are fairly recent in the natural evolution of sensibility.

Hence, to become conscious of this vast ensemble of natural history as it enters into our very beings, to see its place in the graded development of our social history, to recognize that we must develop new sensibilities, technologies, institutions, and forms of experiencing that give expression to this wealth of our inner development and the complexity of our biosocial apparatus is to go along with a deeper grain of evolution and dialectic than is afforded to us by the "epistemological" and "linguistic" turns of recent philosophy.[5] On this score, just as I would argue that science *is* the history of science, not merely its latest "stage," and technology *is* the history of technology, not merely its latest designs, so reason *is* the history of reason, not merely its present analytic and communicative dimensions. Social history includes natural history as a graded dialectic that is united not only in a continuum by a shared logic of differentiation and complementarity; it includes natural history in the socialization process itself, in the natural as well as the social history of experience, in the imperatives of a harmonized relationship between humanity and nature that presuppose new ecotechnologies and ecocommunities, and in the desiderata opened by a decentralized society based on the values of complementarity and community.

The ideas I have advanced to far take their point of departure from a radically different image of nature than the prevailing western one, in which philosophical dualism, economics, sociology, psychology, and even socialism have their roots. As a social ecologist, I see nature as essentially creative, directive, mutualistic, fecund, and marked by complementarity, not "mute," "blind," "cruel," "stingy," or "necessitarian." This shift in focus from a marketplace to an ecological image of nature obliges me to challenge the time-honored notion that the domination of human by human is necessary in order to "dominate nature." In emphasizing how meaningless this rationale for hierarchy and domination is, I conclude—with considerable historical justification, which our own era amply illuminates with its deployment of technology primarily for purposes of social control—that the idea of dominating nature stems from human domination, initially in hierarchical forms as feminists so clearly understand, and later in class and statist forms.

Accordingly, my ecological image of nature leads me to drastically redefine my conception of economics, sociology, psychology, and even socialism, which, ironically, advance a shared dualistic gospel of a radical separation of society from nature even as they rest on a militant imperative to "subdue" nature, be it as "scarce resources," the realm of "animality," "internal nature," or "external nature." Hence, I have tried to re-vision history not only as an account of power over human beings that by far outweighs any attempt to gain power over things, but also as power ramified into centralized states and urban environments, a technology, science, and rationality of social control, and a message of "liberation" that conceals the most awesome features of domination, notably, the traditional socialist orthodoxies of the last century.

At the juncture where nature is conceived either as a ruthless, competitive marketplace or a creative, fecund biotic community, two radically divergent pathways of thought and sensibility emerge, following contrasting directions and conceptions of the human future. One ends in a totalitarian and antinaturalistic terminus for society: centralized, statist, technocratic, corporate, and sweepingly repressive. The other ends in a libertarian and ecological beginning for society: decentralized, stateless, artistic, collective, and sweepingly emancipatory. These are not tendentious words. It is by no means certain that western humanity, currently swept up in a counterrevolution of authoritarian values and adaptive impulses, would regard a libertarian vision as less pejorative than a totalitarian one. Whether or not my own words seem tendentious, the full logic of my view should be seen: the view we hold of the natural world profoundly shapes the image we develop of the social worlds, even as we assert the "supremacy" and "autonomy" of culture over nature.

In what sense does social ecology view nature as a grounding for an ethics of freedom? If the story of natural evolution is not understandable in Locke's atomistic account of a particular species' evolution, if that story is basically an account of ecosystem evolution toward ever more complex and flexible evolutionary pathways, then natural history itself cannot be seen simply as "necessitarian," "governed" by "inexorable laws" and imperatives. Every organism is in some sense "willful," insofar as it seeks to preserve itself, to maintain its identity, to resist a kind of biological entropy that threatens its integrity and complexity. However dimly, every organism transforms the essential attributes of self-maintenance that earn it the status of a distinct form of life into a capacity to choose alternatives that favor its survival and well-being—not merely to react to stimuli as a purely physico-chemical ensemble.

This dim, germinal freedom is heightened by the growing wealth of ecological complexity that confronts evolving life in synchronicity with evolving ecosystems. The elaboration of possibilities that comes with the elaboration of diversity and the growing multitude of alternatives confronting species development opens newer and more fecund pathways for organic development. Life is not passive in the face of these possibilities for its evolution. It drives toward them actively in a shared process of mutual stimulation between organisms and their environment (including the living and non-living environment they create) as surely as it also actively creates and colonizes the niches that cradle a vast diversity of life-forms in our richly elaborated biosphere. This image of active, indeed striving, life requires no Hegelian "Spirit" or Heraklitean *Logos* to explain it. Activity and striving are presupposed in our very definition of metabolism. In fact, metabolic activity is coextensive with the notion of activity as such and imparts an identity, indeed, a rudimentary "self," to every organism. Diversity and complexity, indeed, the notion of evolution as a diversifying history, superadd the dimension of variegated alternatives and pathways to the simple fact of choice—and, with choice, the rudimentary fact of *freedom*. For freedom, in its most germinal form, is also a function of diversity and complexity, of a "realm of necessity" that is diminished by a growing and expanding multitude of alternatives, of a widening horizon of evolutionary possibilities, which life in its ever-richer forms both creates and in its own way "pursues," until consciousness, the gift of nature as well as society to humanity, renders this pursuit willful, self-reflexive, and consciously creative.

Here, in this ecological concept of natural evolution, lies a hidden message of freedom based on the "inwardness of life," to use Hans Jonas's excellent expression, and the ever greater diversification produced by natural evolution. Ecology is united with society in new terms that reveal moral tension in natural history, just as Marx's simplistic image of the "savage" who "wrestles with nature" reveals a moral tension in social history.

We must beware of being prejudiced by our own fear of prejudice. Organismic philosophies can surely yield totalitarian, hierarchical, and eco-fascistic results. We have good reason to be concerned over so-called nature philosophies that give us the notion of *Blut und Boden* and "dialectical materialism," which provide the ideological justification for the horrors of Nazism and Stalinism. We have good reason to be concerned over a mysticism that yields social quietism at best and the aggressive activism of reborn Christianity and certain Asian gurus at worst. We have even better reason to be concerned over the eco-fascism of Garrett Hardin's "lifeboat ethic" with its emphasis on scarce resources and the so-called tragedy of the commons, an ethic which services genocidal theories of imperialism and a global disregard for human misery. So, too, sociobiology, which roots all the savage features of "civilization" in our genetic constitution. Social ecology offers the coordinates for an entirely different pathway in exploring our relationship to the natural world—one that accepts neither genetic and scientistic theories of "natural necessity" at one extreme, nor a romantic and mystical zealotry that reduces the rich variety of reality and evolution to a cosmic "oneness" and energetics at the other extreme. For in both cases, it is not only our vision of the world and the unity of nature and society that suffers, but the "natural history" of freedom and the basis for an objective ethics of liberation as well.

We cannot avoid the use of conventional reason, present-day modes of science, and modern technology. They, too, have their place in the future of humanity and humanity's metabolism with the natural world. But we can establish new *contexts* in which these modes of rationality, science, and technology have their proper place—an *ecological* context that does not deny other, more qualitative modes of knowing and producing which are participatory and emancipatory. We can also foster a new sensibility toward otherness that, *in a nonhierarchical society,* is based on complementarity rather than rivalry, and new communities that, scaled to human dimensions, are tailored to the ecosystem in which they are located and open a new, decentralized, self-managed public realm for new forms of selfhood as well as directly democratic forms of social management.

November 12, 1984

Notes

1. William Trager, *Symbiosis,* New York: Van Nostrand Reinhold Co., 1970, vii.
2. The traditional emphasis on an "active" environment that determines the "survival" of a passive species, altered in a cosmic game of chance by random mutations, is perhaps another reason why the term "environmentalism," as distinguished from social ecology, is a very unsatisfactory expression these days.
3. My use of the word "social" cannot be emphasized too strongly. Words like

"human," "deep," and "cultural," while very valuable as general terms, do not explicitly pinpoint the extent to which our image of nature is formed by the kind of society in which we live and by the abiding natural basis of all social life. The evolution of society out of nature and the ongoing interaction between the two tend to be lost in words that do not tell us enough about the vital association between nature and society and about the importance of defining such disciplines as economics, psychology, and sociology in natural as well as social terms. Recent uses of "social ecology" to advance a rather superficial account of social life in fairly conventional ecological terms are particularly deplorable. Books like *Habits of the Heart* which glibly pick up the term serve to coopt a powerful expression for rather banal ends and tend to compromise efforts to deepen our understanding of nature and society as interactive rather than opposed domains.

4. Claims of hierarchy as a ubiquitous natural fact cannot be ignored by still further widening the chasm between nature and society—or "natural necessity" and "cultural freedom" as it is more elegantly worded. Justifying social hierarchy in terms of natural hierarchy is one of the most persistent assaults on an egalitarian social future that religion and philosophy have made over the ages. It has surfaced recently in sociobiology and reinforced the antinaturalistic stance that permeates so many liberatory ideologies in the modern era. To say that culture is precisely the "emancipation of man from nature" is to revert to Sartre's "slime of history" notion of the natural world that not only separates society from nature but mind from body and subjectivity from objectivity.

5. Our disastrously one-sided and rationalized "civilization" has boxed this wealth of inner development and complexity away, relegating it to preindustrial lifeways that basically shaped our evolution up to a century or two ago. From a sensory viewpoint, we live atrophied, indeed, starved lives compared to hunters and food cultivators, whose capacity to experience reality, even in a largely cultural sense, by far overshadows our own. The twentieth century alone bears witness to an appalling dulling of our "sixth senses" as well as to our folk creativity and craft creativity. We have never experienced so little so loudly, so brashly, so trivially, so thinly, so neurotically. For a comparison of the "world of experience we have lost" (to reword Peter Laslett's title), read the excellent personal accounts of so-called Bushmen, or San people, the Ituri Forest pygmies, and the works of Paul Shepard on food-gatherers and hunters—not simply as records of their lifeways but of their epistemologies.

LIVING BY LIFE: SOME BIOREGIONAL THEORY AND PRACTICE
Jim Dodge

I want to make it clear from the outset that I'm not all that sure what bioregionalism is. To my understanding, bioregionalism is an idea still in loose and amorphous formulation, and presently is more hopeful declaration than actual practice. In fact, "idea" may be too generous: bioregionalism is more properly a notion, which is variously defined as a general idea, a belief, an opinion, an intuition, an inclination, an urge. Furthermore, as I think will prove apparent, bioregionalism is hardly a new notion; it has been the animating cultural principle through 99 percent of human history, and is at least as old as consciousness. Thus, no doubt, the urge.

My purpose here is not really to define bioregionalism—that will take care of itself in the course of things—but to mention some of the elements that I see composing the notion, and some possibilities for practice. I speak with no special privilege on the matter other than my longstanding and fairly studious regard for the subject, a regard enriched by my teachers and numerous bioregional friends. My only true qualification is that I'm fool enough to try.

Bioregionalism" is from the Greek *bios* (life) and the French *region* (region), itself from the Latin *regia* (territory), and earlier, *regere* (to rule or govern). Etymologically, then, bioregionalism means life territory, place of life, or perhaps by reckless extension, government by life. If you can't imagine that government by life would be at least 40 billion times better than government by the Reagan administration, or Mobil Oil, or any other distant powerful monolith, then your heart is probably no bigger than a prune pit and you won't have much sympathy for what follows.

A central element of bioregionalism—and one that distinguishes it from similar politics of place—is the importance given to natural systems, both as the source of physical nutrition and as the body of metaphors from which our spirits draw sustenance. A natural system is a community of interdependent life, a mutual biological integration on the order of an ecosystem, for example. What constitutes this community is uncertain beyond the obvious—that it includes all interacting life forms, from the tiniest fleck of algae to human beings, as well as their biological processes. To this bare minimum, already impenetrably complex, bioregionalism adds the influences of cultural behavior, such as subsistence techniques and ceremonies. Many people further insist—sensibly, I think—that this community/ecosystem must also include the planetary processes and the larger figures of regulation: solar income, magnetism, gravity, and so forth. Bioregionalism is simply biological realism; in natural systems we find the physical truth of our being, the real obvious stuff like the need for oxygen as well as the more subtle need for moonlight, and perhaps other truths beyond those. Not surprisingly, then, bioregionalism holds that the health of natural systems is directly connected to our own physical/psychic health as individuals and as a species, and for that reason natural systems and their informing integrations deserve, if not utter veneration, at least our clearest attention and deepest respect. No matter how great our laws, technologies, or armies, we can't make the sun rise every morning nor the rain dance on the goldenback ferns.

To understand natural systems is to begin an understanding of the self, its common and particular essences—literal self-interest in its barest terms. "As above, so below," according to the old-tradition alchemists; natural systems as models of consciousness. When we destroy a river, we increase our thirst, ruin the beauty of free-flowing water, forsake the meat and spirit of the salmon, and lose a little bit of our souls.

Unfortunately, human society has also developed technologies that make it possible to lose big chunks all at once. If we make just one serious mistake with nuclear energy, for instance, our grandchildren may be born with bones like overcooked spaghetti, or torn apart by mutant rats. Global nuclear war is suicide: the "losers" die instantly; the "winners" inherit slow radiation death and twisted chromosomes. By any sensible measure of self-interest, by any regard for life, nuclear war is abhorrent, unthinkable, and loathsomely stupid, and yet the United States and other nations spend billions to provide that possibility. It is the same mentality that pooh-poohs the growing concentration of poisons in the biosphere. It's like the farmer who was showing off his prize mule to a stranger one day when the mule suddenly fell over sideways and died. The farmer looked at the body in bewildered disbelief: "Damn," he said, "I've had this mule for 27 years and it's the first time he's ever done this." To which the stranger, being a biological realist, undoubtedly replied, "No shit."

While I find an amazing depth of agreement among bioregionalists on what constitutes *bios,* and on what general responsibilities attend our place in the skein of things, there is some disagreement—friendly but passionate—on what actually constitutes a distinct biological region (as opposed to arbitrary entities, like states and counties, where boundaries are established without the dimmest ecological perception, and therefore make for cultural incoherence and piecemeal environmental management). Since the very gut of bioregional thought is the integrity of natural systems and culture, with the function of culture being the mediation of the self and the ecosystem, one might think "bioregion" would be fairly tightly defined. But I think it must be kept in mind that, to paraphrase Poe and Jack Spicer, we're dealing with the grand concord of what does not stoop to definition. There are, however, a number of ideas floating around regarding the biological criteria for a region. I'll mention some of them below, limiting the examples to Northern California.

One criterion for determining a biological region is biotic shift, a percentage change in plant/animal species composition from one place to another—that is, if 15 to 25 percent of the species where I live are different from those where you live, we occupy different biological regions. We probably also experience different climates and walk on different soils, since those differences are reflected in species composition. Nearly everyone I've talked with agrees that biotic shift is a fairly slick and accurate way to make bioregional distinctions; the argument is over the percentage, which invariably seems arbitrary. Since the change in biotic composition is usually gradual, the biotic shift criterion permits vague and permeable boundaries between regions, which I personally favor. The idea, after all, is not to replace one set of lines with another, but simply to recognize inherent biological integrities for the purpose of sensible planning and management.

Another way to biologically consider regions is by watershed. This method is generally straightforward, since drainages are clearly apparent on topographical maps. Watershed is usually taken to mean river drainage, so if you live on Cottonwood Creek you are part of the Sacramento River drainage. The problem with watersheds as bioregional criteria is that if you live in San Francisco you are also part of the Sacramento (and San Joaquin) River drainage, and that's a long way from Cottonwood Creek. Since any long drainage presents similar problems, most people who advance the watershed criterion make intradrainage distinctions (in the case of the Sacramento: headwaters, Central Valley, west slope Sierra, east slope Coast Range, and delta/bay). The west slope of the Coast Range, with its short-running rivers and strong Pacific influence, is often considered as a whole biological area, at least from the Gualala River to the Mattole River or, depending on who you're talking to, from the Russian River to the Eel River, though they aren't strictly west slope Coast Range rivers. The Klamath, Smith, and Trinity drainages are often considered a single drainage system, with the arguable inclusion of the Chetco and the Rogue.

A similar method of bioregional distinction is based upon land form. Roughly, Northern California breaks down into the Sierra, the Coast Range, the Central Valley, the Klamath Range, the southern part of the Cascade Range, and the Modoc Plateau. Considering the relationship between topography and water, it is not surprising that land form distinctions closely follow watersheds.

A different criterion for making bioregional distinctions is, awkwardly put, cultural/phenomenological: you are where you perceive you are; your turf is what you think it is, individually and collectively. Although the human sense of territory is deeply evolved and cultural/perceptual behavior certainly influences the sense of place, this view seems to me a bit anthropocentric. And though it is difficult *not* to view things in terms of human experience and values, it does seem wise to remember that human perception is notoriously prey to distortion and the strange delights of perversity. Our species hasn't done too well lately working essentially from this view; because we're ecological dominants doesn't necessarily mean we're ecological determinants. (In fairness, I should note that many friends think I'm unduly cranky on this subject.)

One of the more provocative ideas to delineate bioregions is in terms of "spirit places" or psyche-tuning power-presences, such as Mount Shasta and the Pacific Ocean. By this criterion, a bioregion is defined by the predominate physical influence where you live. You have to live in its presence long enough to truly feel its force within you and that it's not mere descriptive geography.

Also provocative is the notion that bioregion is a vertical phenomenon having more to do with elevation than horizontal deployment—thus a distinction between hill people and flatlanders, which in Northern California also tends to mean country and city. A person living at 2000 feet in the Coast Range would have more in cultural common with a Sierra dweller at a similar altitude than with someone at sea level 20 miles away.

To briefly recapitulate, the criteria most often advanced for making bioregional distinctions are biotic shift, watershed, land form, cultural/phenomenological, spirit presences, and elevation. Taken together, as I think they should be, they give us a strong sense of where we're at and the life that enmeshes our own. Nobody I know is pushing for a quick definition anyway. Bioregionalism, whatever it is, occupies that point in development (more properly, renewal) where definition is unnecessary and perhaps dangerous. Better now to let definitions emerge from practice than impose them dogmatically from the git-go.

A second element of bioregionalism is anarchy. I hesitate using that fine word because it's been so distorted by reactionary shitheads to scare people that its connotative associations have become bloody chaos and fiends amok, rather than political decentralization, self-determination, and a commitment to social equity. Anarchy doesn't mean out of control; it means out of *their* control. Anarchy is based upon a sense of interdependent self-reliance, the conviction that we as a community, or a tight, small-scale federation of communities, can mind our own business, and can make decisions regarding our individual and communal lives and gladly accept the responsibilities and consequences of those decisions. Further, by consolidating decision making at a local, face-to-face level without having to constantly push information through insane bureaucratic hierarchies, we can act more quickly in relation to natural systems and, since we live there, hopefully with more knowledge and care.

The United States is simply too large and complex to be responsibly

governed by a decision-making body of perhaps 1000 people representing 220,000,000 Americans and a large chunk of the biosphere, especially when those 1000 decision makers can only survive by compromise and generally are forced to front for heavy economic interests
(media campaigns for national office are expensive). A government
where one person represents the interests of 220,000 others is absurd,
considering that not all the people voted for the winning representative
(or even voted) and especially considering that most of those 220,000
people are capable of representing themselves. I think people do much
better, express their deeper qualities, when their actions matter. Obviously one way to make government more meaningful and responsible is to
involve people directly day by day, in the processes of decision, which
only seems possible if we reduce the scale of government. A bioregion
seems about the right size: say close to a small state, or along the lines of
the Swiss canton system or American Indian tribes.

If nothing else, bioregional government—which theoretically would
express the biological and cultural realities of people-in-place—would
promote the diversity of biosocial experimentation; and in diversity is
stability. The present system of national government seems about to
collapse on the weight of its own emptiness. Our economy is dissolving
like wet sugar. Violence is epidemic. The quality of our workmanship—
always the hallmark of a proud people—has deteriorated so badly that
we're ashamed to classify our products as durable goods. Our minds
have been homogenized by television, which keeps our egos in perpetual
infancy while substituting them for a sense of the self. Our information
comes from progressively fewer sources, none of them notably reliable.
We spend more time posturing than we do getting it on. In short,
American culture has become increasingly gutless and barren in our
lifetimes, and the political system little more than a cover for an economics that ravages the planet and its people for the financial gain of
very few. It seems almost a social obligation to explore alternatives. Our
much-heralded standard of living hasn't done much for the quality of our
daily lives; the glut of commodities, endlessly hurled at us out of the vast
commodity spectacle, is just more shit on the windshield.

I don't want to imply that bioregionalism is the latest sectarian addition to the American Left, which historically has been more concerned
with doctrinal purity and shafting each other than with effective practice.
It's not a question of working within the system or outside the system,
but simply of working, *somewhere,* to pull if off. And as I mentioned at
the beginning, I'm not so sure bioregionalism even has a doctrine to be
pure about—it's more a sense of direction (uphill, it seems) than the usual
leftist highway to Utopia . . . or Ecotopia for that matter.

Just for the record, and to give some credence to the diversity of
thought informing bioregionalism, I want to note some of the spirits I see
at work in the early formulation of the notion: pantheists, Wobs, Re-

formed Marxists (that is, those who see the sun as the means of production), Diggers, liberterreans, Kropotkinites (mutual aid and coevolution), animists, alchemists (especially the old school), lefty Buddhists, Situationists (consummate analysts of the commodity spectacle), syndicalists, Provos, born-again Taoists, general outlaws, and others drawn to the decentralist banner by raw empathy.

A third element composing the bioregional notion is spirit. Since I can't claim any spiritual wisdom, and must admit to being virtually ignorant on the subject, I'm reluctant to offer more than the most tentative perceptions. What I think most bioregionalists hold in spiritual common is a profound regard for life—all life, not just white Americans, or humankind entire, but frogs, roses, mayflies, coyotes, lichens: all of it: the gopher snake and the gopher. For instance, we don't want to save the whales for the sweetsie-poo, lily-romantic reasons attributed to us by those who profit from their slaughter; we don't want them saved merely because they are magnificent creatures, so awesome that when you see one close from an open boat your heart roars; we want to save them for the most selfish of reasons; without them we are diminished.

In the bioregional spirit view we're all one creation, and it may seem almost simple-minded to add that there is a connection—even a necessary unity—between the natural world and the human mind (which may be just a fancy way of saying there is a connection between life and existence). Different people and groups have their own paths and practices and may describe this connection differently—profound, amusing, ineluctable, mysterious—but they all acknowledge the importance of the connection. The connection is archaic, primitive, and so obvious that it hasn't received much attention since the rise of Christian dominion and fossil-fuel industrialism. If it is a quality of archaic thought to dispute the culturally enforced dichotomy between the spiritual and the practical, I decidedly prefer the archaic view. What could possibly be of more *practical* concern than our spiritual well-being as individuals, as a species, and as members of a larger community of life? The Moral Majority certainly isn't going to take us in that direction; they're interested in business as usual, as their golden boy, James Watt, has demonstrated. We need fewer sermons and more prayers.

This sense of bioregional spirit isn't fixed to a single religious form or practice. Generally it isn't Christian-based or noticeably monotheistic, though such views aren't excluded. I think the main influences are the primitive animist/Great Spirit tradition, various Eastern and esoteric religious practices, and plain ol' paying attention. I may be stretching the accord, but I also see a shared awareness that the map is not the journey, and for that reason it is best to be alert and to respond to the opportunities presented rather than waste away wishing life would offer some worthy spiritual challenge (which it does, constantly, anyway). Call it whatever seems appropriate—enlightenment, fulfillment, spiritual maturity, happiness, self-realization—it has to be earned, and to be earned it has to be lived, and that means bringing it into our daily lives and working on it. Instant gratifications are not the deepest gratifications, I suspect, though Lord knows they certainly have their charms. The emphasis is definitely on the practice, not the doctrine, and especially on practicing what you preach; there is a general recognition that there are many paths, and that they are a further manifestation of crucial natural diversity. I might also note for serious backsliders that the play is as serious as the work, and there is a great willingness to celebrate; nobody is interested in a spirit whose holiness is constantly announced with sour piety and narrow self-righteousness.

Combining the three elements gives a loose idea of what I take to be bioregionalism: a decentralized, self-determined mode of social organization; a culture predictated upon biological integrities and acting in respectful accord; and a society which honors and abets the spiritual development of its members. Or so the theory goes. However, it's not mere theory, for there have been many cultures founded essentially upon those principles; for example, it has been the dominant cultural mode of inhabitation on this continent. The point is not to go back, but to take the best forward. Renewal, not some misty retreat into what was.

Theories, ideas, notions—they have their generative and reclamative values, and certainly a loveliness, but without the palpable intelligence of practice they remain hovering in the nether regions of nifty entertainments or degrade into more flamboyant fads and diversions like literary movements and hula-hoops. Practice is what puts the heart to work. If theory establishes the game, practice is the gamble, and the first rule of all gambling games has it like this: you can play bad and win; you can play good and lose; but if you play good over the long haul you're gonna come out alright.

Bioregional practice (or applied strategy) can take as many forms as the imagination and nerves, but for purpose of example I've hacked it into two broad categories; resistance and renewal. Resistance involves a struggle between the bioregional forces (who represent intelligence, excellence, and care) and the forces of heartlessness (who represent a greed so lifeless and forsaken it can't even pass as ignorance). In a way, I think it really is that simple, that there is, always, a choice about how we will live our lives, that there is a state of constant opportunity for both spiritual succor and carnal delight, and that the way we choose to live is the deepest expression of who we truly are. If we consistently choose against the richest possibilities of life, against kindness, against beauty, against love and sweet regard, then we aren't much. Our only claim to dignity is trying our best to do what we think is right, to put some heart in it, some soul, flower and root. We're going to fall on our asses a lot, founder on our pettiness and covetousness and sloth, but at least there is the effort, and that's surely better than being just another quivering piece of the national cultural jello. Or so it seems to me.

However, the primary focus of resistance is not the homogeneous American supraculture—that can be resisted for the most part simply by refusing to participate while at the same time trying to live our lives the way we think we should (knowing we'll get no encouragement whatsoever from the colonial overstructure). Rather, the focus of resistance is against the continuing destruction of natural systems. We can survive the ruthless homogeneity of national culture because there are many holes we can slip through, but we cannot survive if the natural systems that sustain us are destroyed. That has to be stopped if we want to continue living on this planet. That's not "environmentalism"; it's ecology with a vengeance. Personally, I think we should develop a Sophoclean appreciation for the laws of nature, and submit. Only within the fractional time frame of fossil-fuel industrialization have we begun to seriously insult the environment and impudently violate the conditions of life. We've done a great deal of damage in a very short time, and only because of the amazing flexibility of natural systems have we gotten away with it so far. But I don't think we'll destroy the planet; she will destroy us first, which is perhaps only to say we'll destroy ourselves. The most crucial point of resistance is choosing not to.

And then we must try to prevent others from doing it for us all, since by allowing monopoly-capital centralized government (which, like monotheism, is not so much putting all your eggs in one basket as dropping your one egg in a blender), we have given them the power to make such remote-control decisions. The way to prevent it is five-fold: by being a model for an alternative; by knowing more than they do; by being politically astute; by protecting what we value; and by any means necessary. (I think it's important to note that there is nearly complete agreement that nonviolence is the best means available, and that the use of violence is always a sad admission of desperation. Besides, they have all the money, guns, and lawyers. People advocating violent means are probably not very interested in living much longer.)

I think political smarts are best applied in the local community and county. Most crucial land use decisions, for instance, are made at the county level by boards of supervisors. The representative-to-constituent ratio is obviously much better in a county than in a country, and therefore informed and spirited constituents have a far greater influence on decisions and policies. Work to elect sympathetic representatives. Put some money where your heart is. Go to your share of the generally boring meetings and hearings. Challenge faulty information (thus the importance of knowing more than they do). Create alternatives. Stand your ground.

Buying land is also a strong political move; "ownership" is the best protection against gross environmental abuse, just as living on the land is the best defence against mass-media gelatin culture, assuming the quality of information influences the quality of thought. Owning land also affords increased political leverage within the present system. Besides, bioregionalism without a tangible land base would be like love without sex; the circuits of association wouldn't be complete. (Of course, it isn't necessary to own land to either appreciate it or resist its destruction, and I hope nobody infers that bioregionalism is for land aristocracy.)

The growth and strength of the "environmental movement" in the past decade has encouraged awareness about the destruction of natural systems and the consequences of such callous disregard. This is all to the good, and we should continue to stay in their faces on critical issues. But it's going to be continual crisis ecology unless we come up with a persuasive economic alternative; otherwise, most people will go on choosing progress over maturity, for progress is deeply equated with payroll, and money, to most people, means life. It's that cold. It's also basically true, and many friends share my chagrin that it took us so long to grasp that truism. It now seems painfully obvious that the economic system must be transformed if we hope to protect natural systems from destruction in the name of Mammon. Economics seems to baffle everyone, especially me. I have no prescriptions to offer, except to note that it doesn't have to be one economic system, and that any economics should include a fair measure of value. What's needed is an economy that takes into true account the cost of biospheric destruction and at the same time feeds the family. People must be convinced that it's in their best economic interest to maintain healthy biological systems. The best place to meet this challenge is where you live—that is, personally and within the community.

It's probably also fairly plain that changing the economic system will involve changing our conception of what constitutes a fulfilled life and cracking the cultural mania for mindless consumption and its attendant waste. To realize what is alive within us, the who of who we are, we have to know what we truly need, and what is enough. As Marshall Sahlins has pointed out, affluence can be attained either through increasing production or reducing needs. Since increased production usually means ravaged natural systems, the best strategy seems the reduction of needs, and hopefully the consequent recognition that enough is plenty. A truly affluent society is one of material sufficiency and spiritual riches.

While we're keeping up this resistance in our daily lives—and I think it is in the quality of daily life rather than monentary thrills that the heart is proven—we can begin repairing the natural systems that have been damaged. Logged and mined watersheds need to be repaired. Streams have to be cleared. Trees planted. Checkdams built to stop gully erosion. Long-term management strategies developed. Tough campaigns waged to secure funding for the work. There's a strong effort in this direction happening in Northern California now, much of it through worker co-ops and citizens' groups, with increasingly cooperative help from local and state agencies. This work has really just begun, and the field is wide open. So far it seems to satisfy the two feelings that prompted it: the sense that we have a responsibility to renew what we've wasted, and the need to practice "right livelihood," or work that provides a living while promoting the spirit.

Natural system renewal (or rehabilitation, or enhancement, or whatever other names it goes by) could well be our first environmental art. It requires a thorough knowledge of how natural systems work, delicate perceptions of specific sites, the development of appropriate techniques, and hard physical work of the kind that puts you to bed after dinner. What finer work than healing the Earth, where the rewards are both in the doing and the results? It deserves our participation and support. For the irrefutable fact of the matter is that if we want to explore the bioregional possibility, we've got to work, got to get dirty—either by sitting on our asses at environmental hearings or by busting them planting trees in the rain. Sniveling don't make it.

The chances of bioregionalism succeeding, like the chances of survival itself, are beside the point. If one person, or a few, or a community of people, live more fulfilling lives from bioregional practice, then it's successful. This country has a twisted idea of success: it is almost always a quantitative judgment—salary, wins, the number of rooms in the house, the amount of people you command. Since bioregionalism by temperament is qualitative, the basis of judgment should be shifted accordingly. What they call a subculture, we call friends.

Most of the people I talk with feel we have a fighting chance to stop environmental destruction within 50 years and to turn the culture around within 800 to 1000 years. "Fighting chance" translates as long odds but good company, and bioregionalism is obviously directed at people whose hearts put a little gamble in their blood. Since we won't live to see the results of this hoped-for transformation, we might as well live to start it right, with the finest expressions of spirit and style we can muster, keeping in mind that there's only a functional difference between the flower and the root, that essentially they are part of the same abiding faith.

The Sun still rises every morning. Dig in.

DWELLERS IN THE LAND
Kirkpatrick Sale

In *The Interpreters,* a book written at the height of the Irish Revolution by the Irish author known as AE, there is a passage in which a group of prisoners, a disparate lot, sit around discussing what the ideal new world should look like. One of them, a philosopher, advances the now-familiar vision of a unitary world order with a global, scientific, cosmopolitan culture. Another, the poet Lavelle, argues fervently against this conception, trying to show that the more the world develops its technological superstructure, the farther it gets from its natural roots. "If all wisdom was acquired from without," he says, "it might be politic for us to make our culture cosmopolitan. But I believe our best wisdom does not come from without, but arises in the soul and is an emanation of the Earth spirit, a voice speaking directly to us dwellers in this land."

It is not difficult to imagine the alternative to the peril the industrio-scientific paradigm has placed us in. It is simply to become "dwellers in the land."

We must try to regain the spirit of the ancient Greeks, once again comprehending the earth as a living creature and contriving the modern equivalent of the worship of Gaea. We must try to learn that she is, in every real sense, *sacred,* and that there is therefore a holy way to confront her and her works, a way of awe and admiration and respect and veneration that simply will not permit despoliation or abuse. We must try to understand ourselves as participants in and not masters over her biotic community—a "reinvention of the human at the species level," in the philosopher Thomas Berry's telling phrase—and take to heart Mark Twain's remark that humans are different from other animals only in that they are able to blush—or need to.

But to become dwellers in the land, to relearn the laws of Gaea, to come to know the earth fully and honestly, the crucial and perhaps only and all-encompassing task is to understand *place,* the immediate specific place where we live. The kinds of soils and rocks under our feet; the source of the waters we drink; the meaning of the different kinds of winds; the common insects, birds, mammals, plants, and trees; the particular cycles of the seasons; the times to plant and harvest and forage—these are the things that are necessary to know. The limits of its resources; the carrying capacities of its lands and waters; the places where it must not be stressed; the places where its bounties can best be developed; the treasures it holds and the treasures it withholds—these are the things that must be understood. And the cultures of the people, of the populations native to the land and of those who have grown up with it, the human social and economic arrangements shaped by and adapted to the geomorphic ones, in both urban and rural settings—these are the things that must be appreciated.

That, in essence, is *bioregionalism.*

Now I would be the last to say that the word "bioregionalism" is one that comes easily to the lips; indeed, let's face it, it is a clumsy word, and difficult, and not only because most people do not instantly grasp a meaning for it. But I believe it to be a concept so accessible and, once understood, so serviceable and even productive, that it is worthwhile using it and explaining its meaning over time.

There is nothing so mysterious about the elements of the word, after all—*bio* is from the Greek word for forms of life, as in *biology* and *biography,* and *region* is from the Latin *regere,* territory to be ruled—and there is nothing, after a moment's thought, so terribly difficult in what they convey together: a life-territory, a place defined by its life forms, its topography and its biota, rather than by human dictates; a region governed by nature, not legislature. And if the concept initially strikes us as strange, that may perhaps only be a measure of how distant we have become from the wisdom it conveys—and how badly we need that wisdom now.

There is another cogent reason for using this word. Since it was first propagated by writer Peter Berg and ecologist Raymond Dasmann more than a decade ago—it is not quite clear who originated the term, but it was those two, working through an organization called Planet Drum and a newspaper irreverently called *Raise the Stakes,* who brought the concept to a wider audience—it has inspired what can fairly be called a movement, albeit still a modest one. As of 1985 there were some sixty groups in North America specifically defining themselves as bioregional, and a nascent continental organization, the North American Bioregional Congress, formed to advance bioregional consciousness and to nurture and link bioregional organizations. Those developments give the word a sufficient lineage, a sufficient currency, to justify its being honored by further usage.

Bioregionalism will define itself more completely in the course of all that follows, but initially it ought to be helpful to get a sense, a feel, of the concept by following some of its natural implications.

Knowing the Land

We may not become as sophisticated about the land we live upon and its resources as the original inhabitants, those who had forty words for snow or knew every tree in the forest. But any one of us can walk the territory and see what inhabits there, become conscious of the birdsongs and waterfalls and animal droppings, follow a brooklet to a stream and down to a river, and learn when to set out tomatoes, what kind of soil is best for celery, and where blueberries thrive. On a more sophisticated level, we can develop a resource inventory for the region, using information from the local Forest Service to map and count the area's trees; checking hydrological surveys to determine waterflows, runoffs, and hydropower sites; collecting biological profiles of the native annual and perennial food plants; learning annual climatic conditions and the full potentials of solar, wind, and water power; and studying human land-use patterns and optimal settlement areas. Out of all that—much of it already available, though not broken down on a bioregional basis—one could ultimately determine with some grandeur the carrying capacity of the region.

Now that does sound a bit bucolic, I realize, and it may be hard to see immediately how it translates into urban terms.[1] But every city is part of a region, after all, and depends on the surrounding countryside for many of its resources and much of its market, and every city is built upon a natural foundation. Knowing place for the urban-dweller, then, means learning the details of the trade and resource-dependency between city and country and the population limits appropriate to the region's carrying capacity. It also suggests exploring the natural *potential* of the land on which the city rests—for though our huge conurbations have largely displaced natural life by diverting rivers, cutting down forests, paving over soils, and confining most animal life to zoos and parks, it is also true that one can discover and measure the possibilities for rooftop gardens, solar energy, recycling, urban silviculture, and the like.

Learning the Lore

Every place has a history, a record of how both the human and natural possibilities of the region have been explored, and this must be studied with new eyes: there is more to discover, as botanist Wes Jackson puts it, than to invent. And though not every place has kept its history properly alive, a fountain of information still exists if we will but tap it—as shown, for example, in the wonderful Foxfire books, the recent collections of Indian lore, and many other projects or oral history and folk knowledge.

Obviously we will not want—or be able—to live as the ancients did. But every serious historical and anthropological exploration of their ways and wisdom shows that earlier cultures, particularly those well-rooted in the earth, knew a number of important things we are only now learning about: the value of herbal medicines, for example, or methods and times of burning prairie grassland, or siting and building houses for maximum passive-solar effect, or the regular and central role of women in tribal decision-making. If nothing else, such history helps us realize that the past was not as bleak and laborious and unhealthy as the high-energy-high-tech proponents try to make out. It was E. F. Schumacher who reminded us that when the modern world organized its thinking "by some extraordinary structure we call objective science," it discarded the "two great teachers" of humanity: "the marvelous system of living nature" and "the traditional wisdom of mankind" by which we know about it. It seems high time to rectify the balance.

Developing the Potential

Once the place and its possibilities are known, the bioregional task is to see how this potential can best be realized *within* the boundaries of the region, using all the biotic and geological resources to their fullest, constrained only by the logic of necessity and the principles of ecology. Fully developing the bioregion allows the full development of the people and communities within it, each section of it able to employ long-neglected processes and long-unused ingenuity but with the full blessing of contemporary knowledge and skills.

Self-reliance, not so much at the individual as at the regional level, is thus inherent in the bioregional concept. We might begin to think of how much of any region's human and material resources are ignored or squandered or left undeveloped because the region looks to far-off sources and depends on extrinsic goods and services instead. We might look at how much of a region's wealth is exported to distant banks or home-offices or absentee owners, instead of watering the gardens at home. And we might try to imagine just what could be done in any region if all its funds, facilities, stocks, and talents were used to their fullest, limited only by the carring capacity of the land and its ecological constraints.

Liberating the Self

Bioregionalism implies also the development of individual potential within the development of the region, along two broad perspectives.

On the one hand, many present constraints on personal freedom and choice from without would be diminished or eliminated—those of distant and impersonal market forces, for example, remote governments and bureaucracies, and unseen corporations dictating consumer choices—while within the bioregion both economic and political opportunities would be inevitably opened up. Also, by living closer to the land one necessarily lives closer to the community, able to enjoy the communitarian values of cooperation, participation, sodality, and reciprocity that enhance individual development.

On the other hand, fully knowing the character of the natural world and being connected to it in a daily and physical way provides that sense of oneness, of *rootedness* that the ancients experienced—and "to be rooted," as philosopher Simone Weil was shrewd enough to know, "is perhaps the most important and least recognized need of the human soul." Moreover, it seems clear from the past that individuals who can best use, because they best understand, the gifts of nature—for food, for energy, for shelter, for crafts—are able to develop and prosper in ways unavailable to those who lack those skills.

Knowing, learning, developing, liberating—these, then, are some of the processes most central to the bioregional idea. Their implications are elaborate and far-reaching, as we shall explore in the chapters that follow.

Obviously, bioregionalism is at once very simple and very complicated. Very simple, because all of its components are *there,* unhidden, right around us, right where we live; because we know that other people, ancient and in our terms perhaps unsophisticated, understood these things and lived for uncomplicated centuries by them. To discover and present the kind of information basic to a bioregional society is not difficult. There are still many old people among us today who know some of the wisdom of our forebears, and the discipline of modern ecology uses contemporary scientific procedures that can help us construct the rest of the bioregional body of knowledge.

Very complicated, because it is so at odds with the conventional way of looking at the world nowadays that it must strike most people at first as either too limiting and provincial, or quaintly nostalgic, or wide-eyed and utopian, or simply irrelevant—or all of those. That is hardly surprising, and the difficulties must be faced frankly.

Obviously it will take a considerable change in attitude before our industrial society begins first to abandon the notion of controlling and remaking the world in the name of a global monoculture and then to realize that maybe what it calls "provincial" is merely the kind of minding-your-own-business attention to local reforms within the limits of the possible that might have a chance of saving the world.

It will take some time before people recognize that the project of understanding place is neither nostalgic nor utopian but rather the realistic sort of occupation anyone can participate in every day that has an immediate and practical chance of curbing our present waste and recklesssness.

It will take some broad and persuasive education to get people to realize that it is not the bioregional task that is irrelevant but precisely the business-as-usual politics of *all* the major parties of *all* the major industrial nations, not one of which has made ecological salvation a significant priority, not one of which is prepared to abandon or even curtail the industrial economy that is imperiling us.

And it will take patience to lead people past their fear and lingering hatred of the natural world, which grows as their ignorance of it grows, and on to appreciation of Gaea as a precious living entity that acts always in reasonable homeostatic ways, violently at times, and unpredictably at times, but for an ultimately benevolent and life-sustaining purpose.[2]

Please understand: I do not underestimate the complications. Yet I am certain that in the bioregional paradigm we have a goal, a philosophy, and a process by which to create a world which is not only *necessary* for the continuation of our species, but is also *desirable* and *possible*.

The first of all of Gaea's daughters was Themis, to whom she entrusted the laws of nature, and it is in the diligent study of those laws that we can best guide ourselves in reconstructing human societies for a bioregional world. To be sure, the laws of nature can sometimes seem confusing and indeed contradictory, and even experts who have spent lifetimes on this sort of work have not always come to the same conclusions. We would be well advised to approach the job with caution.

But after a fairly extensive reading of the literature here, I am struck by what seems to be a wide agreement at least to the broad outlines of what Gaea's laws are and the general directions they suggest for human settlements and systems. I am struck, too, by the extreme variety of the investigators who have arrived at such similar conclusions: ecologists and architects, political scientists and economists, sociologists and naturalists, writers and planners, some carefully "without politics," some frankly conservative, many no more than liberal, and a few forthrightly decentralist and regionalist. I think it is possible to deduce from their work over these past several generations the central principles by which to construct the guiding tenets of an ecological world: the *bioregional paradigm*.

Such a paradigm of course stands in sharp contrast to the industrio-scientific paradigm in almost every aspect. I will examine it in some detail throughout this section, but it might be useful at the start to compare those paradigms and see their differences starkly:

	BIOREGIONAL PARADIGM	INDUSTRIO-SCIENTIFIC PARADIGM
Scale	Region	State
	Community	Nation/World
Economy	Conservation	Exploitation
	Stability	Change/Progress
	Self-sufficiency	World Economy
	Cooperation	Competition
Polity	Decentralization	Centralization
	Complementarity	Hierarchy
	Diversity	Uniformity
Society	Symbiosis	Polarization
	Evolution	Growth/Violence
	Division	Monoculture

There are great complexities here, of course, and overlaps and interconnections that such a chart tends to disguise. In the following pages I will try to develop and examine these concepts and their linkages more carefully, approaching them in the order the chart suggests, focusing on the four basic determinants of any organized civilization: scale, economy, polity, and society. And thus I hope to portray in the round the bioregional paradigm, the means by which we may become "dwellers in the land."

Notes

1. It may be worthwhile to dispel the myth, propagated by the Census Bureau and others, that this nation is predominantly urban: it is in fact largely *non*-urban and getting more so. About two-thirds of the population lives outside even modest cities (50,000 and up), more than a third of that in rural areas and unincorporated villages. Even in so-called "metropolitan areas" some 40 percent of the people live outside the cities proper.

2. Just as a single example of popular fear of the natural, Dr. Lewis Thomas mentions the common paranoia about diseases and bacteria in this society, where we think "we live in a world where the microbes are always trying to get at us, to tear us cell from cell, and we only stay alive and whole through diligence and fear." Actually, he points out, disease and pathogenicity "is not the rule" in nature and indeed "occurs so infrequently and involves such a relatively small number of species, considering the huge population of bacteria on the earth, that it has a freakish aspect."

REVALUING HOME: FEMINISM AND BIOREGIONALISM
Judith Plant

Several years ago, at a conference about regional development, in a workshop with native women, I asked Marie Smallface for some guidance: "What is the best thing for white people to do in the midst of the cultural and environmental havoc *created* by white people?"

She spoke directly and said, "Find a place and stay there." She went on to talk about how she thought it made more sense to be "of" the land you're struggling to save. Ultimately, she meant, staying home.

Bioregionalists express the same idea. Yet, at the same time home has been a very isolated place for women. To be different from this traditional situation, home, as such, needs understanding, valuing, and redefining. Here a partnership between bioregionalism and feminism can provide fertile ground for deep societal changes. For both perspectives value "all our relations"—with nature and with humankind—and both value home.

Without feminism, it seems that the bioregional view is not going to bring about the shift in attitude that is required to live an ecologically harmonious life. We have to put our own house in order. Our relations with the earth reflect our relationships with eath other.

Redefining and Revaluing Home

Bioregional action is based on local control and decentralization; non-violence; sustainable life-styles; and on a revaluing and redefining of home.

In considering the notion of home, bioregionalists turn towards ecology. The word itself comes from the Greek *oikos*, for home—an indication that home is much broader than simply the nuclear family. As it is in the natural world, where all life is connected and inter-related, teeming with diversity and complexities, so it is with human domestic life. Here is the scene of *human* ecology, or what Murray Bookchin refers to as "social ecology." Home becomes the locus of liberation from a culture of violence, because it is here where people really have a measure of control over the creation of nonviolent values. It is where the consequences of political decisions are felt.

Feminism has everything to do with social relations and human ecology. The schism between the personal and the political has kept this valuable information from informing and directing political decisions. Feminists have given this a lot of thought; and not just abstractly, but thought based on experience. Since time-out-of-mind, women have had a history—or herstory—with home. Feminism has helped people understand how women have been isolated at home and, in turn, has articulated the value of women's work at home. This work has been done in the context of a society which has traditionally undervalued both home *and* women.

The Personal As Political

"All the issues are related. Now nobody can deal with all the issues—there isn't energy and time. But we can deal with *our* issues—the ones that affect us immediately—in a way that relates them to all the others.

And I think that we had better because otherwise we're bound to fail."—Joanna Russ, from *Reweaving the Web of Life.*

Dealing with *our* issues is the bioregional method. When bioregionalists talk about Forestry's cut-and-run mentality, they are speaking from their hearts, from their own experience. Clear-cutting the watershed which is the vital artery that supports the environment in which one lives stirs the emotions and the intellect together in a powerful expression. To be an environmentalist takes on a deep, personal meaning.

It is because of this personal connection with political decisions and actions that the bioregional process helps people to see that what is valued personally is the same as what is valued politically. Seems common sense enough but, as many have experienced in political activism (in the alternative politics of the Left in the 60s, for instance), there has been a blind spot in seeing this relationship. So exploitative behavior in the market was viewed as unrelated to exploitative behavior interpersonally. The connection between personal values and political ones was missed. It was because of this blind spot, or inability to make this connection, that many women broke away from Left politics.

Is The Revaluing of Home a Double Bind for Women?

To avoid alienating women again, we have to make sure that bioregionalism does not leave women in a double bind. As bioregionalists place new value on home, on the domestic, everyday life, those values and activities generally associated with women are now believed to be healthy activities that need to be maintained and developed.

At the same time, the historical and, indeed, present reality is that these life activities have been undervalued and have been a source of oppression for women.

> "Women are nurturers: we keep the systems we work in together (the family, service jobs in wage labor) by nurturing. The social relations of our nurturance work account on the one hand for our oppression (sacrificing our own interests for those of men and children) and, on the other hand, for our potential strength as bearers of a radical culture: we support an ethic of sharing, co-operation, and collective involvement that stands in clear opposition to an ethic based on individualism, competition, and private profit."—Ferguson and Folbre, *The Unhappy Marriage of Patriarchy and Capitalism.*

What remains valuable in mainstream society, and deep within our beings, has a dollar sign attached to it, and generally has nothing to do with home. In fact, home is more and more being sacrificed for economic ends. What is important goes on in the public sphere—politics and economics—and a person's worth is gauged in monetary terms. Within this ideology, domestic life has meant that some are subservient to others. Traditionally this has been women, as slaves, servants and wives. Children quickly learn that what goes on at home is unimportant compared to the values "out there."

Out of the Bind

Based on the strong, educated hunches of feminists, the only way out of this bind is to take the view that, culturally, society is in a transformational, transitional phase. We are attempting to move out of culturally-defined sex roles which value one over the other, toward a culture that places positive value on the active involvement of all people in domestic life. For it is here where culture is shaped.

"Societies that do not elaborate the opposition of male and female and place positive value on the conjugal relationships and the involvement of both men and women in the home seem to be most egalitarian in terms of sex roles. When a man is involved in domestic labor, in child care and cooking, he cannot establish an aura of authority and distance. And when public decisions are made in the household, women may have a legitimate public role."—Rosaldo, *Women, Culture, and Society: A Theoretical Overview*.

The polarization of women and men, as either/or, is the social organization from which we have emerged. There has been little, if any, tolerance for gradations or complexities. You are either one or the other. Part of this problem is thinking in pairs of opposites and, as with most dualities, one is thought to be preferred over the other.

In actual fact, human beings have the capacity for a wide range of behaviors. People now know that men are capable of gentleness and women can be assertive. Yet, still, mainstream society persists in valuing tendencies associated with maleness over those associated with femaleness.

The task remains to outsmart ourselves. Harmonizing all our relations, making the connections, is potentially the footing for a quantum leap in evolution. It's not simply a question or rights but of actually saving the species from itself.

It is no easy transition to a valuing of the domestic. For men, it is very difficult to find a place in a sphere of life they have been socialized to avoid and consider unimportant. Similarly for women who are so tempted to prove themselves according to patriarchal society's measuring stick.

Paying consistent attention to how we do things, to process, seems vital to the reconstruction of healthy relationships with the earth and with each other. Bioregionalism and ecology can guide us in our relations with nature, just as feminism can aid in an understanding of our human relationships. These two theories, coupled with inspiration from the natural world, could bring women and men together, with integrity and dignity, in bioregional community.

"To put feminist values of equality, mutual aid, and respect for life in their place requires a society where people are engaged in face-to-face relations and where nature inspires us with the sanctity of life and the need to give back to others that which we receive from them."—Alexandra Devon, *Kick It Over*.

PART II

Radical Ecoactivism and Ecotactics

Introduction

The introduction to this anthology discusses some of the varieties of ecotactics adopted by radical environmental groups in North America and shows how these tactics have evolved in the past two decades. While there is no single thread which sews together all of these forms of behavior as tactics, deep concern about the destruction of the earth and a desire to protect wild animals and natural areas are obviously common motivating factors in most cases. Beyond this, radical groups select specific tactics in order to promote diverse philosophical, ethical, and political goals, and also to bring about specific changes in environmental conditions.

The tactics of radical environmentalists are thus varied in their character and intentional content, and range from the mildest forms of political participation to the strongest types of ecological sabotage. The two forms of direct action that have come under the closest public scrutiny because of their radical character are environmental civil disobedience and ecotage.

Civil disobedience has a long tradition of support in our society. American colonists in the eighteenth century used acts of civil disobedience against the English colonial government. Later in our history, Henry David Thoreau and Martin Luther King, Jr. were two of its more ardent and famous defenders, advocating it as a means of combating injustice in society. It has been practiced for many years by both ordinary citizens and political dissenters to protest such things as unfair taxes, the death penalty, racism, war and militarism, sexism and sex discrimination, nuclear testing and deployment of nuclear weapons, abortion and restrictions on women's rights, animal testing in the cosmetics industry and in scientific laboratories, AIDS policies of the federal government, and such environmental issues as whaling, sealing, and logging in old growth forests.

Typically civil disobedience is understood to be a deliberate and public act of law-breaking that is ethically, religiously, or conscientiously motivated and performed in order to protest some law or policy which the disodients find to be unjust or morally evil. Though there is debate about this, acts of civil disobedience are not supposed to be aimed at overthrowing the government altogether, but are to express fidelity to the law in a fundamental sense and to accept the legitimacy of an existing political system or form of government. Moreover, civil disobedience is to be "civil," which means in part that it should not be violent and destroy property or harm other individuals. Some argue that those who use this tactic must also indicate their willingness to accept the consequences of their law-breaking, by not resisting arrest and by going along with any reasonable legal penalties that are imposed on them. In addition it is sometimes claimed that an act of civil disobedience must be a last resort, undertaken only after all other means of appeal to the legal and political system have been exhausted and failed.[1]

Ecotage, on the other hand, is somewhat different than civil disobedience and should be distinguished from it, though both forms of protest can be defined as forms of "conscientious wrongdoing."[2] One of the major differences is that an act of ecotage is typically done secretly in order to purposely avoid detection and arrest, and is therefore not a public act. Moreover its defenders argue that, while it is never aimed at harming human beings or any other form of life, participants can legitimately use it to damage the machines that are destroying wild animals, plants, and wilderness areas. And, since it may be violent in this respect, this is another way in which it differs from environmental civil disobedience.

As was also explained in the introduction to this anthology, participation in ecotage has often been an important dividing line for distinguishing the practical tactics of one radical group from another. Obviously the more these tactics depart from conventional political and social behavior, the more controversial they become and the more difficult they are to justify in a democratic society. Chapter 10 will look at some of the critical responses that have been made to ecotage, examining the question, What would justify the use of these extreme measures?

Chapters 4 through 8 in this Part present some representative examples of ecotactics, including traditional methods of organizing and pressuring the political system, protest rallies and marches, and environmental civil disobedience and ecotage. These chapters contain selections that show both why radical environmental groups and environmentalists have felt compelled to use these tactics and also what was involved when they used them. However, since the practical goals of some radical groups are not solely directed at protection and restoration of wilderness and wild species, and include broader political strategies, the selection in Chapter 9 on bioregional activism gives an example of a different kind of ecoactivism. In this case, the idea is to attack the basic causes of environmental degradation in our society by fundamentally reorganizing our political and social life. This is a very difficult intellectual and practical task in an industrial system, and bioregionalists understand that it calls for a rethinking of many of our political structures and for implementing new forms of social community.

Notes

1. Useful discussions of civil disobedience can be found in Hugo Adam Bedau, ed., *Civil Disobedience: Theory and Practice* (Indianapolis: Pegasus, 1969); Carl Cohen, *Civil Disobedience: Conscience, Tactics and the Law* (New York: Columbia University Press, 1971); and Peter Singer, *Democracy and Disobedience* (New York: Oxford University Press, 1974).
2. This is an idea borrowed from Michael Martin, "Ecosabotage and Civil Disobedience," *Environmental Ethics* 12 (Winter 1990), pp. 291–310, which is excerpted in Chapter 10 below.

CHAPTER 4

Greenpeace, Warriors of the Rainbow

Introduction to the Selections

Greenpeace has never supported ecotage, though it has been inventive and vigorous in devising and using other unconventional tactics for bringing public attention to the environmentally destructive behavior of corporations, governments, and other organizations in our society. In fact it is more like a transitional group in the history of North American environmentalism, located somewhere between moderate and radical environmentalism. On the one hand it has maintained that conventional tactics are sometimes insufficient to stop or deter such destruction while on the other it has rejected direct sabotage of the machinery of corporate industrialism.

The first selection in Chapter 4 shows how Greenpeace in the 1970s used its interpretation of ecology and ecological laws to support its nonviolent tactics. These laws define the limits of rational human behavior on earth and provide a way to distinguish crimes against the earth from ecologically sound actions. The selections by Bob Hunter and Paul Watson, two important activists in the early Greenpeace movement, present some of the more spectacular acts of civil disobedience for which Greenpeace was known at that time. Hunter discusses Greenpeace efforts to stop underground nuclear testing in the Aleutian Islands by the U.S. government, French atmospheric nuclear tests in the South Pacific, and Russian whaling ventures off the coast of California. Watson describes in more detail one famous Greenpeace campaign to put a halt to harp seal hunting by Canadians and Norwegians off Newfoundland in 1976.

DECLARATION OF INTERDEPENDENCE, 1976
Greenpeace

We have arrived at a place in history where decisive action must be taken to avoid a general environmental disaster. With nuclear reactors proliferating and over 900 species on the endangered list, there can be no further delay or our children will be denied their future.

The Greenpeace Foundation hopes to stimulate practical, intelligent actions to stem the tide of planetary destruction. We are "rainbow people" representing every race, every nation, every living creature. We are patriots, not of any one nation, state or military alliance, but of the entire earth.

It must be understood that the innocent word "ecology" contains a concept that is as revolutionary as anything since the Copernican breakthrough, when it was discovered that the earth was not the center of the entire universe. Through ecology, science has embarked on a quest for the great systems of order that underly the complex flow of life on our planet. This quest has taken us far beyond the realm of traditional scientific thought. Like religion, ecology seeks to answer the infinite mysteries of life itself. Harnessing the tools of logic, deduction, analysis, and empiricism, ecology may prove to be the first true science-religion.

As suddenly as Copernicus taught us that the earth was not the center of the universe, ecology teaches us that mankind is not the center of life on this planet. Each species has its function in the scheme of life. Each has a role, however obscure that role may be.

Ecology has taught us that the entire earth is part of our "body" and that we must learn to respect it as much as we respect ourselves. As we love ourselves, we must also love all forms of life in the planetary system—the whales, the seals, the forests and the seas. The tremendous beauty of ecological thought is that it shows us a pathway back to an understanding of the natural world—an understanding that is imperative if we are to avoid a total collapse of the global ecosystem.

Ecology has provided us with many insights. These may be grouped into three basics "Laws of Ecology" which hold true for all forms of life—fish, plants, insects, plankton, whales, and man. These laws may be stated as follows:

The First Law of Ecology states that all forms of life are interdependent. The prey is as dependent on the predator for the control of its population as the predator is on the prey for a supply of food.

Example: Humans, in their self-interest, often lay plans for the extermination of species that are viewed as "undesirable". There would be few objections raised to a program of mosquito eradication. It would be more difficult, however, to gain acceptance for a program to eradicate swallows, so beautiful as they flit about chasing insects through the sky. But wait, the swallows are eating mosquitoes. Before the mosquitoes are eliminated it would be wise to consider the number of birds that will starve to death as a result.

The Second Law of Ecology states that the stability (unity, security, harmony, togetherness) of ecosystems is dependent on their diversity (complexity). An ecosystem that contains 100 different species is more stable than an ecosystem that has only three species. Thus the complex tropical rain-forest is more stable than the fragile arctic tundra.

Example: Consider a natural ecosystem such as a forest which contains a dozen different species of trees. Each species is susceptible to specific diseases that can kill individual trees. If there are many tree species it is unlikely that they would be attacked at once, and since the trees of any one species are spaced apart, with other species between them, there is less chance of an epidemic that would wipe out every tree of that species. Enter man—the forest is clear-cut for lumber and pulpwood, and is replanted with seedling trees of one species—a species that suits man's needs better than any of the original dozen. Now if a disease that is specific to the new species strikes the forest, all the trees are susceptible and an epidemic is far more likely.

The Third Law of Ecology states that all resources (food, water, air, minerals, energy) are finite and there are limits to the growth of all living systems. These limits are finally dictated by the finite size of the earth and the finite input of energy from the sun.

Example: There are so many examples of our inability to recognize this law that no one instance would explain the severity of the situation. Let it suffice to say that we are now coming up against the limits of many natural resources, including agricultural land, the fisheries, whales, petroleum, minerals, water, and forests. In the process we are creating a desperate situation for other species who also depend on many of these resources for food and energy.

If we ignore the logical implications of these "Laws of Ecology" we will continue to be guilty of crimes against the earth. We will not be judged by men for these crimes, but with a justice meeted out by the earth itself. The destruction of the earth will lead, inevitably, to the destruction of ourselves.

So let us work together to put an end to the destruction of the earth by the forces of human greed and ignorance. Through an understanding of the principles of ecology we must find new directions for the evolution of human values and human institutions. *Short-term economics* must be replaced with actions based on the need for conservation and preservation of the entire global ecosystem. We must learn to live in harmony, not only with our fellow man, but with all the beautiful creatures on this planet.

TAKING ON THE GOLIATHS OF DOOM
Bob Hunter

In 1969, a group of Vancouver-area environmentalists, mostly members of the British Columbia chapter of the Sierra Club, gathered together to form the Don't Make a Wave Committee. Like many other people in B.C., they were deeply concerned about the underground nuclear tests being conducted in the Aleutian Islands by the United States Atomic Energy Commission.

Three such tests had already been carried out at the Amchitka Island site, and four more, each one larger than the last, were reported to be in the planning stages. Reputable geophysicists had stirred public uneasiness by drawing attention to the fact that the Aleutian Islands are the center of some of the worst seismic activity on the planet. They also warned that there was a definite danger of tidal waves being created by large, underground nuclear blasts.

Feelings on the West Coast ran high. In the early part of Sept. 1970, some 6,000 students had blockaded the U.S.-Canada border at Blaine, Washington to protest against the Amchitka tests. These blockades were later to spread across Canada.

Inspired by the Quaker-sponsored voyages of the *Golden Rule* and the *Phoenix* which had attempted to protest nuclear tests by sailing directly into a test zone, the Don't Make a Wave Committee hit upon the idea of sailing a ship across the Gulf of Alaska to Amchitka, a distance of some 2,400 miles from Vancouver. Support for the idea grew quickly, with such normally diverse groups as the Vancouver Real Estate Board and the New Democratic Party endorsing the scheme. Tens of thousands of British Columbians supported the voyage by purchasing anti-Amchitka buttons and bumper stickers. Local ecology groups contributed what they could.

But even with broadly-based support, the Don't Make a Wave Committee took almost two full years organizing the voyage and finding a ship owner. Capt. J. C. Cormack, of Richmond, B.C., who was willing to risk his vessel by sailing into the test zone. Capt. Cormack, a respected fisherman with forty years experience at sea, agreed to charter his 80 foot halibut boat, the *Phyllis Cormack,* to take the protestors to within three miles of the shore of Amchitka Island and remain there throughout the next nuclear test.

Because his ship was Canadian, it created a unique problem for U.S. military authorities. So long as Capt. Cormack remained outside the three mile territorial limit, his vessel could not be seized and removed by the U.S. Navy or Coast Guard.

On Sept. 15th, 1971, the *Phyllis Cormack,* renamed *Greenpeace* for the voyage, set sail from Vancouver. The voyage quickly attracted attention in the media and received a direct endorsement and wishes for a safe voyage from Prime Minister Pierre Elliott Trudeau. The crew—volunteers all—included an ecologist, biologist, lawyers, writers, and three members of the B.C. Sierra Club.

The voyage lasted 42 days. At the end of that time, the battered *Greenpeace* was forced back to Vancouver by a combination of delays in the nuclear test program, worsening autumn weather, and an arrest by the U.S. Coast Guard. Running low on supplies the boat landed on the Aleutian Island of Akutan. The boat was arrested at that point by the coast guard on a technicality involving an old and seldom used tariff regulation.

Back in Vancouver, the Don't Make A Wave Committee hurriedly organized a replacement vessel, the 120-foot converted minesweeper *Edgewater Fortune,* skippered by Hank Johansen with 29 volunteers on board, the *Greenpeace Too* headed out into the first winter storms on the Gulf of Aslaka. Forced several times to retreat by 70-mile-an-hour winds, the *Greenpeace Too* was still 700 miles from Amchitka on November 4th, when the bomb was finally exploded.

In the meantime, enough publicity about the tests had been generated both in Canada and the U.S. so that the Supreme Court was called into a special session to determine whether cancellation of the Amchitka blast should be ordered on environmental grounds. The blast was allowed to go ahead by a margin of only one vote.

The following spring, the U.S. Atomic Energy Commission quietly closed down its Amchitka test site, making the entire island into a bird sanctuary.

In the meantime, the Don't Make a Wave Committee dissolved itself, forming the Greenpeace Foundation, which was duly incorporated under the B.C. Societies Act.

In the early spring of 1972, as soon as word came through that the Amchitka test site had been closed down, the leadership of the Greenpeace Foundation—consisting of individuals who had taken part in the voyages of *Greenpeace* and *Greenpeace Too*—decided to attempt to apply their tactic of seagoing non-violence to French nuclear tests which were being conducted in the atmosphere over Mururoa Atoll, several hundred miles from Tahiti. David McTaggart of Vancouver, a retired businessman and athlete, volunteered to sail his 38-foot ketch, the *Vega*, from New Zealand to Mururoa, a feat which many experienced sailors doubted could be accomplished, given the wind conditions in that part of the South Pacific.

Undaunted, McTaggart and three others set sail at the beginning of June, with the support of New Zealand environmental and anti-nuclear groups, but with most of the financing coming from Vancouver. The *Vega* was renamed *Greenpeace III.*

In July, after entering the French cordon around Mururoa, the *Greenpeace III* was constantly harassed and eventually rammed by a French military vessel. The confrontation was thoroughly recorded in photographs by McTaggart. Despite his meticulous documentation, it took him three years to have his eventual case against the French navy brought before a French civil tribunal in Paris. In June, 1975, the French court ruled that McTaggart had, indeed, been rammed in clear violation of international rules of the sea, and damages were assessed against the French military authorities.

After being rammed, McTaggart's little vessel was towed to Mururoa, given minimal repairs, and towed back out to sea where he limped back to New Zealand. That fall, leaving his boat in New Zealand, McTaggart returned to Vancouver to organize a second voyage to Mururoa and carry on the campaign against nuclear testing. Meanwhile, his voyage had generated headlines all around the world and focussed international attention on the French atmospheric nuclear program, which had been going on for nine years in the South Pacific.

In the wake of the sailing of *Greenpeace III,* a small flotilla of New Zealand registered vessels set out for Mururoa, including the *Boy Roel, Tamure, Magic Isle* and *Wanea.* None succeeded in reaching Mururoa, but they generated a great deal of pressure on the conservative New Zealand government, which subsequently lost a general election that winter. A new party, which had promised to "actively oppose" the French tests, was swept into office. A parallel political event took place that winter in Australia, where slumbering public resentment against the tests had been stirred by McTaggart's voyage. The conservative Australian government also fell and the new administration pledged to take action against the tests.

By the time the Greenpeace Foundation was able to raise sufficient funds for McTaggart to refit his damaged vessel, fly back to New Zealand, and prepare to sail again, the French Nuclear Test Zone had become the center of international press attention. It was summer, 1973. Inspired by the voyage of *Greenpeace III,* the New Zealand government has sent a navy frigate into the zone, backed up by an Australian supply boat, to observe the nuclear tests and remain inside the zone.

An American civilian craft, a former Baltic trader named the *Fri*, with representatives of French anti-nuclear groups on board, had also sailed into the zone. At least five other vessels had set sail from New Zealand and Australia. One by one, the protest vessels were boarded and removed, except for the navy ships which remained only long enough to register a symbolic protest.

By the time the *Greenpeace III* arrived again in the test zone, it was the only vessel in the area remaining between the French military and their plans to explode another series of bombs. In an action that was again documented by McTaggart's crew (and later described in his book, *Outrage: The Ordeal of the Greenpeace III*, J. J. Douglas Ltd.), French commandoes boarded the *Greenpeace III,* and savagely beat both McTaggart and his navigator, a British citizen named Nigel Ingram, with rubber truncheons. As a result of the beating, McTaggart suffered the partial loss of sight in his left eye. (His case against the French navy involved charges of piracy on the high seas, but the same French court which ruled in 1975 that he had, indeed, been rammed declared itself to be "without jurisdiction" in the matter of his beating. McTaggart is now in the process of appealing to the French Supreme Court.)

The second voyage of the *Greenpeace III* brought even more international pressure to bear on the French government. Actions were launched in the International Court of Justice by New Zealand, but the French government refused to recognize the court's "jurisdiction". Greenpeace members from Vancouver meanwhile travelled to France where they established contact with numerous French environmental groups and distributed literature and buttons in French. Other Greenpeacers lobbied with various members of the United Nations in New York in order to introduce a resolution opposing French nuclear tests in the South Pacific.

By the spring of 1974, opposition to the tests had grown in France itself from a trickle to the point where it became a major election issue, with bishops of the Roman Catholic Church publicly debating the French military establishment. The introduction of the nuclear tests issue was attributed by many French observers to the near-defeat of the ruling Gaullist Party at the polls. Immediately after the election, the bully-shaken Gaullists announced that they would carry out their 1974 program of nuclear tests but that they would cease atmospheric testing immediately afterwards, despite statements which had been made by generals at Mururoa the year before to the effect that "France would never agree to cease atmospheric testing."

Beginning in the spring of 1975, the skies over the South Pacific were free of radioactive wastes for the first time in almost a decade. All further French tests would be conducted underground.

Not satisfied, the Greenpeace Foundation funded a small but sturdy ketch, *La Flor,* owned by a German citizen, Rolf Heimann, to sail from Australia to Mururoa in the spring of 1974, while McTaggart pursued his case against the French navy through civil courts in Paris, Heimann's ketch, renamed *Greenpeace IV,* sailed in early May but was delayed by bad weather and mechanical problems, with the result that it did not arrive in the test zone until shortly after the last French blast.

Motivated by its successes at Amchitka and Mururoa, the Greenpeace Foundation announced in January, 1975, that it would turn its attention to the problem of the slaughter of the world's dwindling populations of great whales, now being hunted to the point of extinction by Japanese and Russian whaling fleets, who account for 80 percent of the annual kill.

The tactic of seagoing nonviolent confrontation would again be applied, but this time with a new dimension, Greenpeacers would seek out the whaling fleets on the high seas and attempt to place themselves directly between the harpoons and the whales, making it difficult or impossible for the whalers to make any kills without risking the lives of the protestors in the process. The idea was to put human "shields" between the whalers and their helpless prey.

The undertaking, dubbed "Project Ahab," was envisioned as a mirror image of the mad captain's voyage to destroy Moby Dick. Capt. John C. Cormack's vessel was again chartered for the voyage. The original *Greenpeace,* fitted out with a new engine and $11,000 worth of special electronic equipment designed to communicate music and warning signals to the whales, became the *Greenpeace V.*

In the meantime, David McTaggart had sold his 38-foot ketch, *Vega,* to finance his court case in France. (The Canadian government repeatedly promised to support his case against the French navy but, in fact, did nothing to assist him in his action.) The new owner of the *Vega,* Jacques Longini of Vancouver, a retired law professor, agreed to put his vessel at Greenpeace's disposal for the voyage to save the whales. *Vega,* which had served twice as *Greenpeace III,* became *Greenpeace VI.*

On April 27, 1975, with clear skies in the South Pacific and Amchitka an established bird sanctuary, the two vessels sailed from Vancouver's Jericho Beach, where 23,000 supporters showed up to voice their opposition to whaling, the largest demonstration to have taken place in Vancouver's history.

The voyage of *Greenpeace V* and *Greenpeace VI* lasted 84 days and covered 11,000 miles of coastline from Alaska to California. After 60 days at sea, the *Greenpeace V* succeeded—against odds which retired military advisors had described as "astronomical""—in tracking down the elusive Soviet whaling fleet, 60 miles off the California coast, where it had been operating in secrecy for over a decade.

The fleet was composed of the 350-foot "Factory ship" *Vostok* and nine 150-foot harpoon boats, each equipped with a 50 mm. cannon and 250-pound explosive harpoons.

Using high-speed inflatable rubber dinghies, three Greenpeace crewmen succeeded in positioning themselves directly in front of a Russian killer boat, the *Vlastny,* while it was attempting to run down and harpoon a pod of ten sperm whales. The Greenpeacers were able to effectively block the Soviet harpooner for 45 minutes—an encounter which was thoroughly documented by the Greenpeace photography and film crews—until the Soviets chose to fire regardless of the obvious risk to the Canadians in the small rubber boat.

Disturbed by the confrontation and the presence of cameras, which had already documented the killing of several undersized whales, the Soviet fleet backed off. In the course of their encounter, the Greenpeacers were able to save eight whales.

From that point, the Russians deliberately avoided any further contact with *Greenpeace V.* Moving their entire fleet away at full speed, some 20 knots, they were able to out-distance Capt. Cormack's stout but slower-moving vessel. Although the Greenpeace expedition pursued the Soviet fleet for two weeks afterwards, they were unable to reestablish contact. Eventually, they returned to Vancouver, releasing footage and photographs of the confrontation which generated a tremendous volume of publicity, especially in the United States, against whaling.

At the 1975 meeting of the International Whaling Commission in London, England, while Greenpeace was closing in on the fleet, the Russian delegation pledged that, as a "gesture toward pressure from conservationists," the Soviet Union would "dismantle" one of its whaling fleets. Japan also agreed, reluctantly, to a reduction of 50 percent in their 1976 quotas.

In 1976, the Greenpeace Foundation intends to send a larger, faster vessel out after the Japanese fleet, known to be operating roughly 2,500 miles due west of the Canadian coast, halfway between Hawaii and the Aleutian Islands. It is Greenpeace's analysis that the fleet most likely to be dismantled by the Russians will be the *Vostok* fleet encountered by Greenpeace last summer, primarily because of its vulnerability to exposure by any anti-whaling expedition operating out of North America.

It is entirely likely that the whale slaughter off the West Coast has already been terminated as a result of the widespread publicity given to the encounter. Accordingly, Greenpeace hopes to maintain the pressure on the whaling nations by seeking out the Japanese fleet and attempting to disrupt their activities over an extended period.

No Greenpeace expedition has ever succeeded in achieving its goal by a single mission. Amchitka took two voyages. Mururoa took three. With continued international support, Greenpeace hopes to affect a ten year moratorium on whaling by 1977, but believes that in order for this to be accomplished, public attention must again be drawn to the whale slaughter in 1976. To this end, a campaign is already underway to help finance the voyage of *Greenpeace VII.*

SHEPHERDS OF THE LABRADOR FRONT, TAKING ON THE GOLIATHS OF DOOM
Paul Watson

Monday morning March 15th. The first day of the seal kill. Our two helicopters lift off from the frozen lichen encrusted barrens of Belle Isle, a lonely forsaken chunk of rock between the island province of Newfoundland and the cold rocky coastline of Labrador. We have made of the island an advance base in order to extend our air range over the ice and sea.

On a north easterly course, the vast expanse of salt ice sweeps by a thousand feet beneath us. Within twenty minutes two ships are spotted. The Norwegian owned Canadian registered sealing vessels, "Martin Karlsen" and "Theron". Plunging through the ice, not yet to the whelping grounds.

We change course following the headings of the ships below, rapidly leaving them behind.

Upon the horizon a black speck appears, then another and another. The fleet with eight ships lies before us.

As the ships loom larger their activity is obvious. No longer a blinding white the ice is flowing crimson in blood. Long gashing streams of seal blood, babies blood, coming from all directions and converging into a grotesque pile-up of carcasses. A constellation of scarlet stars tortuously stained into the hard bluish white of granite hard pack ice.

We circle. We land. Two miles from the nearest ship. It will be a long walk. In an effort to halt our protest, the Canadian Ministry of Fisheries passed a series of new regulations aimed specifically at stopping the intended actions of the Greenpeace Foundation. Our present legal barrier being that no aircraft without the permission of the minister of state for fisheries shall fly lower than 2000 feet over or land less than one half mile from any seal.

The new regulations were incredible. In a rather strange Orwellian way, they were referred to by the government as amendments to the Seal Protection Act. The Federal Minister of Fisheries M. Romeo Le blanc had vowed to stop us. By way of an order in council he achieved the means. He would simply have us arrested. It did not matter to him that Canada has no jurisdiction in International waters. He simply assumed jurisdiction. The Canadian government supported him. Other nations said nothing.

Earlier we had planned to disrupt the hunt by arming ourselves with spray cans containing a green organic dye. Our intention was to destroy the commericial value of the seal pelt by applying an irremoveable green cross to each and every baby whitecoat. It was a good tactic, one that atracted much publicity and cries of outrage from the Fisheries department. The plan did however have one basic flaw, we should have kept it secret. Little did we dream that in Canada, "the true north strong and free," that our government would fabricate special laws to stop us, laws that became effective only days before we could put into effect a plan perfectly legal at its inception.

The government had in addition spread false information to the effect that Greenpeace would kill the seals with the dye. Natural predators would find them, their mothers would reject them, they would freeze to death were among the charges they used to justify the new improved Seal Protection Act. Their own research had employed dyes for twenty years. Federal Fisheries Scientists like Dr. H. Dean Fisher and Dr. David Sergeant had advised us that such was the case and the dye would not harm the seals. The only predators were humans and an occasional Orca. The first predator being unnatural, the second a mammal that locates its prey by other means than sight.

When we arrived in Newfoundland we were greeted by open hostility from the people and the media of that province. We were greeted by the Federal leader of the New Democratic Party who denounced us nationally. We entered Newfoundland at Port aux Basques without the support of any political party and without public or media resistance to the new laws brought down in a dictatorial manner.

We were faced with the fact that if we employed the dye we would immediately be apprehended for a violation of a Federal Fishery Regulation. Our dye would be confiscated, our helicopters siezed. The seals would have continued to die. We believe that we made the best possible decision under the circumstances. In fact rather than surrendering, we decided to employ a different tactic. The government had succeeded in turning the majority of the people of Newfoundland against us. We made an attempt to cut off that support and we were successful. We gave up our dyeing plans, asked for and received the support and endorsement of the 9000 member Newfoundland Fisherman, Food and Allied Workers Union. We appealed to the fisherman in the name of conservation, a cause that fishermen are generally sympathetic to. The fact is that the commercial fleets owned by Norwegian companies are wiping out the seal herds. The fact is that the Norwegians destroyed three great herds of seals prior to starting on the Labrador herds in 1947. The fact is that the commercial fleets take only the pelts, leaving the meat on the ice, while the fishermen and Eskimo of Newfoundland and Labrador do eat the meat. With a conservation stand the seals could have a chance. The fishermen are now exerting pressure on the Fisheries to stop the hunt. We siezed the opportunity to grasp a stronger tactic at the cost of sacrificing a weaker now illegal tactic.

On the ice with us now are Newfoundlanders. Across the drifting floes, our crew heads in the direction of the nearest ship. The ice is treacherous and difficult to cross. Baby seals are all around us, beautiful beyond expectation, each a personification of new born perfection. Chubby little bundles of soft white fur, large tear-filled ebony eyes and a cry practically indistinguishable from its human counterpart.

Ahead, the crying is giving way to frightened screaming and the irregular whack and thud of the seal slayer's club.

Norwegians clutching vicious looking hak-a-piks are dispatching the pups in a manner coldly efficient. The ominous hak-a-pik, a club with a dull iron spike on the end, lifts and falls. Each time it descends a vision of innocence is horribly deprived of life, expiring painfully and in many cases slowly.

The Norwegians swear at us. They threaten us. But they do little else. They have been thoroughly lectured. Al Johnson blocks the path of a burly Norwegian, he falls over the sealers intended victim, shielding its little body with his own. The sealers turn away. He approaches another innocent victim. David Garrick cuts him off. Frustrated the sealer returns to his ship.

I pick up a small pup from the ice. Behind me the vessel "Melshorn" rips her way through the ice towards the pup and myself. Each year thousands of seals are crushed by the ships, their numbers not included in the quotas.

With the surprisingly heavy white bundle in my arms, I run to avoid the rampaging steel bow. We are soon safe the baby and I. Finding an isolated area with no sealers about, we part.

It is not a parting without effect. It is now no longer simply a protest of principle on my part. It has suddenly become personal. I had saved that particular pup's life, held its warm body against my own, carried it in my arms.

On all our faces, the tears and the pain of frustrations are obvious. We do all we can and then retreat to our aircraft before dusk descends. Over our heads a Fisheries helicopter and an airplane buzz us and the seals, flying as low as fifty feet overhead.

Friday, March 19th

For three days we have been grounded. An emerging blizzard had heralded the morning of the 16th. We hurriedly evacuated our base camp at Belle Isle. The winds at that time gusted to 40 mph. Returning to the town of St. Anthony we patiently waited out the natural obstacle. Friday, this morning brought calm winds, clear visibility and a rude surprise on return to Belle Isle. Our tents, our personal effects and our equipment had been swept off the island by the storm and out to sea.

Once more, we fly across the floes, now mangled with rafting ice and leads spanning meters of inky black insurpassable North Atlantic chop.

We have chosen a course some thirty miles southward from our last encounter. Instinct is our guide. The position of the sealing fleet is known only to the Fisheries department, a department with a habit of withholding its information.

It was a shot in the dark but it paid off. After eighty miles the fleet once more lay before us. We land. We walk. We encounter a group of Canadian sealers. I try to talk with them but find it unnerving. The man that I'm addressing holds a seal-skinning knife poised a mere three inches from my belly. The knife drips blood. His face and hands are encrusted with the rusty redness of dried blood.

The sealers have been advised by the fisheries officers to not kill seals if any cameras are in the area. They stop and stand around. All about us at a distance other sealers are going about the bloody trade.

Walking on, I find another sealer. Beneath his feet a pup lies slashed open from throat to hind flippers. The heart is exposed expelling steam into the frigid air. The heart still beats weakly.

"Are you proud of your handiwork?" I ask him.

"No bye," a Newfoundlander by his accent, "naught proud t'all, it be me furst year a swiling, I hav nay hart fer it."

This sealer now tells us that he will kill no more seals. He is the only one, the others continue. There are so many of them, so few of us. Another course of action is needed. Perhaps we can stop the ships from moving through the ice. We move across the ice towards an oncoming sealing vessel.

Bob Hunter and myself find a seal twenty feet before the monstrous scarlet ice crushing bow of the "Arctic Endeavor". We hold our position with our backs to the ship.

On the starboard side of the vessel, a crewman is busily attaching and securing winch lines to a bundle of blood soaked pelts. He yells out to us, "Ya betta move b'yes, the ole man a 'int one ta tink twice bout running ya inta the ice".

Bob yells back, "Tell the old bastard to do what he wants, we're not moving."

The ship backs away. We think we've won this round. Then the unexpected. The "Arctic Endeavor" plunges forward picking up speed. Still we look ahead. We feel her coming. We hear her coming. The vibrations of the powerful diesel engines disturb the chilly air and tingle the soles of our feet through our boots. The ice trembles and cracks. Blocks of chunky ice tumble forward before the bow and nudge our feet.

The crewman on the ice screams to the ship's bridge. We can make out his words clearly, "Stop er Cap, stop er, the stupid asses ain't a moving."

The engines are cut and reversed. The ship slowly grinds to a halt, five feet behind our backs.

I pick up the baby whitecoat to remove it to saftey. My way is blocked by a uniformed fisheries officer. He takes my picture. He pulls some papers from his pocket and begins to read me the amendments to the Seal

Protection Act. "Section 21(B) states that it is a Federal offense to remove a seal from one location to another, it is an offense to pick a live seal up from the ice, you are in violation of this regulation."

Incredibly I listen to this man charged with enforcing the Seal Protection Act. "Do you mean to tell me" I ask, "that I'm supposed to leave this baby to be crushed by that ship."

"That's no business of yours," he replies, "the law is the law, I don't make the laws, I just have to enforce them." He leaves me no choice, I ignore the law, I ignore him and carry the seal to safety. I am still amazed that the government of Canada can presume to have jurisdiction within International waters. But the government is the government and the cards both financial and legal are stacked in favour of the Fisheries Ministry.

Once again the approaching evening forces us to retreat to the land. One of our helicopters, low on fuel, battles the strong head winds and just manages to make it back to base with seven gallons of fuel to spare. Captain Jack Wallace tells us that he has never cut it so close in terms of fuel.

Saturday, March 20th

The coldest morning yet. We find the fleet again. The same ships as yesterday. We circle the fleet at 2500 feet, searching for a place where we can land without violating the regulations. After twenty five minutes in the air, we locate a spot. There's not a seal in sight.

As we begin to descend, we are approached by three Fisheries helicopters. They have been waiting for us. We land. They land. An officer approaches our pilot and informs him that he is in violation of the regulation. He claims we flew lower than 2000 feet and that we are presently only a quarter of a mile from a seal. When we inquire as to the location of this seal we are told that it was on the ice when we landed, but that it has now gone back into the water.

The officers are not interested in arguing, they tell us that their word is final. We are told that our helicopters will be seized when we return to base. Too bad, but the law is the law, they tell us.

We leave our pilots to hassle out the regulations with the Fisheries officers. Our crew sets off across the ice in pursuit of the sealers.

We are now about a mile behind and in the wake of the ship "Arctic Explorer". The ship and her crew of deep-sea butchers have left a source of horrific desolation. We follow the edges of the lead opened up by the ship.

We pass hundreds of slaughtered corpses, the skin stripped from their little bodies. The glazed unseeing eyes are hauntingly disturbing us. In many places the bluish white of the snow and ice has all but disappeared under a coating of crimson. The ice is pitted by the heat of the blood as it spilled from the bodies, melted into the floe, coagulated and frozen in puddles.

We approach closer to the ship, greeted occasionally by a single sad-eyed baby survivor. The survivors whimper and attempt to hide their heads in the snow. The ship looms larger.

As we close in, the weather takes a turn. An instant whiteout. Our helicopters come roaring over the ice to pick us up. The Fisheries officers granted them permission to rescue us. The first helicopter lands. Four crew members jump aboard and the aircraft ascends and speeds across the ice headed toward land. The rest of us jump aboard the second machine. The blizzard becomes more dense, more intense. The wind currents thrash us around. As last the welcome cliffs of Newfoundland are in sight.

Ottawa

Saturday, March 20th was the last day we saw the sealing fleets. We could have located the ships on the 21st and the 22nd, but the Fisheries Department had placed a Royal Canadian Mounted Police guard around our machines and grounded them until our pilots could appear before a magistrate on Tuesday morning.

We paid a bond of $10,000 on each helicopter. A trial date was set for May 18th, and the aircraft were free.

Both helicopters took to the sky before noon on Tuesday. We searched for four hours and found nothing. When we returned to St. Anthony for the last time, the superintendent for fisheries told us that he knew before we left that the fleet would be out of range. We had done all that we were physically capable of doing. We were tired and we had more work to do in Ottawa.

Friday, March 26th. The National Press Building across from the Houses of Parliament. A press conference. The Minister of State for Fisheries is invited. He sends two representatives in his stead. He sends Dr. Arthur May, the Director General of the Resource Branch of the Marine and Fisheries Division of the Ministry of Fisheries and Charles Friend, a public relations official to the Fisheries Department.

Dr. May accuses Greenpeace of not doing their homework, and says that the information in regards to harp and hood seal stocks has always been available to the public. Greenpeace states that this is not true. Many requests for information were made, even from the Minister himself. All requests were denied.

Greenpeace Ecologist Dr. Patrick Moore presents a statement to the press and the government officials in attendance. The statement reads:

"The Greenpeace Foundation has found that the Minister of Fisheries and his officers have acted in a manner that is unfitting to persons who have been charged with the responsibility of conserving our natural resources. The policy of the Department of Fisheries has consistently discriminated against the interests of Canadians and in favour of foreign commerical interests. They have misled and misinformed the public in such a way as to reduce the effectiveness of our efforts to preserve a species that is defenseless against the onslaught of man's technological might.

We of the Greenpeace Foundation, demand the immediate resignation of the Minister of Fisheries, M. Romeo Le blanc, on the grounds that he has been negligent in providing leadership in the conservation of Canada's marine resources. We also demand that Canada unilaterally declare a 200 mile limit in order to preserve the integrity of the marine resources on the continental shelf. We further demand that the report on harp seal populations presented to the Department of Fisheries in October of 1975 be made public immediately and that all other information regarding the seal herds be released."

It is time that we realize the inevitability of the crisis that now faces the living ecosystem of our small and fragile planet.

As human power and population expands, the other species are diminished. The balance of nature has become chaotic and this is due, primarily, to human technology and human institutions. It is becoming increasingly obvious that we must correct this imbalance ourselves or accept responsibility for leaving a ruined planet to our children. It is they who will finally judge whether we have betrayed them in search of our own short-term gains, our pleasures and our vanity, or whether we conscientiously concerned ourselves with the welfare of future generations. Our children will be lucky enough to avoid the pangs of hunger, let alone enjoy the luxuries of the present era.

Edward Abbey and the Monkey Wrench Gang

Introduction to the Selections

Edward Abbey has long been seen as one of America's most important, defiant, and entertaining Western novelists and essay writers, defending the American west from what he saw as the idiocies and dangers of modern technology and the authoritarian industrial state. Until his death in 1989, he was also a living inspiration for the Earth First! movement, attending its annual rendezvous and rallies, writing occasional pieces for the *Earth First! Journal,* and generally spurring radical activists on with his gifted and outrageous rhetoric. The selections in Chapter 5 give a taste of his humor, vulgarity, passion, and commitment to defending the earth from corporate industrialism; they are enough to indicate why he has been a thorn in the side of the establishment and has been called a "radical preservationist."

Abbey had graduate training in philosophy at the University of New Mexico and wrote an M.A. thesis on anarchism, arguing that it is a positive philosophy which makes the individual and absolute individual liberty the basis of civil society. Governments he saw to be evils that are corrupted by power. They need to be replaced by self-rule and "decentralized, equally distributed, fairly shared" power arrangements, a view not unlike that to be found in social ecology and bioregionalism. To him anarchism meant maximum democracy, including the dispersal of political, economic, and military power.[1]

The selection from Abbey's book *The Journey Home* has him arguing that a "cancerous industrialism" is threatening life on the planet, and "technological totalitarianism" looms ahead for America. One consequence of this disease is the destruction of wilderness, and since we cannot have individual freedom without wilderness, we thus need more wilderness defenders to preserve it.[2]

Abbey depicts his wilderness defenders at work in the selection from his famous novel *The Monkey Wrench Gang,* published in 1976. "The Raid at Comb Wash" shows a small gang of eco-guerillas "decommissioning" heavy machinery which is being used to build a modern road through the Utah backcountry. This raid has become a legendary model for monkeywrenching activists in the Earth First! movement, and Abbey later argued that the ecotage depicted in it was justified as a form of self-defense against attacks on one's wilderness home.[3] Wilderness destruction was to him an inevitable result of large-scale industrial society, and thus, as he said in another essay, "if we wish to save what is good in our lives and give our children a taste of a good life, we must bring a halt to the ever-expanding economy and put the growth maniacs under medical care."[4] Monkeywrenching is one of his antidotes for industrial cancer.

Notes

1. See Abbey's essay "Theory of Anarchy," in *One Life at a Time, Please* (New York: Henry Holt and Company, 1988), pp. 25–28.
2. The argument for connecting freedom and wilderness can be found in Abbey's essay, "Freedom and Wilderness, Wilderness and Freedom," from *A Journey Home, Some Words in Defense of the American West* (New York: E. P. Dutton, 1977), p. 235.
3. See Abbey's version of this argument in his "Forward!" to *Ecodefense*, second edition, edited by Dave Foreman and Bill Haywood (Tucson: A Ned Ludd Book, 1987), pp. 7–9.
4. "Freedom and Wilderness, Wilderness and Freedom," in *The Journey Home, Some Words in Defense of the American West*, p. 236.

SHADOWS FROM THE BIG WOODS
Edward Abbey

The idea of wilderness needs no defense. It only needs more defenders.

In childhood the wilds seemed infinite. Along Crooked Creek in the Allegheny Mountains of western Pennsylvania there was a tract of forest we called the Big Woods. The hemlock, beech, poplar, red oak, white oak, maple, and shagbark hickory grew on slopes so steep they had never been logged. Vines of wild grape trailed from the limbs of ancient druidical oaks—dark glens of mystery and shamanism. My brothers and I, simple-minded farmboys, knew nothing of such mythologies, but we were aware, all the same, of the magic residing among and within those trees. We knew that the Indians had once been here, Seneca and Shawnee, following the same deer paths that wound through fern, moss, yarrow, and mayapple among the massive trunks in the green-gold light of autumn, from spring to stream and marsh. Those passionate warriors had disappeared a century before we were even born, but their spirits lingered, their shades still informed the spirit of the place. We knew they were there. The vanished Indians were reincarnated, for a few transcendent summers, in our bones, within our pale Caucasian skins, in our idolatrous mimicry. We knew all about moccasins and feathers, arrows and bows, the thrill of sneaking naked through the underbrush, taking care to tread on not a single dry twig. Our lore came from boys' books, but it was the forest that made it real.

My brother Howard could talk to trees. Johnny knew how to start a fire without matches, skin a squirrel, and spot the eye of a sitting rabbit. I was an expert on listening to mourning doves, though not on interpretation, and could feel pleasure in the clapperclaw of crows. The wolf was long gone from those woods, and also the puma, but there were still plenty of deer, as well as bobcat and raccoon and gray fox; sometimes a black bear, or the rumor of one, passed through the hills. That was good country then, the country of boyhood, and the woods, the forest, that sultry massed deepness of transpiring green, formed the theater of our play. We invented our boyhood as we grew along; but the forest—in which it was possible to get authentically lost—sustained our sense of awe and terror in ways that fantasy cannot.

Now I would not care to revisit those faraway scenes. That forest which seemed so vast to us was only a small thing after all, as the bulldozers, earth movers, and dragline shovels have proved. The woods we thought eternal have been logged by methods formerly considered too destructive, and the very mountainside on which the forest grew has been butchered by the strip miners into a shape of crude symmetry, with spoil banks and head walls and right-angled escarpments where even the running blackberry has a hard time finding a roothold. Stagnant water fills the raw gulches, and the creek below runs sulfur-yellow all year long.

Something like a shadow has fallen between present and past, an abyss wide as war that cannot be bridged by any tangible connection, so that memory is undermined and the image of our beginnings betrayed, dissolved, rendered not mythical but illusory. We have connived in the murder of our own origins. Little wonder that those who travel no where but in their own heads, reducing all existence to the space of one skull, maintain dreamily that only the pinpoint tip of the moment is real. They are right: A fanatical greed, an arrogant stupidity, has robbed them of the past and transformed their future into a nightmare. They deny the world because the only world they know has denied them.

Our cancerous industrialism, reducing all ideological differences to epiphenomena, has generated its own breed of witch doctor. These are men with a genius for control and organization, and the lust to administrate. They propose first to shrink our world to the dimensions of a global village, over which some technological crackpot will erect a geodesic dome to regulate air and light; at the same time the planetary superintendent of schools will feed our children via endless belt into reinforcement-training boxes where they will be conditioned for their functions in the anthill arcology of the future. The ideal robot, after all, is simply a properly processed human being.

The administrators laying out the blueprints for the technological totalitarianism of tomorrow like to think of the earth as a big space capsule, a machine for living. They are wrong: The earth is not a mechanism but an organism, a being with its own life and its own reasons, where the support and sustenance of the human animal is incidental. If man in his newfound power and vanity persists in the attempt to remake the planet in his own image, he will succeed only in destroying himself—not the planet. The earth will survive our most ingenious folly.

Meanwhile, though, the Big Woods is gone—or going fast. And the mountains, the rivers, the canyons, the seashores, the swamps, and the deserts. Even our own, the farms, the towns, the cities, all seem to lie helpless before the advance of the technoindustrial juggernaut. We have created an iron monster with which we wage war, not only on small peasant nations over the sea, but even on ourselves—a war against all forms of life, against life itself. In the name of Power and Growth. But the war is only beginning.

The Machine may seem omnipotent, but it is not. Human bodies and human wit, active here, there, everywhere, united in purpose, independent in action, can still face that machine and stop it and take it apart and reassemble if—if we wish—on lines entirely new. There is, after all, a better way to live. The poets and the prophets have been trying to tell us about it for three thousand years.

THE RAID AT COMB WASH
Edward Abbey

... One fine day in early June, bearing west from Blanding, Utah, on their way to cache more goods, the gang paused at the summit of Comb Ridge for a look at the world below. They were riding four abreast in the wide cab of Seldom Seen Smith's truck. It was lunchtime. He pulled off the dusty road—Utah State Road 95—and turned south on a jeep track that followed close to the rim. Comb Ridge is a great monocline, rising gradually on the east side, dropping off at an angle close to 90 degrees on the west side. The drop-off from the rim is about five hundred feet straight down, with another three hundred feet or more of steeply sloping talus below the cliff. Like many other canyons, mesas and monoclines in southeast Utah, Comb Ridge forms a serious barrier to east-west land travel. Or it used to. God meant it to.

Smith pulled the truck up onto a shelf of slickrock within twenty feet of the rim and stopped. Everybody got out, gratefully, and walked close to the edge. The sun stood high in the clouds; the air was still and warm. Flowers grew from cracks in the rock—globe mallow, crownbeard, gilia, rock cress—and flowering shrubs—cliff rose, Apache plume, chamisa, others. Doc was delighted.

"Look," he said, "*Arabis pulchra. Fallugia paradoxa. Cowania mexicana,* by God."

"What's this?" Bonnie said, pointing to little purplish things in the shade of a pinyon pine.

"*Pedicularis centranthera.*"

"Yeah, okay, but what is it?"

"What is it?" Doc paused. "What it is, no man knows, but men call it . . . wood betony."

"Don't be a wise-ass."

"Also known as lousewort. A child came to me saying, 'What is the lousewort?' And I said, 'Perhaps it is the handkerchief of the lord.' "

"Nobody loves a wise-ass."

"I know," he admitted.

Smith and Hayduke stood on the brink of five hundred feet of naked gravity. That yawning abyss which calls men to sleep. But they were looking not down at death but southward at life, or at least at a turmoil of dust and activity. Whine of motors, snort and growl of distant diesels.

"The new road," Smith explained.

"Uh huh." Hayduke raised his field glasses and studied the scene, some three miles off. "Big operation," he mumbled. "Euclids, D-Nines, haulers, scrapers, loaders, backhoes, drills, tankers. What a beautiful fucking layout."

Doc and Bonnie came up, flowers in their hair. Far off south in the dust, sunlight flashed on glass, on bright steel.

"What's going on down there?" Doc said.

"That's the new road they're working on," Smith said.

"What's wrong with the old road?"

"The old road is too old," Smith explained. "It crawls up and down hills and goes in and out of draws and works around the head of canyons and it ain't paved and it generally takes too long to get anywhere. This new road will save folks ten minutes from Blanding to Natural Bridges."

"It's a county road?" Doc asked.

"It's built for the benefit of certain companies that operate in this county, but it's not a county road, it's a state road. It's to help out the poor fellas that own the uranium mines and the truck fleets and the marinas on Lake Powell, that's what it's for. They gotta eat too."

"I see," said Doc. "Let me have a look, George."

Hayduke passed the field glasses to the doctor, who took a long look, puffing on his Marsh-Wheeling.

"Busy busy busy," he said. He returned the glasses to Hayduke. "Men, we have work to do tonight."

"Me too," Bonnie said.

"You too."

One thin scream came floating down, like a feather, from the silver-clouded sky. Hawk. Redtail, solitaire, one hawk passing far above the red reef, above the waves of Triassic sandstone, with a live' snake clutched in its talons. The snake wriggled, casually, as it was borne away to a different world. Lunchtime.

After a little something themselves the gang got back in Smith's truck and drove two miles closer, over the rock and through the brush, in low range and four-wheel drive, to a high point overlooking the project more directly. Smith parked the truck in the shade of the largest pinyon pine available, which was not big enough to effectively conceal it.

Netting, Hayduke thought; we need camouflage netting. He made a note in his notebook.

Now the three men and the girl worked their way to the rim again, to the edge of the big drop-off. Out of habit Hayduke led the way, crawling forward on hands and knees, then on his belly the last few yards to their observation point. Were such precautions necessary? Probably not, so early in their game; the Enemy, after all, was not aware yet that Hayduke & Co. existed. The Enemy, in fact, still fondly imagined that he enjoyed the favor of the American public, with no exceptions.

Incorrect. They lay on their stomachs on the warm sandstone, under the soft and pearly sky, and peered down seven hundred vertical feet and half a mile by line of sight to where the iron dinosaurs romped and roared in their pit of sand. There was love in neither head not heart of Abbzug, Hayduke, Smith and Sarvis. No sympathy. But considerable involuntary admiration for all that power, all that controlled and directed superhuman force.

Their vantage point gave them a view of the heart, not the whole, of the project. The surveying crews, far ahead of the big machines, had finished weeks earlier, but evidence of their work remained: the Day-Glo ribbon, shocking pink, that waved from the boughs of juniper trees, the beribboned stakes planted in the earth marking center line and shoulder of the coming road, the steel pins hammered into the ground as reference points.

What Hayduke and friends could and did see were several of the many phases of a road-building project that follow the survey. To the far west, on the rise beyond Comb Wash, they saw bulldozers clearing the right-of-way. In forested areas the clearing job would require a crew of loggers with chain saws, but here in southeast Utah, on the plateau, the little pinyon pines and junipers offered no resistance to the bulldozers. The crawler-tractors pushed them all over with nonchalant ease and shoved them aside, smashed and bleeding, into heaps of brush, where they would be left to die and decompose. No one knows precisely how sentient is a pinyon pine, for example, or to what degree such woody organisms can feel pain or fear, and in any case the road builders had more important things to worry about, but this much is clearly established as scientific fact: a living tree, once uprooted, takes many days to wholly die.

Behind the first wave of bulldozers came a second, blading off the soil and ripping up loose stone down to the bedrock. Since this was a cut-and-fill operation it was necessary to blast away the bedrock down to the grade level specified by the highway engineers. Watching from their comfortable grandstand bleachers, the four onlookers saw drill rigs crawl on self-propelled tracks to the blasting site, followed by tractors towing air compressors. Locked in position and linked to the compressors, the drill steel bit into the rock with screaming teconite bits, star-shaped and carbide-tipped. Powdered stone floated on the air as the engines roared. Resonant vibrations shuddered through the bone structure of the earth. More mute suffering. The drill rigs moved on over the hill to the next site.

The demolition team arrived. Charges were lowered into the bore holes, gently tamped and stemmed, and wired to an electrical circuit. The watchers on the rim heard the chief blaster's warning whistle, saw the crew move off to a safe distance, saw the spout of smoke and heard the thunder as the blaster fired his shot. More bulldozers, loaders and giant trucks moved in to shovel up and haul away the debris.

Down in the center of the wash below the ridge the scrapers, the earthmovers and the dump trucks with eighty-ton beds unloaded their loads, building up the fill as the machines beyond were deepening the cut. Cut and fill, cut and fill, all afternoon the work went on. The object in mind was a modern high-speed highway for the convenience of the trucking industry, with grades no greater than 8 percent. That was the immediate object. The ideal lay still farther on. The engineer's dream is a model of perfect sphericity, the planet Earth with all irregularities removed, highways merely painted on a surface smooth as glass. Of course the engineers still have a long way to go but they are patient tireless little fellows; they keep hustling on, like termites in a termitorium. It's steady work, and their only natural enemies, they believe, are mechanical breakdown or "down time" for the equipment, and labor troubles, and bad

weather, and sometimes faulty preparation by the geologists and surveyors.

The one enemy the contractor would not and did not think of was the
band of four idealists stretched out on their stomachs on a rock under the
desert sky.

Down below the metal monsters roared, bouncing on rubber through
the cut in the ridge, dumping their loads and thundering up the hill for
more. The green beasts of Bucyrus, the yellow brutes of Caterpillar,
snorting like dragons, puffing black smoke into the yellow dust.

The sun slipped three degrees westward, beyond the clouds, beyond
the silver sky. The watchers on the ridge munched on jerky, sipped from
their canteens. The heat began to slacken off. There was talk of supper,
but no one had much appetite. There was talk of getting ready for the
evening program. The iron machines still rolled in the wash below, but it
seemed to be getting close to quitting time.

"The main thing we have to watch for," Hayduke said, "is a night
watchman. They just might keep some fucker out here at night. Maybe
with a dog. Then we'll have problems."

"There won't be any watchman," Smith said. "Not all night, anyhow."

"What makes you so sure?"

"It's the way they do things around here; we're out in the country.
Nobody lives out here. It's fifteen miles from Blanding. This here project
is three miles off the old road, which hardly nobody drives at night
anyhow. They don't expect any trouble."

"Maybe some of them are camping out here," Hayduke said.

"Naw," Smith said. "They don't do that kind of thing either. These
boys work like dogs all day long; they wanta get back to town in the
evening. They like their civilized comforts. They ain't campers. These
here construction workers don't think nothing of driving fifty miles to
work every morning. They're all crazy as bedbugs. I worked in these
outfits myself."

Doc and Hayduke, armed with the field glasses, kept watch. Smith and
Bonnie crawled down from the ridge, keeping out of sight, until they
were below the skyline. Then they walked to the truck, set up the
campstove and began preparing a meal for the crew. The doctor and
Hayduke, poor cooks, made good dishwashers. All four were qualified
eaters, but only Bonnie and Smith cared enough about food to cook it
with decency.

Smith was right; the construction workers departed all together long
before sundown. Leaving their equipment lined up along the right-of-
way, nose to tail, like a herd of iron elephants, or simply *in situ*, where
quitting time found them, the operators straggled back in small groups to

their transport vehicles. Far above, Doc and Hayduke could hear their voices, the laughter, the rattle of lunch buckets. The carryalls and pick-ups driven by men at the eastern end of the job came down through the big notch to meet the equipment operators. The men climbed in; the trucks turned and ground uphill through the dust, into the notch again and out of sight. For some time there was the fading sound of motors, a cloud of dust rising above the pinyon and juniper; then that too was gone. A tanker truck appeared, full of diesel fuel, groaning down the grade toward the machines, and proceeded from one to the next, the driver and his helper filling the fuel tanks of each, topping them off. Finished, the tanker turned and followed the others back through the evening toward the distant glow of town, somewhere beyond the east-ward bulge of the plateau.

Now the stillness was complete. The watchers on the rim, eating their suppers from tin plates, heard the croon of a mourning dove far down the wash. They heard the hoot of an owl, the cries of little birds retiring to sleep in the dusty cottonwoods. The great golden light of the setting sun streamed across the sky, glowing upon the clouds and the mountains. Almost all the country within their view was roadless, uninhabited, a wilderness. They meant to keep it that way. They sure meant to try. *Keep it like it was.*

The sun went down.

Tactics, materials, tools, gear.

Hayduke was reading off his checklist. "Gloves! Everybody got his gloves? Put 'em on now. Anybody goes fucking around down there without gloves I'll chop his hands off."

"You haven't washed the dishes yet," Bonnie said.

"Hard hat! Everybody got his hard hat?" He looked around at the crew. "You—put that thing on your head."

"It doesn't fit," she said.

"Make it fit. Somebody show her how to adjust the headband. Jesus Christ." Looking back at his list. "Bolt cutters!" Hayduke brandished his own, a 24-inch pair of cross-levered steel jaws for cutting bolts, rods, wire, most anything up to half an inch in diameter. The rest of the party were equipped with fencing pliers, good enough for most purposes.

"Now, you lookouts," he went on, addressing Bonnie and Doc. "Do you know your signals?"

"One short and a long for warning, take cover," Doc said, holding up his metal whistle. "One short and two longs for all clear, resume op-erations. Three longs for distress, come help. Four longs for . . . what are four longs for?"

"Four longs mean work completed, am returning to camp," Bonnie said. "And one long means acknowledgment, message received."

"Don't much like them tin whistles," Smith said. "We need something more natural. More eco-logical. Owl hoots, maybe. Anybody hears them tin whistles will know there's two-legged animals slinkin' around. Lemme show you how to hoot like a owl."

Training time. Hands cupped and close, one little opening between thumbs, shape the lips, blow. Blow from the belly, down deep; the call will float through canyons, across mountainsides, all the way down in the valley. Hayduke showed Dr. Sarvis; Smith showed Abbzug, personally, holding her hands in the necessary way, blowing into them, letting her blow into his. She picked it up quickly, the doctor not so fast. They rehearsed the signals. For a while the twilight seemed full of great horned owls, talking. Finally, they were ready. Hayduke returned to his checklist.

"Okay, gloves, hats, wire cutters, signals, Now: Karo syrup, four quarts each. Matches. Flashlights—be careful with those: keep the light close to your work, don't swing it around, shut it off when you're moving. Maybe we should work out light signals? Naw, later. Water. Jerky. Hammer, screwdriver, cold chisel—okay, I got them. What else?"

"We're all set," Smith said. "Let's get a move on."

They shouldered their packs. Hayduke's pack, with most of the hardware in it, weighed twice as much as anyone else's. He didn't care. Seldom Seen Smith led the way through the sundown gloom. The others followed in single file, Hayduke at the rear. There was no trail, no path. Smith picked the most economic route among the scrubby trees, around the bayonet leaves of the yucca and the very hairy prickly pear, across the little sandy washes below the crest of the ridge. As much as possible he led them on the rock, leaving no tracks.

They were headed south by the stars, south by the evening breeze, toward a rising Scorpio sprawled out fourteen galactic worlds wide across the southern sky. Owls hooted from the pygmy forest. The saboteurs hooted back.

Smith circumvented an anthill, a huge symmetric arcologium of sand surrounded by a circular area denuded of any vestige of vegetation. The dome home of the harvester ants. Smith went around and so did Bonnie but Doc stumbled straight into it, stirring up the formicary. The big red ants swarmed out looking for trouble; one of them bit Doc on the calf. He stopped, turned and dismantled the anthill with a series of vigorous kicks.

"Thus I refute R. Buckminster Fuller," he growled. "Thus do I refute Paolo Soleri, B. F. Skinner and the late Walter Gropius."

"How late was he?" Smith asked.

"Doc hates ants," Bonnie explained. "And they hate him."

"The anthill," said Doc, "is sign, symbol and symptom of what we are about out here, stumbling through the gloaming like so many stumblebums. I mean it is the model in microcosm of what we must find a way to oppose and halt. The anthill, like the Fullerian foam fungus, is the mark of social disease. Anthills abound where over-grazing prevails. The plastic dome follows the plague of runaway industrialism, prefigures technological tyranny and reveals the true quality of our lives, which sinks in inverse ratio to the growth of the Gross National Product. End of mini-lecture by Dr. Sarvis."

"Good," Bonnie said.

"Amen," said Smith.

The evening gave way to night, a dense violet solution of starlight and darkness mixed with energy, each rock and shrub and tree and scarp outlined by an aura of silent radiation. Smith led the conspirators along the contour of the terrain until they came to the brink of something, an edge, a verge, beyond which stood nothing tangible. This was not the rim of the monocline, however, but the edge of the big man-made cut *through* the monocline. Below in the gloom those with sufficient night vision could see the broad new roadway and the dark forms of machines, two hundred feet down.

Smith and friends proceeded along this new drop-off until they reached a point where it was possible to scramble down to the crushed rock and heavy dust of the roadbed. Looking northeast, toward Blanding, they saw this pale raw freeway leading straight across the desert, through the scrub forest and out of sight in the darkness. No lights were visible, only the faint glow of the town fifteen miles away. In the opposite direction the roadbed curved down between the walls of the cut, sinking out of view toward the wash. They walked into the cut.

The first thing they encountered, on the shoulder of the roadbed, were survey stakes. Hayduke pulled them up and tossed them into the brush.

"Always pull up survey stakes," he said. "Anywhere you find them. Always. That's the first goddamned general order in the monkey wrench business. Always pull up survey stakes."

They walked deeper into the cut to where it was possible, looking down and west, to make out though dimly the bottom of Comb Wash, the fill area, the scattered earth-moving equipment. Here they stopped for further consultation.

"We want our first lookout here," Hayduke said.

"Doc or Bonnie?"

"I want to wreck something," Bonnie said. "I don't want to sit here in the dark making owl noises."

"I'll stay here," Doc said.

Once more they rehearsed signals. All in order. Doc made himself comfortable on the operator's seat of a giant compactor machine. He toyed with the controls. "Stiff," he said, "but it's transportation."

"Why don't we start with this fucker right here?" Hayduke said, meaning Doc's machine. "Just for the practice."

Why not? Packs were opened, tools and flashlights brought out. While Doc stood watch above them his three comrades entertained themselves cutting up the wiring, fuel lines, control link rods and hydraulic hoses of the machine, a beautiful new 27-ton tandem-drummed yellow Hyster C-450A, Caterpillar 330 HP diesel engine, sheepsfoot rollers, manufacturer's suggested retail price only $29,500 FOB Saginaw, Michigan. One of the best. A dreamboat.

They worked happily. Hard hats clinked and clanked against the steel. Lines and rods snapped apart with the rich *spang!* and solid *clunk!* of metal severed under tension. Doc lit another stogie. Smith wiped a drop of oil from his eyelid. The sharp smell of hydraulic fluid floated on the air, mixing uneasily with the aroma of Doc's smoke. Running oil pattered on the dust. There was another sound, far away, as of a motor. They paused. Doc stared into the dark. Nothing. The noise faded.

"All's clear," he said. "Carry on, lads."

When everything was cut which they could reach and cut, Hayduke pulled the dipstick from the engine block—to check the oil? not exactly—and poured a handful of fine sand into the crankcase. Too slow. He unscrewed the oil-filler cap, took chisel and hammer and punched a hole through the oil strainer and poured in more sand. Smith removed the fuel-tank cap and emptied four quart bottles of sweet Karo syrup into the fuel tank. Injected into the cylinders, that sugar would form a solid coat of carbon on cylinder walls and piston rings. The engine should seize up like a block of iron, when they got it running. If they could get it running.

What else? Abbzug, Smith and Hayduke stood back a little and stared at the quiet hulk of the machine. All were impressed by what they had done. The murder of a machine. Deicide. All of them, even Hayduke, a little awed by the enormity of their crime. By the sacrilege of it.

"Let's slash the seat," said Bonnie.

"That's vandalism," Doc said. "I'm against vandalism. Slashing seats is petty-bourgeois."

"So okay, okay," Bonnie said. "Let's get on to the next item."

"Then we'll all meet back here?" Doc said.

"It's the only way back up on the ridge," Smith said.

"But if there's any shit," Hayduke said, "don't wait for us. We'll meet at the truck."

"I couldn't find my way back there if my life depended on it," Doc said. "Not in the dark."

Smith scratched his long jaw. "Well, Doc," he said, "if there's any kind of trouble maybe you better just hightail it up on the bank there, above the road, and wait for us. Don't forget the hoot owl. We'll find you that way."

They left him there in the dark, perched on the seat of the maimed and poisoned compactor. The one red eye of his cigar watched them depart. The plan was for Bonnie to stand watch at the far west end of the project, alone, while Hayduke and Smith worked on the equipment down in the wash. She murmured against them.

"You ain't afraid of the dark, are you?" Smith asked.

"Of course I'm afraid of the dark."

"You afraid to be alone?"

"Of course I'm afraid to be alone."

"You mean you don't want to be lookout?"

"I'll be lookout."

"No place for women," Hayduke muttered.

"You shut up," she said. "Am I complaining? I'll be lookout. So shut up before I take your jaw off."

The dark seemed warm, comfortable, secure to Hayduke. He liked it. The Enemy, if he appeared, would come loudly announced with roar of engines, blaze of flares, an Operation Rolling Thunder of shells and bombs, just as in Vietnam. So Hayduke assumed. For the night and the wilderness belong to *us*. This is Indian country. Our country. Or so he assumed.

Downhill, maybe a mile, in one great switchback, the roadway descended through the gap to the built-up fill across the floor of Comb Wash. They soon reached the first group of machines—the earthmovers, the big trucks, the landscape architects.

Bonnie was about to go on by herself. Smith took her arm for a moment. "You stay close, honey," he told her, "only concentrate on looking and listening; let me and George do the hard work. Take the hard hat off so you can hear better. Okay?"

"Well," she agreed, "for the moment." But she wanted a bigger share of the action later. He agreed. Share and share alike. He showed her where to find the steps that led to the open cab of an 85-ton Euclid mountain mover. She sat up there, like a lookout in a crow's nest, while he and Hayduke went to work.

Busywork. Cutting and snipping, snapping and wrenching. They crawled all over a Caterpillar D-9A, world's greatest bulldozer, the idol of all highwaymen. Put so much sand in the crankcase that Hayduke couldn't get the dipstick reinserted all the way. He trimmed it short with the rod-and-bolt cutter. Made it fit. Sand in the oil intake. He climbed into the cab, tried to turn the fueltank cap. Wouldn't turn. Taking hammer and chisel he broke it loose, unscrewed it, poured four quarts of good high-energy Karo into the diesel fuel. Replaced the cap. Sat in the driver's seat and played for a minute with the switches and levers.

"You know what would be fun?" he said to Smith, who was down below hacking through a hydraulic hose.

"What's that, George?"

"Get this fucker started, take it up to the top of the ridge and run it over the rim."

"That there'd take us near half the night, George."

"Sure would be fun."

"We can't get it started anyhow."

"Why not?"

"There ain't no rotor arm in the magneto. I looked. They usually take out the rotor arm when they leave these beasts out on the road."

"Yeah?" Hayduke takes notebook and pencil from his shirt pocket, turns on his flashlight, makes notation: *Rotor arms.* "You know something else that would be fun?"

Smith, busy nullifying all physical bond between cylinder heads and fuel injection lines, says, "What?"

"We could knock a pin out of each tread. Then when the thing moved it would run right off its own fucking tracks. That would really piss them."

"George, this here tractor ain't gonna move at all for a spell. It ain't-a-goin' *nowheres.*"

"For a spell."

"That's what I said."

"That's the trouble."

Hayduke climbed down from the cab and came close to Smith, there in the black light of the stars, doing his humble chores, the pinpoint of his flashlight beam fixed on a set screw in an engine block the weight of three Volkswagen buses. The yellow Caterpillar, enormous in the dark, looms over the two men with the indifference of a god, submitting without a twitch of its enameled skin to their malicious ministrations. The down payment on this piece of equipment comes to around $30,000. What were the men worth? In any rational chemico-psycho-physical analysis? In a nation of two hundred and ten million (210,000,000) bodies? Getting cheaper by the day, as mass production lowers the unit cost?

"That's the trouble," he said again. "All this wire cutting is only going to slow them down, not stop them. Godfuckingdammit, Seldom, we're wasting our time."

"What's the matter, George?"

"We're wasting our time."

"What do you mean?"

"I mean we ought to really blast this motherfucker. This one and all the others. I mean set them on fire. Burn them up."

"That there's arson."

"For chrissake, what's the difference? You think what we're doing now is much nicer? You know damn well if old Morrison-Knudsen was out here now with his goons he'd be happy to see us all shot dead."

"They ain't gonna be too happy about this, you're right there. They ain't gonna understand us too good."

"They'll understand us. They'll hate our fucking guts."

"They won't understand why we're doin' this, George. That's what I mean. I mean we're gonna be misunderstood."

"No, we're not gonna be misunderstood. We're gonna be hated."

"Maybe we should explain."

"Maybe we should do it right. None of this petty fucking around."

Smith was silent.

"Let's *destroy* this fucker."

"I don't know," Smith said.

"I mean roast it in its own grease. I just happen to have a little siphon hose here in my pack. Like I just happen to have some matches. I mean we just siphon some of that fuel out of the tank and we just sort of slosh it around over the engine and cab and then we just sort of toss a match at it. Let God do the rest."

"Yeah, I guess He would," Smith agreed. "If God meant this here bulldozer to live He wouldn't of filled its tank with diesel fuel. Now would He of? But George, what about Doc?"

"What about him? Since when is he the boss?"

"He's the one bankrolling this here operation. We need him."

"We need his money."

"Well, all right, put it this way: I like old Doc. And I like that little old lady of his too. And I think all four of us got to stick together. And I think we can't do anything that all four of us ain't agreed to do beforehand. Think about it that way, George."

"Is that the end of the sermon?"

"That's the end of the sermon."

Now Hayduke was silent for a while. They worked. Hayduke thought. After a minute he said, "You know something, Seldom? I guess you're right."

"I thought I was wrong once," Seldom said, "but I found out later I was mistaken."

They finished with the D-9A. The siphon hose and the matches remained inside Hayduke's pack. For the time being. Having done all they could to sand, jam, gum, mutilate and humiliate the first bulldozer, they went on to the next, the girl with them. Smith put his arm around her.

"Miss Bonnie," he says, "how do you like the night shift?"

"Too peaceful. When's my turn to wreck something?"

"We need you to look out."

"I'm bored."

"Don't you worry about that none, honey. We're gonna have enough excitement pretty soon to last you and me for the rest of our lives. If we live that long. How do you think old Doc is doing back there all by his lonesome?"

"He's all right. He lives inside his head most of the time anyway."

Another giant machine looms out of the darkness before them. A hauler; they chop it up. Then the next. Bonnie watches from her post in the cab of a nearby earthmover. Next! The men go on.

"If only we could start up the motors on these sombitches," Hayduke said. "We could drain the oil out, let the motors run and walk away. They'd take care of themselves and we'd be finished a lot faster."

"That'd do it," Smith allowed. "Drain the oil and let the engines run.

They'd seize up tighter'n a bull's asshole in fly time. They never would get them buggers prised open."

"We could give each one a try anyhow." And acting on his words, Hayduke climbed to the controls of a big bulldozer. "How do you start this mother?"

"I'll show you if we find one ready to go."

"How about a hot wire? Maybe we could start it that way. Bypass the ignition."

"Not a caterpillar tractor. This ain't no car, George, you know. This is a D-Eight. This here's heavy-duty industrial equipment; this ain't the old Farmall back home."

"Well, I'm ready for driving lessons anytime."

Hayduke climbed down from the operator's seat. They worked on the patient, sifting handfuls of fine Triassic sand into the crankcase, cutting up the wiring, the fuel lines, the hydraulic hoses to fore and aft attachments, dumping Karo into the fuel tanks. Why Karo instead of plain sugar? Smith wanted to know. Pours better, Hayduke explained; mixes easier with the diesel, doesn't jam up in strainers. You sure about that? No.

Hayduke crawled under the bulldozer to find the drain plug in the oil pan. He found it, through an opening in the armored skid plate, but needed a big wrench to crack it loose. They tried the toolbox in the cab. Locked. Hayduke broke the lock with his cold chisel and hammer. Inside they found a few simple and massive instruments: an iron spanner three feet long; a variety of giant end wrenches; a sledgehammer; a wooden-handled monkey wrench; nuts, bolts, friction tape, wire.

Hayduke took the spanner, which looked like the right size, and crawled again underneath the tractor. He struggled for a while with the plug, finally broke it loose and let out the oil. The great machine began to bleed; its lifeblood drained out with pulsing throbs, onto the dust and sand. When it was all gone he replaced the plug. Why? Force of habit—thought he was changing the oil in his jeep.

Hayduke surfaced, smeared with dust, grease, oil, rubbing a bruised knuckle. "Shit," he said, "I don't know."

"What's the matter?"

"Are we doing this job right? That's what I don't know. Now the operator gets on this thing in the morning, tries to start it up, nothing happens. So the first thing he sees is all the wiring cut, all the fuel lines cut. So putting sand in the crankcase, draining the oil, isn't going to do any good till they get the motor to run. But when they fix all the wiring and lines they're gonna be checking other things too. Like the oil level, naturally. Then they find the sand. Then they see somebody's drained the oil. I'm thinking if we really want to do this monkey wrench business right, maybe we should hide our work. I mean keep it simple and sophisticated."

"Well, George, you was the one wanted to set these things on fire about a minute ago."

"Yeah. Now I'm thinking the other way."

"Well, it's too late. We already showed our hand here. We might as well go on like we started."

"Now think about it a minute, Seldom. They'll all get here about the same time tomorrow morning. Everybody starts up the engine on his piece of equipment, or tries to. Some'll discover right away that we cut up the wiring. I mean on the machines we already cut. But look, on the others, if we let the wiring alone, let the fuel lines alone, so they can start the engines, then the sand and the Karo will really do some good. I mean they'll have a chance to do the work we want them to do: ruin the engines. What do you think about that?"

They leaned side by side against the steel track of the Cat, gazing at each other through the soft starlight.

"I kind of wish we had figured all this out before," Smith said. "We ain't got all night."

"Why don't we have all night?"

"Because I reckon we ought to be fifty miles away from here come morning. That's why."

"Not me," Hayduke said. "I'm going to hang around and watch what happens. I want that personal fucking satisfaction."

A hoot owl hooted from the earthmover up ahead. "What's going on back there?" Bonnie called. "You think this is a picnic or something?"

"Okay," Smith said, "let's keep it kinda simple. Let's put these here cutters away for a while and just work on the oil and fuel systems. God knows we got plenty of sand here. About ten thousand square miles of it." Agreed.

They went on, quickly and methodically now, from machine to machine, pouring sand into each crankcase and down every opening which led to moving parts. When they had used up all their Karo syrup, they dumped sand into the fuel tanks, as an extra measure.

All the way, into the night, Hayduke, Smith, they worked their way to the end of the line. Now one, now the other, would relieve Bonnie at the lookout post so that she could participate fully in field operations. Team work, that's what made America great: teamwork and initiative, that's what made America what it is today. They worked over the Cats, they operated on the earthmovers, they gave the treatment to the Schramm air compressors the Hyster compactors the Massey crawler-loaders the Joy Ram track drills the Dart D-600 wheel loaders not overlooking one lone John Deere 690-A excavator backhoe, and that was about all for the night; that was about enough; old Morrison-Knudsen had plenty of equipment all right but somebody was due for headaches in the morning when the sun came up and engines were fired up and all those little particles of sand, corrosive as powdered emery, began to wreak earth's vengeance on the cylinder walls of the despoilers of the desert.

When they reached the terminus of the cut-and-fill site, high on the folded earth across the wash from Comb Ridge, and had thoroughly sand-packed the last piece of road-building equipment, they sat down on a juniper log to rest. Seldom Seen, reckoning by the stars, estimated the time at 2 A.M. Hayduke guessed it was only 11:30. He wanted to go on, following the surveyors, and remove all the stakes, pins and flagging that he knew was waiting out there, in the dark, in the semi-virgin wilds beyond. But Abbzug had a better idea; instead of destroying the survey crew's signs, she suggested, why not relocate them all in such a manner as to lead the right-of-way in a grand loop back to the starting point? Or lead it to the brink of, say, Muley Point, where the contractors would confront a twelve-hundred-foot vertical drop-off down to the goosenecks of the San Juan River.

"Don't give them any ideas," Hayduke said. "They'd just want to build another goddamned bridge."

"Them survey markings go on west for twenty miles," Smith said. He was against both plans.

"So what do we do?" Says Bonnie.

"I'd like to crawl into the sack," Smith said. "Get some sleep."

"I like that idea myself."

"But the night is young," Hayduke said.

"George," says Smith, "we can't do everything in one night. We got to get Doc and get back to the truck and haul ass. We don't want to be around here in the morning."

"They can't prove a thing."

"That's what Pretty-Boy Floyd said. That's what Baby-Face Nelson said and John Dillinger and Butch Cassidy and that other fella, what's his name—?"

"Jesus," Hayduke growls.

"Yeah, Jesus Christ. That's what they all said and look what happened to them. Nailed."

"This is our first big night," Hayduke said. "We ought to do as much work as we can. We're not likely to get more easy operations like this. Next time they'll have locks on everything. Maybe booby traps. And watchmen with guns, shortwave radios, dogs."

Poor Hayduke: won all his arguments but lost his immortal soul. He had to yield.

They marched back the way they'd come, past the quiet, spayed, medicated machinery. Those doomed dinosaurs of iron, waiting patiently through the remainder of the night for buggering morning's rosy-fingered denouement. The agony of cylinder rings, jammed by a swollen piston, may be like other modes of sodomy a crime against nature in the eyes of *deus ex machina;* who can say? . . .

CHAPTER **6**

The Sea Shepherd Society, Direct Action on the High Seas

Introduction to the Selections

Chapter 4 claims that Paul Watson was a leading activist in Greenpeace during the 1970s, helping it in its expeditions against whaling and harp seal hunting. In the first selection of Chapter 6, Watson explains that his activism began to cause him trouble in the Canadian branch of Greenpeace, and he was eventually expelled from the group in 1977. Apparently he had become too much of a vigilante for their taste and had to move on. In the first selection, taken from his book *Sea Shepherd, My Fight for Whales and Seals*, Watson reformulates the laws of ecology that were part of the Greenpeace Declaration of Interdependence, then indicates his reservations about a completely nonviolent approach to eco-action. As he says earlier in the book, "Few changes on this planet have taken place solely because of nonviolent action. To remain nonviolent totally is to allow the perpetuation of violence against people, animals and the environment."[1] Since Greenpeace stood for nonviolence even with respect to machines, their differing views about ecotactics obviously led them along different paths.

Watson eventually formed his own ecotactical group, the Sea Shepherd Society, and purchased an ocean-going boat with the help of Cleveland Amory's Fund for Animals. Working with donations and donated help, and little bureaucratic organization, this society has managed to carve out a niche for itself in the radical environmentalist movement by taking direct action on the oceans to save marine mammals— especially whales but also dolphins and sea turtles, among others. The Sea Shepherds have become so notorious for their fearlessness and their willingness to damage the machines and other technological devices used to capture and destroy marine mammals that they have been dubbed "the Kamikaze conservationists" by the Japanese press.

Watson doesn't mince any words: he thinks that whaling is an atrocity

167

that must be stopped. It is a crime against international law, a crime against nature, and a crime against future generations, he says in the second selection in Chapter 6. That selection gives his version of the efforts of two Sea Shepherd activists, with his full support, to sabotage an Iceland whale processing plant and scuttle Iceland's three whaling ships in the Reykjavik harbor in 1986. He also articulates the ethical guidelines for direct Sea Shepherd action in the field. The guidelines show why Sea Shepherd ecotage is a compromise between using violence against nature destroyers and using no violence against humans or machines. Watson believes that there is a clear difference between attacking the machines that are destroying sea mammals and harming the individuals who are whaling, sealing, and fishing. He also has argued that Sea Shepherd interference with whaling on the oceans is not a violation of law, since his society is enforcing international law in a world where there is no other enforcement against illegal whaling. Watson claims that he could not logically be violating the law anyway since the only laws that are valid in this case are the laws of ecology, and when the laws of nations permit whaling they violate ecological laws and become invalid themselves. It is the whalers, then, who are the civilly disobedient ones and not the Sea Shepherds.[2]

The final selection in this chapter gives another illustration of ecotage by the Sea Shepherd Society in the summer of 1990. In this case, Watson explains how the society mounted an attack against the crime of drift netting by ramming and disabling Japanese drift netting ships in the Pacific. At the time, drift netting had not been declared firmly illegal by international law or by compacts between nations. But to Watson it was still a violation of ecological law, and nothing was being done about the massive, incidental killing of sea birds and marine mammals in these powerful nets. Waston believes then that his group was justified in stepping in and doing something about these atrocities.

Notes

1. *Sea Shepherd, My Fight for Whales and Seals* (New York: W. W. Norton & Company, 1982), p. 26.
2. This is an argument that Watson made in a talk before the L.A.W. Environmental Law Conference at the University of Oregon Law School, Eugene, Oregon, in March 1988.

GOODBYE TO GREENPEACE
Paul Watson

. . . Things were coming to a boil between the leadership of Greenpeace and me when we returned to Vancouver. There was the usual fuss about paying off debts, and then I was hauled on the carpet by Pat Moore. I was, he felt, too much of an activist. He had told me that if he were elected president of Greenpeace, he would move to kick me out, and he was making good on that private campaign pledge.

But away from the foundation's internal politics, our work was having an impressive impact. I was astonished, for example, at the heart-warming turnout of students at the University of California in Berkeley to hear my report on the 1977 harp seal hunt. About seven hundred people gathered that April 7 on the steps of Sproul Hall, and, led by me and Gary Zimmerman, president of Greenpeace America, most marched to the Art Museum, where Prime Minster Pierre Trudeau was having lunch. Trudeau was visibly shaken when he emerged to a bilingual demonstration, with people chanting:

"Stop the slaughter!"

"*Cessez le massacre!*"

Support came too, from the state legislature in Hawaii. The Hawaiian Senate applauded the resolution introduced by Rep. Leo J. Ryan (D-California) and passed by the U.S. House of Representatives, and another in the U.S. Senate by Sen. Spark M. Matsunaga (D-Hawaii) calling on Canada to "reassess its present policy of permitting the killing of new-born harp seals." The Hawaiian Senate, by its own resolution, gave full support to the Ryan-Matsunaga effort against what it called "the brutal and merciless slaughter of the seals."

And so it seemed to me that progress was being made, however slowly, and that this growing world concern was far more important than fighting over who sits above or below the salt in the Greenpeace hierarchy. What we were in danger of forgetting was why we undertook to protest the seal hunt in the first place. That decision was made primarily because, in addition to the possibility of saving seals, we could also call attention to the plight of all sea mammals. We saw the seals as a symbol through which we could dramatize the depletion and wholesale mismanagement of entire marine ecosystems. Ironically, the major result of our two anti-sealing expeditions was that the Canadian government, which more or less ignored Newfoundland as a rule, was now directing federal grants and programs toward the chronically poor people of that rocky out cropping in the Labrador Sea—and the slaughter of the harp seals went on.

In any event, the people in Vancouver who were running the Greenpeace Foundation decided I was one founder of the organization they could do without. Apparently, the ultimate transgression was that I had picked up a sealer's club and had thrown it into the water. I was voted out of Greenpeace. I vowed not to be bitter, and not even to look back, but to keep on going as my conscience dictated, to continue to be nonviolent and yet to defy authority whenever I considered it wrong— and whenever its policies worked against the sea mammals.

"You have no right to make yourself judge and jury," the Greenpeacers had told me, as I stood before them. "You have no right to appoint yourself a one-man vigilante squad."

That struck me as both extreme and unfair. But the attention of the organization seemed directed more now at working out little boxes and charts and creating an international complex of Greenpeacers that would be controlled out of a super-headquarters in Vancouver. Thus, it appeared, Greenpeace would spend so much of its time organizing and fund-raising that its efforts to conserve our planet would be dissipated. A million dollars in newly raised funds would not make a man or a woman face up to clubs and harpoons. That takes heart. And, as for the judge-and-jury charge, I told the Greenpeace board of directors something to this effect:

"Informed judgment of reasonable and humane people is the jury, and that verdict has been in for a long time. What is lacking is a police force to make the verdict stick.

"I guess I plead guilty to being a vigilante, but I can tell you something. If there are no police, then vigilantes will appear, because there will always be somebody to see to it that crime is never given a free rein."

It was an emotional parting. All of us had given too much of ourselves over too many years for there to be dispassionate goodbyes. Those in control at Greenpeace were going one way, others of us were going another. Soon after I was sacked, David Garrick sent in his resignation— not as a result of my departure, but because he was protesting creation of an international board to oversee policy and funding of all Greenpeace campaigns.

"This is the last straw," Garrick said. Like me, he cared little for form and everything for substance. No man had a better friend or stauncher ally than David Garrick, and I was gratified, though hardly surprised, to see him turn away from the direction in which Greenpeace was headed.

Severing my Greenpeace connections, as painful as it was, in no way diminished my activity. In fact, I felt more at liberty to pursue my own goals. The complications arising from Greenpeace's success were those I felt I should avoid at all cost. Thoreau had said, "Simplify, simplify, simplify," and I agreed with that. Some years earlier, I had put down three fundamental laws of ecology, and I reviewed them now as bench-marks in the struggle.

1. All forms of life are interdependent. The prey is as dependent upon the predator for control of its population as the predator is upon the prey for supply of food. Many people feel that eliminating mosquitoes is necessary for humans, but what of the swallows feeding on them? Do we want to do away with swallows, too?

2. Diversity promotes stability. An ecosystem with hundreds of different species is far less likely to decline and disappear than one that has only a handful. The complex rain forest is more stable than the sparse Arctic tundra.

3. All resources are finite. As mankind uses the things of the earth, sometimes seemingly endless in our closed system, it is easy to lose sight of the immutable truth that everything has an end. Examples are almost too numerous and familiar to dwell upon—such as our energy and fuel shortage, and, of course, our ever-growing lists of endangered species.

There are other such laws, of course, and we ignore them all at our peril. Short-term economics must be made to give way to these rules of conservation and preservation. We must learn to live in harmony, not only with our fellow man, but with all the wonderful creatures of our planet.

This is really not as difficult a job as we tend to make it out to be. It is far too much to expect one person, or even a small group, to take on the job of assuring continued existence for all that is endangered in our world. But some good can be done, even by a small band, if it is made up of determined individuals—call them vigilantes, even—who devote their lives to the issue of survival, as I have devoted my life to saving whales and other sea mammals.

Those of us who do this kind of work are treated at times like escapees from a sideshow—weirdos who care more for animals than for humans. We are seen as vigilantes and radicals, revolutionaries and nonconformists, who, figuratively if not literally, are at peace with ourselves only when causing conflict.

I do not feel like a freak. I feel normal. And sometimes I wonder if the rest of the world is normal, especially that part of it that goes around plundering the natural world. It is at such times that the opposing philosophies of violence and nonviolence tear at me. I know violence is morally wrong and nonviolence is morally right. But what about results? Nonviolent action alone has seldom produced beneficial change on our planet. I continue to fret over this point. I compromise by allowing myself violence against property but never against life, human or otherwise. . . .

RAID ON REYKJAVIK
Paul Watson

Hold it right there. Before you begin to read my incredibly interesting narrative which follows, I want to get something straight. If you are a self-righteous tight-ass who gets morally indignant about correct tactics, you know, the "I agree with your motives, I just can't accept your methods" type—if you are one of THEM, then do yourself and us a favour and read *Time* or the *Greenpeace Examiner* instead. This article does not contain scenes of excessive violence nor does it contain sexually explicit material (unfortunately). It does however advocate the destruction of property because, and pardon me for my old-fashioned ways, I believe that respect for life takes precedence over respect for property which is used to take lives.

Let's get something else straight. The killing of whales in 1986 is a crime. It is a violation of international law, but more importantly it is a crime against nature and a crime against future generations of humanity. Moreover, whaling is a nasty form of anti-social behaviour and an atrocity which should be stamped out. So, I don't want any crappy letters about tradition, livelihood or Icelandic rights.

With that said, we can get into the story.

August 1985: The "Sea Shepherd" makes a stop in Reykjavik while on route to the Faroe Islands. We berth directly behind the Greenpeace ship "Sirius." Across the harbour, we can see the Icelandic whaling fleet tied together. Our plan is to take on provisions before heading to the Faroes. At the same time, many pictures are taken, port facilities surveyed, security measures observed and a few crew tour the site of a whale processing plant 50 miles from the city.

Our arrival did not go unnoticed. The Icelandic police post a 24 hour guard at our gangway and police divers investigate the hulls of the whalers every few hours. Some of this activity is the fault of our reputation and some of it results from a Greenpeace conference where we were accused of being terrorists. Greenpeace wanted to make it clear that they were not associated with us in any way. We hold our own press conference to say that we are not associated with the wimps on the "Sirius" in any way. A bunch like that can give us a bad name. At the same time, we deliver a warning to Iceland through the media.

I tell them that we have not come to interfere with Icelandic whaling at the moment; but that if Iceland intends to violate the moratorium on commercial whaling set to begin in 1986, then Iceland can expect to see the enforcement of International Whaling Commission (IWC) regulations.

We then left Iceland and Greenpeace. Greenpeace workers were relieved to see us leave. They were "networking" with the whalers. That meant they were giving tours of their ship and sharing beer with whale-killers. My crew, by the way, were not allowed to tour the Greenpeace ship or share the beer. When we left, Greenpeace warned us to stay out of Icelandic waters. Quaking in our deck-boots, we scurried away from Iceland in mortal fear and proceeded to the Faroe Islands to save a few whales.

June 1986: Malmo, Sweden. The "Sea Shepherd" sails from Plymouth, England, to Sweden. We berth a few blocks from where the meeting of the IWC is taking place. Ben White is our official observer at the meeting. He is not happy. "The whalers intend to keep whaling. They say that Icelandic and Norwegian whaling is not commercial and must continue for scientific purposes."

The objective for continuation of scientific whaling would be almost funny were it not so tragic. The Icelanders requested a scientific permit to kill whales so as to determine the reasons for a decline in Fin and Sei Whale populations in the North Atlantic. The proposal was rejected by the scientific committee. One committee member stated, "Iceland is seeking to prostitute science in an attempt to mask a commercial venture."

Iceland left the meeting vowing to kill whales despite IWC disapproval. The established approach had failed. A decade of work to bring about a moratorium was all for nothing. With the moratorium in effect, whales continued to be slaughtered by the Soviet Union, Japan, Iceland, Norway, and South Korea. We were ready to act against these pirates; but, still, the forces of moderation screamed, "We still have an ace in the hole, the Packwood-Magnusson Amendment."

The Packwood-Magnusson Amendment is a wonderful piece of legislation which seeks to protect whales by advocating the implementation of economic sanctions against nations which do not comply with IWC regulations. This meant that Iceland, Norway, Japan and South Korea would have to stop whaling or face the ire of the US. To keep whaling would be to lose fishing rights in US waters and to lose the right to market fish in the US. Sounds too good to be true, and it was. President Reagan shot the Amendment down by announcing that the US would not impose sanctions on a NATO ally. By choosing to discriminate in the application of the law, the President made a mockery of the law and sacrificed the whales on the altar of NATO. To add insult to injury, the President then struck a deal with the Icelanders that would allow them to market 49% of their whale meat to Japan without US interference. The price—permission to use Iceland as a staging platform for the Soviet-US summit.

July 1986: the North Atlantic. On route back to Britain after our second summer of interfering with Pilot Whale killing in the Faroe Islands, the kid approaches me. You might remember the kid from the last article I wrote for *Earth First!*. Rod Coronado is a young Californian, an articulate, dedicated whale warrior. He is apparently not satisfied with being jailed and shot at in the Faroe Islands. He has a plan and a damn good one to boot—a commando raid of Reykjavik.

We don't discuss details, tactics, or strategy. If the kid had an idea, that was good enough for me and that was all the detail I wanted to know. We did review, however, the Sea Shepherd Society guidelines for direct action in the field. We have five rules: 1) No explosives. 2) No utilization of weapons. 3) No action taken that even has a remote possibility of causing injury to a living thing. Respect for life must always be our primary consideration. 4) If apprehended, do not resist arrest in a violent manner. 5) Be prepared to accept full responsibility and suffer the possible consequences for your actions. Could he operate within the guidelines? Yes. End of discussion. He and David Howitt were not on their own as Sea Shepherd field operatives.

October 15, 1986: Rod and David arrive in Reykjavik and book into the Salvation Army Youth hostel. Hey, our guys travel first class. They find employment in the local fish processing plant. There are more jobs than citizens in Iceland, so securing employment as a noncitizen is relatively easy.

Three weeks were spent on scouting the sites and determining the schedule of the security watches. They waited for an opportunity.

November 8: A stormy day and night in Iceland. Rod and David drive the 50 miles to the whale processing plant. It was Saturday night and the watchman went home in the evening, leaving the station abandoned.

The two Sea Shepherd agents break into the plant. The tools are there—sledge hammers, acid and, ah yes, a couple monkeywrenches. The objective is to inflict as much economic destruction as possible. Both men apply themselves to the job for the next eight hours.

The refrigeration machinery was destroyed, followed by dismantling of six diesel engines and destruction of the plant's pumps. Engine parts were tossed into the deep waters of the fjord along with a collection of flensing knives and tools. The laboratory was demolished. The computers were trashed thoroughly and cyanic acid poured into the diskette files and filing cabinets. After eight hours, the plant looked as if it had suffered a bomb blast. Damage was later estimated to be about 1.8 million US dollars.

Our two merry eco-commandos then drive back to Reykjavik in the early morning. They go directly to the three whaling ships tied in the harbour. A fourth is in dry dock. Both men go through all the cabins on board the ships. On the third ship, they locate a sleeping watchman. A decision is made to spare the third ship so as to avoid possible injury to the watchman. The wind is howling and the water is choppy and the noise provided by nature covers the activities of the two men below decks. They spend nearly two hours in preparation. The removal of 14 bolts from the salt water sea valve flange results in a massive volume of water spewing into the engine compartment of the ship. The other ship is dealt with in a similar manner a few moments later. The third ship is cut adrift so as not to be dragged down with the two now mortally wounded killer boats.

The crew then calmly walked down the dock and drove to the airport at Kleflavik 30 miles away. The ships sank within 40 minutes. The police discovered the results at 0600 hours.

At about the same time, our crew were stopped by a routine roadblock on route to the airport. Both men were questioned and given a breath analyzer test to determine if they had been drinking. They had not and were allowed to proceed. They boarded an Icelandic airlines flight to Luxembourg. The plane left at 0745 hours.

Back in Vancouver, early Sunday morning: My phone rings. It is Sarah Hambley, our director for the United Kingdom. Calmly she says, "Paul, we have two on the bottom."

The raid on Reykjavik had been a success. Rod and David had brought the Icelandic whaling industry to its knees and then had kicked it in the teeth. The damage to the ships was later estimated to be $2.8 million, to add to the $1.8 million of damage to the plant. The Hvalur of Hvalfjordur whaling company had just received a reprimand to their pirate whaling activities which has cost them $4.6 million, in addition to canceling their insurance, and increasing their future security costs. The destruction of the refrigeration unit had spoiled the stockpile of whale meat. The Japanese were not happy to discover that the Icelanders had refrozen the thawed meat and were attempting to sell it nonetheless.

The news of the raid on Reykjavik was greeted enthusiastically throughout most of the world. Of course, we had our critics. The ever dependable Greenpeace crowd condemned the act as terroristic, foolish, simplistic . . . *ad nauseum*. They only stopped critizing when they ran out of adjectives. I understand their position. After all, there are more anti-whalers employed in the world than there are whalers; and shucks, being serious about actually ending whaling might lead to, "shudder," no more work for anti-whalers. One has to feel sorry for all the Greenpeace Fuller Brush men who would suffer. They have a good thing going—hundreds of salesmen knocking on doors throughout North America, peddling eco-business for 35% of the take. I say, throw the bums out. A more realistic reaction came from Dr. Roger Payne, one of the world's leading whale researchers. Speaking a week after the incident, Dr. Payne said, "I have given up thinking it (whaling) can be handled through international agreements. These whaling nations are willing to cheat, lie, use the name of science—whatever is necessary. They're completely unethical."

Another positive result of Sea Shepherd activities is that people have been aroused from their complacency and apathy over whaling. Most people thought whaling was a thing of the past. After all, didn't we have a moratorium in effect? Our actions shook the world awake on this issue and delivered a message: Whaling continues despite international regulations. The whaling nations of Iceland, Norway, South Korea, Japan, and the Soviet Union are in contempt of international regulations.

Norway responded to the raid in Iceland by throwing a fit of paranoia. Believing that Sea Shepherd hit squads were poised for attack, the country increased their security budget, thus increasing their costs and cutting into illegal whaling profits. The security won't help. When the first opportunity arises, the whaling ships of Norway will be converted to submersibles by Sea Shepherd agents.

Rod has returned to the US. David is back in merry old England. Iceland has issued warrants for their arrest through Interpol but extradition is not possible due to the illegality of Iceland's whaling operation. I am being investigated by Canadian authorities for possible conspiracy charges, but I'm not losing any sleep over the noise from Ottawa. Our legal ass is covered.

We have important things to do, including further enforcement of international regulations against offending whaling nations. We are also preparing an expedition to the North Pacific in the summer of 1987 to confront the drift net fishermen of Japan, Korea and Taiwan. Each summer, they send about 2000 ships to the North Pacific to set monofilament nets that range from 8 to 35 miles in length. The incidental kills in these nets include approximately 150,000 marine mammals and one to two million sea birds; plus they have a severe impact on populations of salmon, billfish, squid and other finny types.

I will end this article with a disgusting plea for funds. If you support this battle to protect our oceans and our aquatic friends, then for Gaia's sake, send some loot. We don't have a megabuck fund-raising machine or door to door salesmen. We can only take advantage of opportunities to plug ourselves for free, like in this here paper. I can tell you what your money will buy—fuel, oil, supplies and assorted nautical knick-knacks that will enable us to get a ship up to the North Pacific to kick ass and take names, if you get my drift. Also, a few bucks might buy an airline ticket or two; don't worry, we only travel in steerage. Your hard earned dollar could sent one of our commando types on a worthwhile mission.

TORA! TORA! TORA!
Paul Watson

Ed. note: On 13 August 1990, Paul Watson and his crew of 23 on the Sea Shepherd II rammed two Japanese drift net fishing boats and chased the fleet of six out of the North Pacific fishing grounds. Here the Captain tells the story.

On December 7, 1941, the Imperial Japanese First Naval Air fleet launched a surprise attack against the US Naval base at Pearl Harbor on the Hawaiian island of Oahu.

As the Japanese planes swooped in low, their wing commander gave his orders. The Japanese words "tora, tora, tora" crackled through the cockpits of the torpedo bombers.

"Attack, attack, attack." Such was the battle cry of a people who had mastered the martial strategies of Asia. The attack was swift, surprising, ruthless, and effective.

As an ecological strategist, I have faced the Japanese as adversaries on numerous occasions. For this reason, I have studied Japanese martial strategy, especially the classic work entitled *A Book of Five Rings* written by Miyamoto Musashi in 1648. Musashi advocated the "twofold way of pen and sword," which I interpret to mean that one's actions must be both effective and educational.

In March 1982, the Sea Shepherd Conservation Society successfully negotiated a halt to the slaughter of dolphins at Iki Island in Japan. Contributing to this success was our ability to quote Musashi and talk to the Japanese fishermen in a language they could understand—the language of no compromise confrontation.

During our discussion, a fisherman asked me, "what is of more value, the life of a dolphin or the life of a human?"

I answered that, in my opinion, the life of a dolphin was equal in value to the life of a human.

The fisherman then asked, "if a Japanese fisherman and a dolphin were both caught in a net and you could save the life of one, which would you save?"

All the fishermen in the room smirked. They had me pegged a liberal and felt confident that I would say that I would save the fisherman, thus making a mockery of my declaration that humans and dolphins are equal.

I looked about the room and smiled. "I did not come to Japan to save fishermen; I am here to save dolphins."

They were surprised but not shocked by my answer. All the fishermen treated me with respect thereafter.

Why? Because the Japanese understand duty and responsibility. Saving dolphins was both my chosen duty and my responsibility.

Sea Shepherd had already established a reputation in Japan as the "Samurai protector of whales." This came in an editorial that appeared in the Tokyo daily *Asahi Shimbun* in July 1979, a few days after we rammed and disabled the Japanese owned pirate whaler, the *Sierra*, off the coast of Portugal.

That incident ended the career of the most notorious outlaw whaler. In February of 1980, we had the *Sierra* sunk in Lisbon harbor. A few months later, in April, our agents sank two outlaw Spanish registered whalers, the *Isba I* and the *Isba II,* in Vigo Harbor in northern Spain.

We then gave attention to two other Japanese pirate whalers, the *Susan* and the *Theresa*. Given the controversy of the *Sierra*, and the fact that the *Susan* and the *Theresa* were owned by the same Japanese interests, the South Africans, who had just publicly denounced whaling did not want the stigma of harboring illegal whaling ships. The South African Navy confiscated and sank the *Susan* and *Theresa* for target practise after we publicly appealed to them to do so, in 1980.

The last of the Atlantic pirate whalers, the *Astrid* was shut down after I sent an agent to the Spanish Canary Islands with a reward offer of $25,000 US to any person who would sink her. The owners saw the writing on the wall and voluntarily retired the whaler.

Because of these actions many have labeled us pirates ourselves. Yet we have never been convicted of a criminal charge not have we ever caused injury or death to a human. Nor have we attempted to avoid charges. On the contrary, we have always invited our enemies to continue the fight in the courts. Most times they have refused and the few times that they complied, they lost.

Vigilante buccaneers we may well be but we are policing the seas where no policing authority exists. We are protecting whales, dolphins, seals, birds, and fish by enforcing existing regulations, treaties and laws that heretofore have had no enforcement.

In November 1986, when two Sea Shepherd agents, Rod Coronado and David Howitt, attacked the Icelandic whaling industry, they were enforcing the law. The International Whaling Commission (IWC) had banned commercial whaling, yet Iceland continued to whale without a permit. We did not wish to debate the issue of legality with the Icelanders. We acted instead. Coronado and Howitt destroyed the whaling station and scuttled half the Icelandic whaling fleet.

Iceland refused to press charges. I traveled to Reykjavik to insist that they press charges. They refused and deported me without a hearing. They only legal case to result from the incident is my suit against Iceland for illegal deportation.

In March of 1983, the crew of the *Sea Shepherd II* were arrested under the Canadian Seal Protection Regulations, an Orwellian set of rules which actually protected the sealing industry. The only way to challenge these unjust rules was to break them. We did and at the same time we chased the sealing fleet out of the nursery grounds of the Harp Seals. We beat the charges and in the process helped the Supreme Court of Canada in its decision to dismiss the Seal Protection Act as unconstitutional.

In the years since, we have intervened against the Danish Faeroese fishermen in the North Atlantic to save the Pilot Whales they kill for sport. We have shut down seal hunts in Scotland, England and Ireland. We have confronted Central American tuna seiners off the coast of Costa Rica in an effort to rescue dolphins.

In 1987, we launched our first campaign to expose drift net operations in the North Pacific. Our ship the *Divine Wind* voyaged along the Aleutian chain documenting the damage of the drift nets and ghost nets (abandoned nets). We helped convince Canada to abandon plans to build a drift net industry.

For new supporters who do not know what drift nets are, I will briefly explain. Drift nets are to the Pacific Ocean what clearcuts are to the Amazon Rainforest or the Pacific Northwest Temperate Rainforest. Drift-netting is strip-mine fishing.

From May until late October, some 1800 ships each set a net measuring from 10 to 40 miles in length! These monofilament nylon gill nets drift freely upon the surface of the sea, hanging like curtains of death to a depth of 26 or 34 feet. Each night, the combined fleet sets between 28,000 and 35,000 miles of nets. The nets radiate across the breadth of the North Pacific like fences marking off property. The nets are efficient. Few squid and fish escape the perilous clutches of the nylon. Whales and dolphins, seals and sea lions, sea turtles, and sea birds are routinely entangled. The death is an agonizing ordeal of strangulation and suffocation.

Drifts nets take an annual incidental kill of more than one million sea birds and a quarter of a million marine mammals each year, plus hundreds of millions of tons of fish and squid. A few short years ago, the North Pacific fairly teemed with dolphins, turtles, fur seals, sea lions, dozens of species of birds and uncountable schools of fish. Today it is a biological wasteland.

The Japanese say their nets are taking fewer incidental kills now than a few years ago. This is true, but the reason the kills are down is simply that there are now fewer animals to kill.

For many years, governments and environmental groups have talked about the problem. Nobody actually did anything about it. Sick of talk, the Sea Shepherd Conservation Society decided to take action.

The *Sea Shepherd II* moved to Seattle, Washington, in September 1989 to prepare for an expedition to intercept the Japanese North Pacific drift net fleet. We set our departure date for June 1990. Overhauls and refitting were completed by May to meet the targeted date.

We were unable to leave Seattle. One of our crew was a paid infiltrator working, we believe, for the Japanese fishing industry. He successfully sabotaged our engine by pouring crushed glass into our oil, destroying our turbo-charger, and destroying electrical motors. Although we discovered the damage and identified the saboteur, we faced extensive repairs.

The saboteur fled to Britain. We asked Scotland Yard to track him down and investigate the incident. However, the damage was done and we were hardly in a position to cry foul. After all, we had already been responsible for destroying six whaling ships ourselves. The enemy had succeeded in striking a blow—it was as simple as that. We were down, but not for long.

We immediately set to work to repair the damage. Thanks to an appeal to Sea Shepherd Society members, funds were raised to purchase a replacement turbo-charger.

The *Sea Shepherd II* was prepared for departure again on August 5. We left Seattle and stopped briefly in Port Angeles on the Olympic Peninsula. Port Angeles resident and Sea Shepherd veteran David Howitt stopped by to visit us. He could not bring himself to leave. The ship departed with David on board. He had left his job and an understanding wife on the spur of the moment. We needed him and he knew it and that was reason enough to return to the eco-battles. He took the position of 1st Engineer.

It was with confidence that I took the helm of our ship and headed out the Strait of Juan de Fuca for the open Pacific beyond. I had a good crew, including many veterans.

Myra Finkelstein was 2nd Engineer. A graduate zoologist, Myra had worked for weeks in the bowels of the engine room to repair the damage to the engine. She was a veteran of the 1987 drift net campaign and the 1989 tuna dolphin campaign. In addition she had been a leader of the Friends of the Wolf campaign in northern British Columbia where she had parachuted into the frigid and remote wilderness to interfere with a government sponsored wolf kill.

Sea Shepherd Director Peter Brown was on board with the camera gear to document the voyage. Peter was also helmsman and my deputy coordinator for the expedition.

Marc Gaede, who had sailed with us a year ago on the campaign off the coast of Costa Rica, returned as our photographer. Trevor Van Der Gulik, my nephew, a lad of only 15 from Toronto, Canada, became—by virtue of his skills—our 3rd Engineer. Trevor had helped to deliver the *Sea Shepherd* from Holland to Florida in 1989.

Also sailing with us this summer was Robert Hunter. Bob and I had both been founders of Greenpeace and he had been the first President of the Greenpeace Foundation. Both had been the dynamic force behind the organization and ultimate success of Greenpeace. Like myself, he had been forced out of Greenpeace by the marauding bureaucrats who in the late 1970s ousted the original activists and replaced us with fundraisers and public relations people.

With Bob on board, I felt a little of the old spirit which got us moving in the early 70s. We had no doubts: we would find the drift net fleets.

Five days out to sea, we saw a military ship on the horizon, moving rapidly toward us. We identified her as a large Soviet frigate. The frigate hailed us and asked us what we were about. I replied that we were searching for the Japanese drift net fleet and asked if they had seen any Japanese fishing vessels.

The Russians said they thought the Japanese were a few days to the west. Then, surprisingly, the Soviet officer, who spoke impeccable English, said, "Good luck, it is a noble cause that you follow. We are with you in spirit."

Eco-glasnost? Only a few years ago we battled the Russian whalers. In 1975 Bob Hunter and I had survived a Russian harpoon fired over our heads by a Soviet whaler we had confronted. In 1981, we had invaded Siberia to capture evidence on illegal whaling by the Russians. We had narrowly escaped capture. Now, here we were being hailed by the Soviets with a statement of support. We have indeed made progress.

In fact, the Soviets were allies in more than just words. On 29 May 1990, the Russians had seized a fleet of North Korean fishing boats with drift nets in Soviet waters. Japan was diplomatically embarrassed when it was discovered that the 140 supposedly North Korean fishermen in Soviet custody were in fact Japanese.

On the eighth day out from Seattle, I put the *Sea Shepherd II* on a course of due west and decided not to correct the drift. I felt that the drift would take us to the outlaws. Slowly we began to drift north on the course line. Forty-eight hours later, my intuition proved itself right. The sea herself had taken us directly to a drift net fleet.

At 2030 Hours on August 12, we sailed into the midst of six Japanese drift netters. The fleet had just completed laying their nets—more than 200 miles of net in the water. The Japanese ships were each about 200 feet long, equal in size to our own.

As we approached, the Japanese fishermen warned us off, angrily telling us to avoid their nets. Our ship is a large 657 ton North Atlantic trawler with an ice strengthened bow and a fully enclosed protected prop. We were able to cruise harmlessly over the lines of floating nets. We made close runs on the vessels to inspect them closely.

With darkness rapidly closing in, we decided to wait until morning before taking action against the ships. The Japanese vessels had shut down for the night. They drifted quietly. We waited out the night with them.

An hour before dawn they began to move. We moved with them. For three hours, we filmed the hauling in of mile after mile of net from the vessel *Shunyo Maru #8*. We watched the catch of two foot long squids being hauled into the boat along with incidental kills of sharks, sea-birds and dolphins. The catching of the sea birds violated the Convention for the Protection of Migratory Birds, a treaty signed between the US and Japan in March 1972. The nets impact more than 22 species of birds, 13 of which are protected by the treaty. It was to enforce this treaty that our ship and crew had made this voyage.

The fishing boats were brilliantly illuminated and the work on the deck could be adequately filmed. As the power blocks pulled in the nets, the bodies of squid, fish and birds fell from the nets to the deck or back into the sea.

We had the evidence we needed. We had seen the bodies of protected species in the net. For the next step we needed more light. It was painful to continue watching but it was imperative that we wait for dawn and the light we needed to properly film events.

At 0540 Hours, there was enough light. We prepared the deck and the engine room for confrontation. We positioned our cameramen and photographers. I took the wheel. We brought the engine up to full power and charged across the swells toward the *Shunyo Maru #8* whose crew were still hauling in nets. Our objective was to destroy the net retrieval gear. To do so, we had to hit her on an angle on her port mid-side.

We sounded a blast on our horn to warn the Japanese crew that we were coming in. I piloted the *Sea Shepherd II* into position. We struck where intended. The ships ground their hulls together in a fountain of sparks amidst a screeching cacophony of tearing and crushing steel. The net was severed, the power blocks smashed. We broke away as the Japanese stood dumbfounded on their decks.

One fisherman, however, hurtled his knife at photographer Marc Gaede. The knife missed Marc and hit the sea. The same fisherman grabbed a second knife and sent it flying at cameraman Peter Brown. Peter's camera followed it as it came toward the lens. It fell at Peter's feet.

As we pulled away, I looked with satisfaction on the damage we had inflicted. One ship down for the season. On board our own ship, a damage control party reported back that we had suffered minimal injury. The Japanese ships were no match for our ice-strengthened steel reinforced hull.

We immediately targeted a second ship, the *Ryoun Maru #6*. The Japanese were attempting to cut a large shark out of the net. Looking up, they saw us bearing down at full speed upon them. Eyes wide, they ran toward the far deck.

We struck where intended. Again to the roaring crescendo of tortured metal, the power blocks and gear were crushed; the deck and gunnels buckled. The net was severed.

We broke off and immediately set out for the third ship. By now, the Japanese realized what was happening. The first and second ships had been successfully Pearl Harbored. The third was not to be surprised. As we approached, she dropped her net and fled. We pursued.

We then turned and targeted a fourth ship. She also fled, dropping her net in panic. We stopped and pulled up alongside the radio beacon marking the abandoned net. We confiscated the beacon. We then grappled the net, secured a ton of weight to one end and dropped it, sending the killer net to the bottom, two miles beneath us. We watched the cork line drop beneath the surface, the floats disappearing in lines radiating out from our ship toward the horizon.

On the bottom the net would be rendered harmless. Small benthic creatures would literally cement it to the ocean floor over a short period of time.

We cleaned up the remaining nets and then returned to the chase. For the next twenty hours, we chased the six ships completely out of the fishing area.

The next morning, we could look at what we had achieved with pleasure. Two ships completely disabled from further fishing, a million dollars worth of net sunk and destroyed and all six ships prevented from continued fishing and running scared.

We had delivered our message to the Japanese fishing industry. Our tactics had been both effective and educational. Effective in that we directly saved lives by shutting down a fleet, and educational in that we informed the Japanese fishing industry that their greed will no longer be tolerated.

Our ship was only slightly damaged. Most importantly, there were no injuries on any of the ships involved.

I turned the bow of our ship southward to Honolulu to deliver the documentation to the media and to begin again the tedious task of fund-raising which will allow us to mount further attacks against these mindless thugs slaughtering our oceans.

As we headed south, we stopped repeatedly to retrieve drifting remnants of nets. In one we found 54 rotting fish. In another a large dead mahi-mahi. In another a dead albatross. These "ghost nets" present an additional problem for life in the sea. Each day the large fleets lose an average or six miles of net. At present an estimated 10,000 plus miles of ghost nets are floating the seas. These non-biodegradable nets kill millions of fish and sea creatures each year. Decaying fish attract more fish and birds . . . a vicious cycle of death and waste.

Arriving in Honolulu, we berthed at pier eleven, ironically just in front of two fishery patrol vessels, one from Japan, the other from Taiwan. The crew of each scowled at us.

We were prepared for the Japanese to attempt to lay charges against us or failing that to publicly denounce us. Instead, they refused to even recognize that an incident took place.

We contacted the Japanese Consulate and declared that we had attacked their ships and had destroyed Japanese property. We informed the Consulate that we were ready to contest charges, be they in the Internation Court at the Hague or in Tokyo itself. The Consulate told us he had no idea about what we talking about.

The Japanese realize they have nothing to gain by taking us to court and much to lose. Which means that we must return to the oceans and must escalate the battle.

The Taiwanese drift netters are beginning to move into the Caribbean Sea. We must head them off. We must continue to confront the Japanese fleets, and we must take on the Koreans.

Each net we sink will cost the industry a million dollars. Each vessel we damage will buy time for the sea animals. Each confrontation we mount will embarrass the drift net industry.

This summer, we won a battle. However, the war to end high seas drift netting continues.

The Japanese, Taiwanese, and Korean drift net fleets can be driven from the oceans. We need only the will, the courage, and the financial support to do so.

CHAPTER 7

Earth First!

Introduction to the Selections

The Sea Shepherd Society directs its ecotage against the machines that are destroying marine mammals, while Earth First! is a land-based group that is most known for its support of monkeywrenching ecotactics in the wilderness areas of the western United States. Dave Foreman, author of the first two selections in this chapter, is a founder of Earth First! and, until recently, a leading member in this loosely knit "nonorganization." The first selection, written by Foreman in 1981, indicates that he and several other activists were dissatisfied with the behavior of mainline environmental groups in the late 1970s and decided to create a new group which would adopt a more militant, uncompromising stance in defense of Mother Earth. Why was this necessary? Foreman gives several answers to this question in the first selection, mentioning the importance of wilderness preservation as the keystone to preserving "the integrity, stability, and beauty of the biotic community."[1] To Foreman, wilderness is the "most radical idea in human thought," and wilderness has a right to exist for its own sake regardless of human benefit. This latter idea is of course one of the biocentric insights of deep ecology and is now widely accepted by many environmentalists.

Foreman argues that radical environmental action is the key to preserving and restoring wilderness. In fact radical activism is more important than the philosophical hairsplitting and endless refining of dogma, characteristic, he implies, of ecophilosophy. Radicals have been too quiet, too calm, too dispassionate in their defense of wilderness, and the time has come to express rage at its destruction. Foreman ends the selection by discussing the skeptical assertion that no one can stop the forces of industrialism in their consumption of wilderness. In reply he says that the point isn't necessarily that Earth First! will succeed in stopping this destruction but that it may thwart and delay it through monkeywrenching acts.

The second selection by Foreman gives his official definition of monkeywrenching. The term itself is a rather loose one and his book *Ecodefense* describes a great variety of tactics, from the mundane and conventional forms of political action such as letter writing and political lobbying, to less standard forms of political protest such as guerilla theater demonstrations at government resource agency offices, to acts of environmental civil disobedience such as forest road blockades or tree sitting, to more direct forms of monkeywrenching such as survey stake pulling in backcountry areas, tree spiking, billboard trashing, and heavy equipment sabotage. Although Foreman describes monkeywrenching as nonviolent and ethical, others have argued otherwise, as will be clear in Chapter 10.

The point is that the tactics of Earth First!ers are quite diverse, and monkeywrenching is only one tactic among many. Since monkeywrenching is illegal and sometimes dangerous, Foreman does not recommend it for just anyone and does not describe it as an obligatory behavior for radicals. It is a tool that can sometimes work to make resource extraction corporations and resource agencies pay the financial costs of their destruction of wilderness. And it is an option that individuals must assess within the bounds of their own ethical frameworks. For some Earth First!ers, it has clearly been a tactic that they believe in. It represents "the final step in the defense of the wild, the deliberate action taken by the Earth defender when all other measures have failed, the process whereby the wilderness defender becomes the wilderness acting in self-defense."[2] To others, however, it has brought discredit to this radical group and has violated the principles of nonviolent reverence for all life.

Chapter 7 also contains two examples of Earth First! activism, in both cases actions in which members joined with other groups to commit civil disobedience against the logging of old growth forests in Oregon and California. The first example explains the Middle Santiam blockade in the Willamette National Forest in western Oregon in June 1984 and includes a manifesto from the main protest group, the Cathedral Forest Action Group. Mike Roselle, a long-time and well-known Earth First!er, helped to lead and participate in this protest, along with a few other members of Earth First! The second example gives an account of the Redwood Summer action undertaken during 1990, again through the eyes of Earth First!ers. Here Earth First! cooperated with several groups to protest the destruction of California's last unprotected stands of old growth redwood. The action involved the use of a variety of nonviolent tactics over several months' time in Northern California, including marches, demonstrations, and civil disobedience. And, while it was not successful in stopping the cutting of all old growth redwoods in the area, as is clear from the article by Zack Stenz, one participant, Karen Pickett, in her retrospective on the action, judges it a success nevertheless. In particular, environmental protests of old growth logging have brought this issue to the attention of the American public and have put the pressure on national political forces to reevaluate this timber practice.

Notes

1. This idea is taken directly from Aldo Leopold's famous essay on the land ethic in *A Sand County Almanac* (Oxford: Oxford University Press, Inc., 1949).
2. "Earth First!, An Introductory Guide to the Earth First! Movement," *The Earth First! Journal*, n.d., p. 4.

EARTH FIRST!
Dave Foreman

. . . Maybe—some of us began to feel, even before Reagan's election—it was time for a new joker in the deck: a militant, uncompromising group unafraid to say what needed to be said or to back it up with stronger actions than the established organizations were willing to take. This idea had been kicking around for a couple of years; finally last year several of us (including, among others, Susan Morgan, formerly educational director for the Wilderness Society: Howie Wolke, former Wyoming representative for Friends of the Earth: Bart Koehler, former Wyoming representative for the Wilderness Society, and myself) decided that the time for talk was past. We formed a new national group. EARTH FIRST! We set out to be radical in style, positions, philosophy, and organization in order to be effective and to avoid the pitfalls of co-option and moderation which we had already experienced.

What, we asked ourselves as we sat around a campfire in the Wyoming mountains, were the advantages, the reasons for environmental radicalism?

- To state honestly the views held by many conservationists.
- To demonstrate that the Sierra Club and its allies were raging moderates, believers in the system, and to refute the Reagan/Watt contention that they were "extremist environmentalists."
- To balance such anti-environmental radicals as the Grand County commission and provide a broader spectrum of viewpoints.
- To return some vigor, joy, and enthusiasm to the allegedly tired environmental movement.
- To keep the established groups honest. By stating a pure, non-compromise pro-Earth position, we felt EARTH FIRST! could help keep the other groups from straying too far from their philosophical base.

- To give an outlet to many hard-line conservationists who were no longer active because of disenchantment with compromise politics and the co-option of environmental organizations.
- To provide a productive fringe since it seems that ideas, creativity, and energy spring up on the fringe and later spread into the middle.
- To inspire others to carry out activities straight from the pages of *The Monkey Wrench Gang* even though EARTH FIRST!, we agreed, would itself be ostensibly law-abiding.
- To question the system; to help develop a new world view, a biocentric paradigm, an Earth philosophy. To fight, with uncompromising passion, for Mother Earth.

The name—EARTH FIRST!—was chosen deliberately because it succinctly summed up the one thing on which we could all agree: That in *any* decision, consideration for the health of the Earth must come first, or, as Aldo Leopold said, "A thing is right when it tends to preserve the integrity, stability, and beauty of the biotic community. It is wrong when it tends otherwise."

In a true Earth-radical group, concern for wilderness preservation must be the keystone. The idea of wilderness, after all, is the most radical in human thought—more radical than Paine, than Marx, than Mao. Wilderness says: Human beings are not dominant, Earth is not for *Homo sapiens* alone, human life is but one life form on the planet and has no right to take exclusive possession. Yes, wilderness for its own sake, without any need to justify it for human benefit. Wilderness for wilderness. For grizzlies and whales and titmice and rattlesnakes and stink bugs. And . . . wilderness for human beings. Because it is the laboratory of three million years of human evolution—and because it is home.

It is not enough to protect our few remaining bits of wilderness. The only hope for Earth (and humanity for that matter) is to withdraw huge areas as inviolate natural sanctuaries from the depredations of modern industry and technology. Keep Cleveland, Los Angeles. Contain them. Try to make them habitable. But identify areas—big areas—that can be restored to a semblance of natural conditions, reintroduce the griz and wolf and prairie grasses, and declare them off limits to modern civilization.

In the United States pick an area for each of our major ecosystems and recreate the American wilderness—not in little pieces of a thousand acres but in chunks of a million or ten million. Move out the people and cars. Reclaim the roads and plowed land. It is not enough any longer to say no more dams on our wild rivers. We must begin tearing down some dams already built—beginning with Glen Canyon, Hetch Hetchy, Tellico, and New Melones—and freeing shackled rivers.

This emphasis on wilderness is not to ignore other environmental issues or to abandon the people who suffer because of them. In the

United States blacks and Chicanos of the inner cities are the ones most affected by air and water pollution, the ones most trapped by the unnatural confines of urbanity. So we decided that not only should ecomilitants be concerned with these human environmental problems; we should also make common ground with other progressive elements of society whenever possible.

Obviously, for a group more committed to Gila monsters and mountain lions than to people, there will not be a total alliance with the other social movements. But there are issues where Earth radicals can cooperate with feminist, Indian rights, anti-nuke, peace, civil rights, and civil liberties groups. The inherent conservatism of the conservation community has made it wary of snuggling too close to these questionable (in their minds) leftist organizations. We hoped that the way might be paved for better cooperation from the entire conservation movement.

We believed that new tactics were needed—something more than commenting on dreary environmental impact statements and writing letters to members of Congress. Politics in the streets. Civil disobedience. Media stunts. Holding the villains up to ridicule. Using music to charge the cause.

Action is the key. Action is more important than philosophical hairsplitting or endless refining of dogma (for which radicals are so well known). Let our actions set the finer points of our philosophy. And let us recognize that diversity is not only the spice of life, it is also the strength. All that would be required to join us, we decided, was a belief in Earth first. Apart from that, EARTH FIRST! would be big enough to contain street poets and cowboy bar bouncers, agnostics and pagans, vegetarians and raw steak eaters, pacifists and those who think that turning the other cheek is a good way to get a sore face.

Radicals frequently verge toward a righteous seriousness. But we felt that if we couldn't laugh at ourselves we would be merely another bunch of dangerous fanatics who should be locked up (like the oil companies). Not only does humor preserve individual and group sanity, it retards hubris, a major cause of environmental rape, and it is also an effective weapon. Additionally, fire, passion, courage, ad emotionalism are called for. We have been too reasonable, too calm, too understanding. It's time to get angry, to cry, to let rage flow at what the human cancer is doing to Mother Earth, to be uncompromising. For EARTH FIRST! it is all or nothing. Win or lose. No truce or cease fire. No surrender. No partitioning of the territory.

Ever since the Earth goddesses of ancient Greece were supplanted by the macho Olympians, repression of women and Earth has gone hand in hand with imperial organization. EARTH FIRST! decided to be nonorganizational: no officers, no bylaws or constitution, no incorporation, no tax status; just a collection of women and men committed to the Earth. At the turn of the century William Graham Sumner wrote a famous essay entitled "The Conquest of the United States by Spain." His thesis was that Spain had ultimately won the Spanish-American War because the United States took on the imperialism and totalitarianism of Spain as a result. We felt that if we took on the organization of the industrial state, we would soon accept their anthropocentric paradigm (much as Audubon and the Sierra Club already had).

In keeping with that view, EARTH FIRST! took the shape of a circle, a group of thirteen women and men around the country who more or less direct the movement, and a collection of regional contacts. We also have local affiliates (so far in Alaska, Montana, Wyoming, Colorado, Arizona, New Mexico, Utah, Arkansas, Maine, and Virginia). We publish a newsletter eight times a year and are developing position papers on a range of issues from automobiles to overgrazing. We also send out press releases. Membership is free, although we do encourage members to kick in ten bucks or more, if they can afford it, to help with expenses. We have not sought any grants or funding with strings attached, nor do we plan to have paid staff (although we hope to have field organizers receiving expenses in the tradition of the Wobblies).

And, when we are inspired, we *act*.

Massive, powerful, like some creation of Darth Vader's. Glen Canyon Dam squats in the canyon of the Colorado River on the Arizona-Utah border and backs the cold dead waters of Lake Powell some 180 miles upstream, drowning the most awesome and magical canyon on Earth. More than any other single entity, Glen Canyon Dam is the symbol of the destruction of wilderness, of the technolgical rape of the West. The finest fantasy of *eco*-warriors in the West is the destruction of the dam and the liberation of the Colorado. So it was only proper that on March 21, 1981—on the Spring Equinox, the traditional time of rebirth—EARTH FIRST! held its first national gathering at Glen Canyon Dam.

On that morning, seventy-five members of EARTH FIRST! lined the walkway of the Colorado River Bridge 700 feet above the once free river and watched five compatriots busy at work with an awkward black bundle on the massive dam just upstream. Those on the bridge carried placards reading "Damn Watt, Not Rivers," "Free the Colorado," and "Let It Flow." The four men and one woman on the dam attached ropes to a grill on the dam, shouted out "Earth first!" and let 300 feet of black plastic unfurl down the side of the dam, creating the impression of a growing crack. Those on the bridge returned the cheer.

A few minutes later, Edward Abbey, author of *The Monkey Wrench Gang,* a novel of environmental sabotage in the Southwest, told the protesters of the "green and living wilderness" that was Glen Canyon only nineteen years ago:

"And they took it away from us. The politicians of Arizona, Utah, New Mexico, and Colorado, in cahoots with the land developers, city developers, industrial developers of the Southwest, stole this treasure from us in order to pursue and promote their crackpot ideology of growth, profit, and power—growth for the sake of power, power for the sake of growth."

Speaking toward the future, Abbey offered this advice: "Oppose. Oppose the destruction of our homeland by these alien forces from Houston, Tokyo, Manhattan, Washington, D.C., and the Pentagon. And if opposition is not enough, we must resist. And if resistance is not enough, then subvert."

Abbey than launched a nationwide petition campaign demanding the dismantling of Glen Canyon Dam. Hardly had he finished speaking when Park Service police and Coconino County sheriff's deputies arrived on the scene. While they questioned the organizers of the illegal assembly and tried to disperse it, outlaw country singer Johnny Sagebrush led the demonstrators in song for another twenty minutes.

The Glen Canyon Dam caper brought EARTH FIRST! an unexpected degree of media attention. Membership in our group has spiraled to more than a thousand with members from Maine to Hawaii. Even the Government is interested—according to reliable reports, the FBI dusted the entire Glen Canyon Dam crack for fingerprints!

Last Fourth of July more than 200 EARTH FIRST!ers gathered in Moab, Utah, for the first Sagebrush Patriot Rally to express support for Federal public lands and to send a message to anti-Earth fanatics that there are Americans who are patriotic about *their* wilderness.

When a few of us kicked off EARTH FIRST! we sensed a growing environmental radicalism in the country but we did not expect the response we have received. Maybe EARTH FIRST! is in the right place at the right time. Tom Turner, editor of Friends of the Earth's *Not Man Apart,* recently wrote to us to say:

"Russ Train once said, 'Thank God for Dave Brower—he makes it so easy for the rest of us to appear reasonable.' Youze guys are about to make Dave Brower look reasonable, and more power to you!"

The cynical may smirk. "But what can you really accomplish? How can you fight Exxon, Coors, David Rockefeller, Japan, and the other great corporate giants of the Earth? How, indeed, can you fight the dominant dogmas of Western Civilization?"

Perhaps it *is* a hopeless quest. But is that relevant? Is that important? No, what is important is that one who loves Earth can do no less. Maybe a species will be saved or a forest will go uncut or a dam will be torn down. Maybe not. A monkey wrench thrown into the gears of the machine may not stop it. But it might delay it. Make it cost more. And it feels good to put it there.

STRATEGIC MONKEYWRENCHING
Dave Foreman

... It is time for women and men, individually and in small groups, to act heroically and admittedly illegally in defense of the wild, to put a monkeywrench into the gears of the machine destroying natural diversity. This strategic monkeywrenching can be safe, it can be easy, it can be fun, and—most importantly—it can be effective in stopping timber cutting, road building, overgrazing, oil and gas exploration, mining, dam building, powerline construction, off-road-vehicle use, trapping, ski area development and other forms of destruction of the wilderness, as well as cancerous suburban sprawl.

But it must be strategic, it must be thoughtful, it must be deliberate in order to succeed. Such a campaign of resistance would follow these principles:

Monkeywrenching is Non-Violent

Monkeywrenching is non-violent resistance to the destruction of natural diversity and wilderness. It is not directed toward harming human beings or other forms of life. It is aimed at inanimate machines and tools. Care is always taken to minimize any possible threat to other people (and to the monkeywrenchers themselves).

Monkeywrenching is Not Organized

There can be no central direction or organization to monkeywreching. Any type of network would invite infiltration, *agents provocateurs* and repression. It is truly individual action. Because of this, communication among monkeywrenchers is difficult and dangerous. Anonymous discussion through this book and its future editions, and through the Dear Ned Ludd section of the *Earth First! Journal*, seems to be the safest avenue of communication to refine techniques, security procedures and strategy.

Monkeywrenching is Individual

Monkeywrenching is done by individuals or very small groups of people who have known each other for years. There is trust and a good working relationship in such groups. The more people involved, the greater are the dangers of infiltration or a loose mouth. Earth defenders avoid working with people they haven't known for a long time, those who can't keep their mouths closed, and those with grandiose or violent ideas (they may be police agents or dangerous crackpots).

Monkeywrenching is Targeted

Ecodefenders pick their targets. Mindless, erratic vandalism is counterproductive. Monkeywrenchers know that they do not stop a specific logging sale by destroying any piece of logging equipment which they come across. They make sure it belongs to the proper culprit. They ask themselves what is the most vulnerable point of a wilderness-destroying project and strike there. Senseless vandalism leads to loss of popular sympathy.

Monkeywrenching is Timely

There is a proper time and place for monkeywrenching. There are also times when monkeywrenching may be counterproductive. Monkeywrenchers generally should not act when there is a non-violent civil disobedience action (a blockade, etc.) taking place against the opposed project. Monkeywrenching may cloud the issue of direct action and the blockaders could be blamed for the ecotage and be put in danger from the work crew or police. Blockades and monkeywrenching usually do not mix. Monkeywrenching may also not be appropriate when delicate political negotiations are taking place for the protection of a certain area. There are, of course, exceptions to this rule. The Earth warrior always thinks: Will monkeywrenching help or hinder the protection of this place?

Monkeywrenching is Dispersed

Monkeywrenching is a widespread movement across the United States. Government agencies and wilderness despoilers from Maine to Hawaii know that their destruction of natural diversity may be met with resistance. Nationwide monkeywrenching is what will hasten overall industrial retreat from wild areas.

Monkeywrenching is Diverse

All kinds of people in all kinds of situations can be monkeywrenchers. Some pick a large area of wild country, declare it wilderness in their own minds, and resist any intrusion against it. Others specialize against logging or ORVs in a variety of areas. Certain monkeywrenchers may target a specific project, such as a giant powerline, construction of a road, or an oil operation. Some operate in their backyards, others lie low at home and plan their ecotage a thousand miles away. Some are loners, others operate in small groups.

Monkeywrenching is Fun

Although it is serious and potentially dangerous activity, monkeywrenching is also fun. There is a rush of excitement, a sense of accomplishment, and unparalleled camaraderie from creeping about in the night resisting those "alien forces from Houston, Tokyo, Washington, DC, and the Pentagon." As Ed Abbey says, "Enjoy, shipmates, enjoy."

Monkeywrenching is Not Revolutionary

It does *not* aim to overthrow any social, political or economic system. It is merely non-violent self-defense of the wild. It is aimed at keeping industrial "civilization" out of natural areas and causing its retreat from areas that should be wild. It is not major industrial sabotage. Explosives, firearms and other dangerous tools are usually avoided. They invite greater scrutiny from law enforcement agencies, repression and loss of public support. (The Direct Action group in Canada is a good example of what monkeywrenching is *not*.) Even Republicans monkeywrench.

Monkeywrenching is Simple

The simplest possible tool is used. The safest tactic is employed. Except when necessary, elaborate commando operations are avoided. The most effective means for stopping the destruction of the wild are generally the simplest: spiking trees and spiking roads. There are obviously times when more detailed and complicated operations are called for. But the monkeywrencher thinks: What is the simplest way to do this?

Monkeywrenching is Deliberate and Ethical

Monkeywrenching is not something to do cavalierly. Monkeywrenchers are very conscious of the gravity of what they do. They are deliberate about taking such a serious step. They are thoughtful. Monkeywrenchers—although non-violent—are warriors. They are exposing themselves to possible arrest or injury. It is not a casual or flippant affair. They keep a pure heart and mind about it. They remember that they are engaged in the most moral of all actions: protecting life, defending the Earth.

A movement based on these principles could protect millions of acres of wilderness more stringently than any Congressional act, could insure the propagation of the grizzly and other threatened life forms better than an army of game wardens, and could lead to the retreat of industrial civilization from large areas of forest, mountain, desert, plain, seashore, swamp, tundra and woodland that are better suited to the maintenance of natural diversity than to the production of raw materials for over-consumptive technological human society.

If loggers know that a timber sale is spiked, they won't bid on the timber. If a Forest Supervisor knows that a road will be continually destroyed, he won't try to build it. If seismographers know that they will be constantly harassed in an area, they'll go elsewhere. If ORVers know that they'll get flat tires miles from nowhere, they won't drive in such areas.

John Muir said that if it ever came to a war between the races, he would side with the bears. That day has arrived.

The Middle Santiam Protest

MIDDLE SANTIAM HEATS UP; 15 ARRESTED—MORE TO COME
Mike Roselle

Monday. June 4, 1984. It was raining hard. We sat around the coffee shop while people slowly filtered in. By 8 AM there were 22 of us gathered for the action, the same number as for the previous action of May 4th. Many members of the earlier group were unable to attend this event due to school finals or other pressing responsibilities. There were, however, many new faces, and everyone was eager despite the weather. The coffee was good.

Not being an Oregonian, I thought the weather sucked. Others advised me that it would clear up any minute. They always say that. We left the coffee shop and had a circle/meeting in front of the Siuslaw National Forest headquarters. The action was to take place in the Willamette National Forest. We thought this would confuse them. There were lots of curious Freddies peeking out of the windows and wondering what we were doing. A few of us went in to ask for maps. We then loaded into two trucks and drove off.

Two hours later we arrived at a remote logging site about a mile from Pyramid Creek, near the Middle Santiam River. We had another circle. (It may seem to the casual observer that we have a lot of circles; we do.) Omar (Omar Sheriff—the law) was on the scene. Someone must have tipped him off, possibly the press. There was no alarm since we had planned for the possibility. You always take risks when you alert a large portion of the media.

Under the eyes of the police and the newspaper reporters, we began to walk casually down the road to where the logging was taking place. We talked and sang some blockade songs from Australia as we walked. It was still raining.

The workers were at lunch, sitting in their crummies and listening to Paul Harvey. The deputies were staying out of sight for the moment. We arrived at the bridge and proceeded to occupy it. There were 26 of us now, a rag-tag outfit in our variously colored raingear. This was our wilderness boundary and no vehicles would be allowed to pass.

When the logging trucks returned from the mill for the fresh carcasses, they stopped at the bridge. We refused to move. The driver made no attempt to run over us or threaten us. He had his Thermos ready. (Next action, by god, I'm bringing my Thermos. I could have used some hot coffee.) The deputies arrived on the scene. Thinking most of us would disperse when asked to leave, as in the last action, one informed us that we were breaking the law. We informed him that we were here to protect and defend the wilderness, and that we were not leaving "until all work was stopped.

The officer eyed our determined group and asked in slight disbelief, "None of you are moving?" "That's correct," was our reply. This seemed to surprise the deputies since they had two Blazers in which to put us. It would take two hours to get another vehicle up to the site. We sat down. The officers unloaded their spare tires and other assorted cop equipment from the back of their Blazers and put them in a Willamette Industries truck. They came back and placed us all under arrest. One by one they proceeded to carry us off the bridge to the waiting Blazers. It was slow work and they were careful not to hurt anyone. A total of 15 people were arrested and squeezed into the two vehicles. The rest left the bridge voluntarily and were not arrested. The police thought the action was over, but in reality, it had just begun.

It was a one hour ride over rain-soaked logging roads to the mobile booking station they had set up at a closed-down restaurant on Hwy 20. At the previous action, protesters were cited and released here. The Freddies tried to down play the seriousness of our last action to the press by stating that there were no arrests made and no one was taken to jail. This time it was different. Everyone refused to give their names or any other information. The cops were not going to get to use their nifty little mobile booking station. We were all taken the 51 miles to the Linn County Jail.

They didn't want to take us to the jail. It wasn't because they liked us, but because there wasn't any room in the jail. In fact, the jail was seriously overcrowded, and they were already facing legal challenges due to the poor conditions. We were aware of this, but wished to see for ourselves.

Many officers were on hand to receive us, hoping to process us as quickly as possible and go home. We discovered that they don't receive extra pay for working overtime. This is probably why they were mad when we still refused to give them any information. It was sort of a stand-off. I was rather enjoying the whole thing and was in no great hurry. They tried yelling at us. They tried being indifferent. They even tried being nice and almost pleading with us to give our names so they could book us and go home. We finally agreed.

We were mugshot and finger printed and the 15 of us were stuffed into two 4 person cells, 8 women in one cell and 7 men in the other. They put me in the wrong cell. I was put in the men's.

Although conditions were less than ideal, the night we spent wasn't too terribly uncomfortable. The food was bad, however. We were taken to court at noon the next day. The women were taken in separately, and protested, insisting we all be charged together. The court refused their demands. They refused bail and were taken back to their cells. The Judge was mad. The D.A. was mad. The Sheriff was mad. Now it was our turn. They led us into the courtroom.

After trying to intimidate the women had backfired on them, they were much nicer to us. After a long discussion with the Judge, who was trying to hide his impatience, and many objections from the D.A. and the Sheriff, all but two of us men signed release agreements. There was no bail. The only condition was that we remain law abiding citizens. We could return to the logging site. Two of the men, however, refused to sign and were taken back to their cells.

At the time of this writing, everyone has signed the release agreement except Sarah Barton, who told the Judge that her conscience would not let her sign anything that would prevent her from interfering with the ongoing destruction in the Middle Santiam. The struggle will continue. We need your support.

On Tuesday, June 5, other protesters sat in the lobby of the Willamette National Forest office in Eugene, demanding to see Forest Supervisor Mike Kerrick. Kerrick stalled for an hour. Then EF!ers were directed to a conference room. Kerrick finally entered to face protesters, charges of false promises, the press, and a sign that read: 'Kerrick Stop Plundering America's Heritage.'

He had promised several weeks earlier that the Cathedral Forest Action Group would be notified before any more cutting was done. But the group was notified AFTER the cuts happened this past week. The gist of Kerrick's reply to questions about this was that he didn't know what was going on up there. He insisted he was breaking no laws. Brian Heath told him: "It's hardly justice to be cutting trees down while the courts are making decisions as to whether or not to cut the trees down."

The protesters' heated, emotional, but formidable questions were met by bland bureaucrates. Finally, David Zupan asked Kerrick:

"Who are you working for?"

"I work for my boss."

"You represent a minority—people who are going to make a profit from this crime. Why don't you call a spade a spade? *Say* you're working for the timber industry."

"I won't say that."

CATHEDRAL FOREST ACTION GROUP FIGHTS FOR OREGON OLD GROWTH
George Draffan

After months of rumors and promises, environmentalists are nervous about the imminent Oregon Wilderness Bill. In April a group of Oregon Earth First!ers (some of them veterans of the Bald Mountain blockades last summer) met at Cecelia Ostrow's cabin on Big Creek on the Oregon coast. Big Creek's Roosevelt elk and silverspotted butterflies are threatened with a multi-million dollar resort financed by tax-exempt state bonds. Logging around the Kalmiopsis Wilderness continues. Old growth trees at Wassen Creek, Hardesty Mountain, Drift Creek, and the Middle Santiam are being cut or threatened. Less than 20% of the 4.5 million unprotected roadless acres are listed in the Oregon "wilderness" bill. It is hard to decide where to begin to protect these millions of acres. Heartfelt commitment and energy are flowing but the logistics are overwhelming. Many environmental advocates have worked long and hard on the legislative process, lobbying, filing timber appeals and lawsuits, for years on end. For many of us the resulting piece of legislation, probably the last omnibus wilderness bill in Oregon, is a great disappointment. Congress is giving protection to an infinitesimal remnant of the Northwest's great forests and then accusing environmentalists of ruining the economy and refusing to compromise. The politicos in Washington, D.C. are washing their bloody hands of the dirty issue.

The infamous RARE II is moot and little stands in the path of the Forest Service's timber sales to the pockets of old growth that remain. There are many small areas that deserve protection and large areas that need reclaiming. The largest old growth Douglas fir forest remaining in Oregon is in the Middle Santiam drainage east of Eugene in the Willamette National Forest. There are trees 5–8 feet in diameter, 200–300 feet tall and 250–700 years old. It is the last large reserve in Oregon for old growth-dependent wildlife species and may be the densest stand of living biological material on earth except for the redwoods, even surpassing tropical rainforests. There have been numerous timber sales in the area, ten of them on Pyramid Creek, which empties into the Middle Santiam, the longest stretch of wild unroaded river in the western Oregon Cascades. The Pyramid Creek road (USFS 2041), intended for hauling out the trees, has been moved numerous times from under massive landslides and now sits on the Middle Santiam floodplain. Steep, unstable slopes are being undercut by miles of roads and clearcuts and end up as silt in the creeks and rivers. Some of the slides are down to bedrock and will recover only on a geological time scale.

In 1981 a Pyramid timber sale appeal by the Middle Santiam Wilderness Committee was denied. In 1982 the MSWC filed a suit claiming the Pyramid sales and the rerouting of USFS Road 2041 were illegal, based on insufficient RARE II considerations. The MSWC wanted 35,000 acres of the Middle Santiam protected. The House version of the Oregon Wilderness Bill proposed 25,000 acres, and then reduced that figure to 19,500 acres to accomodate existing timber sales. Senator Mark Hatfield's version proposes a miserly 7500 acres in the Santiam and 4800 acres in the nearby Menagerie. In 1983, the MSWC, with the Oregon Natural Resources Council and the Sierra Club, asked for a temporary restraining order to halt construction activities on USFS 2041; the request was denied. A summary judgment filed by the MSWC was also denied, as were 7 more timber sale appeals.

This year the Sweet Home District Ranger quit the Forest Service to take an executive position with Clear Lumber Company, which operates in the area. The acting district ranger lied to the MSWC, saying no operations were occuring in the Pyramid sale area, when in fact cutting was underway. The MSWC and others filed for a stay of action: U.S. District Court Judge Panner ruled against them. The appeal was placed on an "expedited schedule." Meanwhile the clearcutting and roadbuilding continued.

On May 5, the Cathedral Forest Action Group was formed by members of the MSWC, Oregon Earth First!ers, and other concerned citizens. Twenty-two members then sat on boxes of dynamite which were to be used to blast a hillside to provide rock that would be crushed and spread on the logging road. Cecelia Ostrow, Leo Hund, Brian Heath, Linda Sebring, Mike Oswald and Steve Petersson were arrested for disorderly conduct, and later sentenced to perform 20 hours of community service. On May 7, thirty angry CFAG members occupied the Willamette National Forest headquarters in Eugene and confronted Supervisor Mike Kerrick, who admitted clearcutting the old growth but claimed he was following the law of the land. A week later CFAG confronted Regional Forester Jeff Sirmon in Portland. He would say only that he was there to listen; he refused to follow Kerrick's lead in admitting poor forest management. Road shows with slides of the Santiam by Steve Walti, music by Cecelia and Windsong, and expert information by Brian Heath were held in Portland, Eugene and Corvallis. By the Memorial Day weekend the Cathedral Forest Action Group had grown to a hundred members. A memorial wake was held for the trees that have fallen and strategy for future actions were considered.

The Cathedral Forest Action Group in making its stand in the Santiam Cathedral Forest, an 80,000 acre wilderness which includes both the Middle Santiam and the Old Cascades Wilderness proposals. We stand for:

1. A complete moratorium on cutting and roadbuilding in our old growth ecosystems;

2. An immediate closure of USFS Road 2041 in the Middle Santiam drainage. This is an illegal road constructed on a flood plain in front of a massive moving landslide;

3. Preservation of the entire 80,000 acre Santiam Cathedral Forest;

4. A fundamental restructuring of Forest Service policy in the Pacific Northwest. The Forest Service should protect our forests, not cut them.

We remember the great forests of the Pacific Northwest. We will protect what remains of them.

CATHEDRAL FOREST WILDERNESS DECLARATION

The last significant stands of Oregon's old growth cathedral forests are being destroyed. The so-called 1984 Oregon Forest Wilderness Bill not only fails to protect the major remaining forested wilderness in Oregon, but opens it to accelerated development by removing even the flimsy protection of the RARE II planning process: therefore, we offer our own protection for these lands.

We believe that all things are connected; that whatever we do to the earth, we do to ourselves. If we destroy our remaining wild places, we will ultimately destroy our identity with the earth: wilderness has values for humankind which no scientist can synthesize, no economist can price, and no technological distraction can replace.

We believe that we should protect in perpetuity these wild places, not only for our own sake, but for the sake of the plants and animals and for the good of the sustaining earth. The forests, like us, are living things: wilderness should exist intact solely for its own sake; no human justification, rationale, or excuse is needed.

We perceive the earth is dying. We pledge ourselves to turning this process around, to stopping the destruction, so that the earth can become alive, clean, and healthy once again.

We call on the United States government to preserve the forests of the

Pacific Northwest as some of many irreplaceable treasures of our great continent.

On behalf of all citizens of the earth community, we declare the Oregon Cathedral Forest—all that which remains of Oregon's old growth ecosystems—an inviolable wilderness for all time.

"Redwood Summer" Action

TWO THOUSAND RALLY AT FORT BRAGG

"The timber companies treat the loggers and millworkers the same way they treat the forests—as objects to exploit for maximum profit."—*Judi Bari, October 1989*

In the entire timber industry, no company demonstrates the above like Georgia-Pacific. G-P, whose Northern California operations are based at Fort Bragg, is not only a primary culprit in the destruction of ancient forests, but has announced plans to eliminate thousands of North Coast jobs by moving its processing facilities to Mexico. This maneuver will not only give the company access to a fresh pool of non-union, low-paid labor, but turn Northern California into a timber colony, looted of its resources and jobs.

On Saturday, July 21, two thousand Redwood Summer activists targeted G-P with a rally in Fort Bragg, followed by a march to the pulp mill. The day of protest, organized by Industrial Workers of the World, Seeds of Peace, Earth Action Network, and Earth First!, began at 10 a.m. with music and speeches.

A counter-demonstration, organized by the industry-sponsored Yellow Ribon coalition, took place on the opposite end of town.

At 2 p.m., Redwood Summer demonstrators paraded to the California Department of Forestry building and on to the pulp mill. Although occasionally confrontational, there was no violence and only six arrests.

There, marchers deeded the mill to those whose it really is: the people of Fort Bragg. At the same time, Redwood Summer organizers insisted that the mill not just reduce, but eliminate its emissions of dioxin and other deadly toxics. Two timber workers were invited to speak, and shared concern with the crowd about log exports, sustained yield logging and their families' future.

44 ARRESTED AT L-P MILL

In the first major action of Redwood Summer, California Earth First! forced a partial shutdown of Louisiana-Pacific's lumber mill in the coastal town of Samoa, CA, on June 20. Their action kicked off the campaign to save the world's last unprotected stands of old growth redwood. Forty-four activists were arrested at the demonstration, which was attended by over 750 activists and 200 members of the press, in what the Santa Rosa *Press Democrat* called "a perfect protest."

While lumber company PR types and the corporate press were whipping up a frenzy of anticipation over the likelihood of violence, Redwood Summer organizers held meetings with timber companies, mill workers and law enforcement agencies, defusing tension and educating them about nonviolence. The result was a peaceful and powerful demonstration that brought together a wide spectrum of people ranging from loggers and mill workers to Veterans for Peace, students and activists from all over the country. Speakers included columnist Alexander Cockburn, Oakland bombing victim Darryl Cherney, Earth Day organizer Denis Hayes, and Rainforest Action Network director Randy Hayes. A solar-powered sound system filled the air with reggae music by Clan Dyken, accompanied by Cherney.

After the speeches, rally participants walked into the four-lane access road that also serviced L-P's giant pulp mill/lumber dock and the Simpson timber and pulp mills. Police in riot gear were on hand from every law enforcement agency with jurisdiction in Humboldt County.

The police, who initially anticipated a massive rush through the main gate, were the first to block the entrance to the mill. Soon hundreds of activists were in the road, some sitting and some dancing to the rhythms of a highly energetic drum ensemble. Vehicles were slowly let through the blockade until a log truck arrived. A large affinity group linked arms in a circle directly in front, blocking its passage. People hung banners and danced on top of the truck. As the drums beat on, police eventually broke up the blockade and arrested 44 people. All were charged with obstructing a public place, unlawful assembly, and refusing to disperse. Log trucks were backed up for eight miles as nearly a thousand people danced and swayed on the highway to the music on a warm sunny day.

The Samoa action proved that EF! could mobilize the support needed to make Redwood Summer a reality, and could organize a peaceful non-violent protest in a community currently under the grip of a timber industry terror campaign. Media coverage was international and included articles in *Newsweek, Time* and the *New York Times*.

Of the women and men who ensured the success of the Samoa action by placing their bodies on the line, 17 remained in jail until the following

Friday. 26 pleaded no contest, and received a 180-day suspended sentence, one year of probation, and fines ranging from $325 to $550. This means that if they are arrested again within the next year, they must spend six months in jail.

The remaining 18 defendants pled not guilty. They will have the opportunity to state their case and motives in front of a jury, and to protest the harsh sentence of the others. They will probably use the "necessity defense," and state that they had an ethical responsibility to act.

OSPREY GROVE FALLS
Zack Stentz

O sprey Grove is dead. The old growth redwood stand that Navarro Ridge neighbors and Redwood Summer activists spent all summer defending has largely ceased to exist, and none of our lamentations or Louisiana Pacific's lame "apologies" can alter the fact. In this article I aim to set the record straight on what actually transpired in the Grove and hopefully extract some lessons from the experience that may help us save some of the north coast's other residual pockets of old growth forest. In writing this, I'm also trying to come to terms with some of the grief and shock that I still feel from witnessing the Osprey Grove destruction, for though the acreage cut was small, the magnitude of the crime committed there cannot be understated. But before I cover the events of September 12 and 13 in detail, I should briefly review the first battle for Osprey Grove.

Osprey Grove I

Osprey Grove was the name hastily stuck to an approximately 10 acre stand of old growth redwood and Douglas-fir trees plugged into a steep ravine on the side of Navarro Ridge in Mendocino County. The grove was part of a larger area of second growth forest belonging to Louisiana Pacific, who, while negotiating with the neighbors over details of the cut, neglected to inform them of the old growth existence. Instead, the neighbors learned of the old growth on July 16, when they heard the unmistakable crash of an ancient redwood being felled. Enraged by L-P's deceit, some of the neighbors formed Friends of the Osprey Grove (named for an osprey nest located in the grove) and vowed to stop the logging in the courts.

In the meantime, they called in Redwood Summer activists to help. The activists put wave after wave of nonviolent demonstrators into the grove over a three day period. They halted the logging with their bodies long enough for the court to issue a Temporary Restraining Order to prevent further cutting, though thirty-nine demonstrators were arrested and several assaulted and injured by Lee Susan, L-P's registered Professional Deforester.

Though the motion to stop the cutting of Osprey Grove was eventually defeated in court, the combined pressure forced L-P to enter into negotiations with Save the Redwoods League to see Osprey Grove and fifty surrounding acres for conversion into parkland. Negotiations continued for almost two months, with Save the Redwoods League sending a letter the week of September 2–8 offering to buy Osprey Grove and surrounding timberland for "fair market value." Meanwhile, we all thought Osprey Grove was safe. Navarro Ridge neighbors heard the sound of machines coming from the woods below, but were assured that it was only Bob Pardini's crew removing the trees that had been cut down in July.

Osprey Grove II

On the morning of September 12, the sound of chainsaws was heard again in Osprey Grove. Neighbor Steve Heckeroth went with his video camera to the Grove and was met with a torrent of verbal abuse from Pardini's loggers, who were in the process of cutting it. The neighbors put out a call for assistance. We were taken by surprise and were still recovering from Redwood Summer exhaustion. We were only able to muster about a dozen people, and only two of us ventured into the woods. I arrived at about 9 a.m. and attempted to persuade the loggers to stop cutting. Like Steve, I was rewarded with threats and insults "Where are you from?" asked one logger.

"Fort Bragg," I answered.

"Yeah, well I'll be looking for you," he said icily.

I spent the morning darting through the upper half of the Grove, while one logging crew cursed me and others tried to encircle me. When they came perilously close I would exit out the side of the Grove, wait a few minutes, then re-enter the woods and start the chase over again. It didn't stop the cutting, but I hoped it would slow them down a bit, as each minute the loggers chased me was one minute they weren't cutting an ancient redwood. Finally the top border of the Grove was ringed with loggers and security people and owner Robert Pardini, who dared me to re-enter the Grove, presumably so he could beat the living daylights out of me. "Come on," Pardini said, "I'll even let you have the first punch." I kindly declined his offer and on the advice of the neighbors and fellow Earth First!ers, I didn't re-enter the woods alone that day.

Logging stopped about 3 p.m., though whether from our actions or the brisk winds that sprang up that afternoon is unknown. From the top of Osprey Grove the damage didn't look very severe; logging had been concentrated toward the bottom of the Grove (and up to 200 feet outside the area marked on the timber harvest plan, as it turned out). That evening three of us entered Osprey Grove to inspect the damage. It was disheartening; over sixty percent of the grove had been pulled out. The living forest we had defended in July with its abundant wildlife and rich, multi-layered canopy was now a wasteland, the soil ripped by machines and open to the sky. The opposite side of the valley, also once lush with greenery, was now in open view, revealing the scarred hillsides of an older timber cut; one clearcut staring at another. As I looked up at the blue sky I saw a lone osprey circling overhead, surveying the remains of the forest named in its honor.

I spent the predawn hours of September 13 with my mother, Anna Marie, on the edge of Osprey Grove observing the lights of the guards within and waiting for reinforcements to arrive. Only three more people showed up, but we were determined to do what we could, so the five of us spread out along the top of the Grove. Again we tried to speak with the loggers and again we were verbally abused and threatened. Though we were at times perilously close to the trees being cut, the loggers showed no sign of slowing down. I don't know what was more horrifying, watching the ancient trees being cut or witnessing the attitude of the people cutting them. They enjoyed what they were doing, and wanted us to know it. "The joy of malice," one person called it, and I had to agree. Did they care that they were destroying some of Mendocino County's last old growth? "There's millions of board feet set aside in parks," a logger said. He couldn't bring himself to use the word *trees* or *forest* to describe redwood ecosystems, only cold hard economic terms like "board feet" or "standing inventory."

The carnage we witnessed and the callousness of the people perpetrating it took its toll on us—we all cried. When we left the Grove we encountered Robert Pardini and our old nemesis Lee Susan, lounging against a tree with a smirk on his face. "How's Judi's pelvis?" Pardini asked, then laughed. Did we respond in an abusive manner? Yes, but I don't think anyone could blame us at that point. Given the enormity of Susan's and Pardini's crimes, against the forest, against the neighbors, and against the demonstrators (Susan had beaten one young man with an axe handle back in July) our verbal abuse was a restrained response.

At that point some of us then proceeded to Steve's house to check the status of the legal case. An appeal had been filed in San Francisco that morning, and word on its result was expected any moment. A matter of minutes would determine if there was anything left to save. In the meantime, Anna Marie and another activist had returned to the Grove, with Kay Rudin videotaping the proceedings. Susan and L-P's security men, Jack Sweeley and Richard Goss, went after them, at which point Anna Marie dove into the hollowed out interior of a giant redwood while Kay warned the men that they had no legal right to touch the demonstrators. Legally, the men were obligated to stop the logging and have the Sheriff's Department come and remove the demonstrators. They refused to do so.

When I arrived, Kay and Anna Marie were arguing with the men, while another demonstrator kept running around another part of the Grove, distracting loggers. "I'd like to drill him a third eye," a logger said. When I saw three men grouped threateningly around my mother, I got extremely agitated. Though Sweeley and Susan were unbelievably hateful, I persuaded Goss to let me in to see my mother "to talk her out." And indeed I asked her if she wished to leave; when she refused, I sat down in the tree and stayed with her.

The loggers continued to log, sometimes barely twenty feet from our faces. We stayed put, determined to save at least the tree we were sitting in. We got depressed. We cried. We tried to lift our spirits by singing, but all we could remember were "The Internationale" and "Happy Birthday" (it was my twenty-first birthday that day).

Then Steve returned with the first good news of the day. Supervisor Liz Henry had spoken with L-P vice president Joe Wheeler and had persuaded him to stop cutting. The logging had to stop. When Goss was told of the order he replied, "I have to hear it from him."

"Go call him," Steve replied, and Goss left. He returned shortly and by then, logging had stopped. We all breathed a little easier, and when a logger walked in front of an old growth tree fifteen feet away, we assumed it was to urinate. Then he fired up his chainsaw, and twenty minutes later a four hundred year old tree was changed from a living organism to a length of dead wood while we all watched incredulously. "I love it, I fuckin' love it" a logger yelled as the tree fell. Then Goss gave the word for work to stop.

The men turned to leave and on their way out, a man fired up his chainsaw to another ancient redwood; this time, our paralysis dissolved. My mother and I ran down the hill and jumped between the chainsaw and the tree. "What are you gonna do?" the logger asked, revving his saw.

"Stay right here," Anna Marie replied.

"Be a hell of a mess," Lee Susan said. But the logger shut down his saw and left. He fired up his saw one more time, making a shallow cut in a tree on the hill above us while another logger yelled "down below," threatening to fall the tree on us. "One last act of terrorism," was how a demonstrator described it. That afternoon legal word came in: the logging of Osprey Grove was illegal. But by that time it was almost too late. Of the original grove, only twelve old redwoods and one old Douglas fir remained.

Aftermath

So what lessons can we glean from Osprey Grove? First and foremost, never trust the timber companies. The whole affair from beginning to end was marked by L-P's lies and deceptions. We can't depend on negotiations to save the forest. We need to be ready at all times to challenge a logging cut legally and with direct action if necessary.

Second, we need to be able to put activists into the woods on very short notice. Five people couldn't stop Osprey Grove from being killed but thirty, twenty, or even fifteen could have. Mendocino and Humboldt Counties need to form an emergency response network, a sort of environmental SWAT team of activists willing to go into the woods on short notice. A network like this is already being set up. If you're interested in joining, call Anna Marie at 961–0302.

Finally, we need to know where the remaining old growth is so we can keep an eye on it and defend it, when necessary. There's precious little old growth left in Mendocino County, and we shouldn't discover a particular patch of it because a neighbor heard a giant tree fall. Again, if you know of any old growth, call 961-0302. When only 4% of the original redwoods remain, it's ludicrous for it to continue to be cut.

But of course, it's too late for Osprey Grove. That piece of ancient forest now exists only on Kay Rudin's videotape and in the minds of the people who were there. I spent the night of September 13 in San Francisco, drinking with my friends and having a proper birthday celebration, marred only by my eyes being swollen and infected from exposure to redwood dust. For the most part, I had no trouble blocking the events of the day from my mind. Except whenever I shut my eyes, I saw Osprey Grove falling over and over again.

REDWOOD SUMMER RETROSPECTIVE
Karen Pickett

The Redwood Summer poster said, "*It's been said the 90s will make the 60s look like the 50s ... (and) THIS IS WHERE THE 90S BEGIN ...*" Was Redwood Summer a success? More importantly—did it live up to the poster?

The 60s was a decade when a new kind of protest was born and people fomenting change hit the streets in record numbers. At one point during the summer I took a 2 hour break from Redwood Summer madness and went to see the movie "Berkeley in the 60s". I remember wondering, watching the crowds surge down Telegraph Avenue to defend People's Park, what *happened* to all those people—why aren't they in the streets and woods fighting for the earth? I think we know where most of them are—entrenched in yuppiedom and chained to internal combustion engines and a job in a concrete tower with no windows. But the environmental movement *needs* that many people—and many more—waking up to the fact that the planet is being killed and that the people killing it have names and addresses (as Utah Phillips said) and that we too are complicit unless we *do* something about it.

Bringing the fight to save the last old growth forests into the consciousness of the public and involving them was part of Redwood Summer's success. Watching over 2000 people march down Highway 1 in Ft. Bragg yelling "Save the Old Growth! Earth First!," fists in the air, sent chills down my spine. Sure we need to do more than march and sure it feels symbolic at the moment, but we have to look deeper to really see the impact of Redwood Summer. Redwood Summer is unlike any campaign we've done before, and it only makes sense to keep tying new ways to be more effective on all fronts. How do we measure the success of a campaign? Certainly not by simply "winning" or "losing." Redwood Summer is a campaign that is infinitely easy to criticize, and I've heard many criticisms. Goddess knows, the self-criticism and assessment *are* important. We haven't won yet.

But *my* take on Redwood Summer is that it was successful—very much so. Did we achieve our goals? Well, our goals were rather ambitious—to slow logging in Northern California down to sustained yield and to save the Redwood ecosystem from extinction. We did slow logging, not to sustained yield, but we did obstruct them in a big way. A third goal was to bring national attention to the plight of the forests, particularly in Northern California. Redwood Summer did that. The Corporate plunder of old growth forests made it into the pages of *Newsweek*, the *Washington Post*, the *N.Y. Times*, the *London Times* and many other national and international journals; footage from Redwood Summer is turning into several documentary films and our message was widely broadcast over TV and radio airwaves.

In terms of raising the level of the debate, raising the general level of consciousness, Redwood Summer kicked butt. We brought in several thousand people from all over the country, put tools of activism in their hands and sent many home with a new understanding of forestry issues, of bio-diversity, of the environmental movement, and of direct action. Yes, in base camp there were flakes and hangers-on and people who never did figure out why they were there.

You throw a party, announce it over the radio and some people are going to show up just for the free food. Earth First! is known for its good parties. But overall, many people were radicalized; many people learned about direct action and took that home with them to fight their town's toxic waste dump or Forest Service logging plan. Many people already involved with EF! found themselves catapulted to leadership positions by the tidal wave of activity so that now there are considerably more people in our midst who can write a press release, do re-con, blather coherently to the TV cameras . . . That process of empowerment should translate into more effective activists, more campaigns, more actions in defense of the old growth and biodiversity. More of what we need to do. Redwood Summer participants took home to their communities something valuable to the environmental movement at large.

Of course, Redwood Summer was designed as a campaign, not a training ground; but some of the benefits and successes will be indirect and/or come about as a delayed reaction. If Save the Redwood League buys the grove of old growth in Mendocino, *they* will get the credit for saving the trees. But they would never have known about it, much less had their interest piqued had it not been for EF! direct action in the forest. Campaigns waged in Minnesota or Massachusetts or Florida by activists who honed their skills during Redwood Summer will not bear the RS banner. Some of the radicalizing, raising of consciousness or effects of the burrs placed in the side of the corporate timber beast or the Forest Service will take a while to kick in. But EF!'s role has always been that of a catalyst. We often *don't* take the credit and run, and so it will be with Redwood Summer.

This is true for EF!'s relationship to/in Redwood Summer as well. Redwood Summer is not characteristic of some "new EF!". Not at all. Redwood Summer had a life of its own right from the beginning. Earth First! was just a player, albeit a key player. It was an EF! campaign; Earth First! (as a slogan) was the inspiration; EF! as an organization (uh oh! the O-word!) was the catalyst. But besides the fact that it was a coalition (Seeds of Peace, Earth Action Network, IWW, local watershed groups, the Mendocino Environmental Center and others as well as EF!) it was truly its own creature. Redwood Summer was also an experiment. It was an experiment to see if we could garner support from other corners for old growth in a hard hitting no-compromise campaign, an experiment to see if without a structure or a process we could stage continuous waves of direct actions aimed at slowing the logging to see how far our networking tentacles reached, to see how organized a non-organization could attempt to be before things began to get diluted.

As an experiment it put those involved to a test—stretching the skills and endurance of the organizers, who endeavored to keep their sense of humor about the "Redwood Hell" we found ourselves in. But in my mind the biggest success of Redwood Summer *was that it happened at all.* I haven't said it publicly, but the truth is when my psyche was first digesting the horror of the bombing of Judi and Darryl, I thought Redwood Summer was doomed. (Oh well. Maybe next year.) That doldrums perspective didn't last long, and the campaign regrouped in a truly amazing way *without* the key organizers; regrouped in a way that put a clear message out about the commitment to keep the front line battle going to defend the planet.

The critical eye must look from a perspective that recognizes that there were some very strong forces working against Redwood Summer; that it did happen is a testament to the fact that it had a life of its own. It's true, as the Montanans observed when they arrived at base camp, that the scene was "short on organizers and tall on massage circles". That's why we put out a call for EF! organizers from all over the country to come and be part of the campaign. As we all know (media stories and the image we present to the Freddies et al. notwithstanding), we *are* a small group, and the percentage of long time California EF!ers who were either physically or psychically injured or consumed by political and legal bullshit and fallout from the bombing and FBI infiltration was high.

Redwood Summer was prolific in what it gave birth to. With a support system in place, many local watershed groups sprang up and they remain committed to direct action as a tactic. We achieved a level of scrutiny and monitoring of timber harvest plans heretofore unrealized. We developed relationships with groups like Greenpeace and Seeds of Peace that I believe will yield future benefits (read: effective campaigns) without compromising the EF! position; we developed an amazing communications network (6–10 offices at any given time, eco-net hook-ups, borrowed fax machines and burning phone lines) wherein news of cointelpro books, National Lawyers Guild tips on dealing with the FBI, car pools and funny stories were exchanged as well as pertinent info regarding THPs, CDF activity, action reports, legal maneuvers and planning for actions. Weekly Redwood Summer updates went out on Berkeley's 50,000 watt Pacifica radio station, and a S.F. paper ran weekly pieces on Redwood Summer activity.

We found we could do some things that initially seemed damn near impossible. We found we could mobilize hundreds of people around preservation of biodiversity and old growth forest ecosystems. We could find funding and outreach tools for a huge campaign without much of a process, hardly any bureaucracy and no hierarchy.

When all is said and done, the sheer size and scope of the campaign and level of activity is staggering—as the northcoast's environmental rag put it: "*scores* of protests, *hundreds* of arrests, *thousands* of demonstrators, *millions* made aware of timber abuse . . ." There were several actions a week; there was *something* happening nearly every day for the entire summer. There's a lot that's not included in the accompanying chronology. There was nearly a crisis a day—Judi's police guard being pulled without notice from her hospital room; the truck hauling the kitchen to base camp breaking down; the porta john contract being canceled; funding crises; base camp being evicted (twice) . . . On the positive side are the many actions, benefits and events in *other* locales around the country in support of and in solidarity with Redwood Summer. Information centers for RS operated in New York, Minnesota, Pennsylvania and several other states. But most importantly there were people out there every day, in the woods, in the courts, in the CDF offices, at the corporate offices, standing up for the old growth.

What kind of score does that add up to in terms of the spotted owl, the 2000 year old redwood tree, the marbled murrelet? While they are still not ensured of their survival in the long term, RS did up the ante in the timber wars for *everyone*—for the Sierra Club, for Save the Redwoods League, for the politicians, for the timber communities. RS not only raised the issues for people in Iowa and Connecticut, but it demonstrated that thousands of people will come out and stand up for old growth and endangered species and the earth.

In the short term the campaign probably polarized the timber communities even more than they had been. But it's like voting for Nixon to bring on the revolution—the level of controversy needs to be raised before it can be quieted.

Even though the polarization sometimes translated into violence and also into non-cooperation from police agencies (who didn't investigate or prosecute incidents of violence), the dialogue and interaction, hostile though it may have been, was significant in the big picture. The interaction with loggers is not a matter of taking on the cause of the loggers—or even seeing the parallels—that the locals see us as the villains, as the reason the mills are closing, is an obstacle to our work because it throws a smokescreen over the realities of corporate greed and over cutting. But there *is* a parallel between the loggers who blame the environmentalists and the environmentalists who blame the loggers while in the background the corporate dogs rake in the bucks and the trees go down. While I don't think we made many new friends this summer in the Northern California counties, the interaction was part of what needs to happen if we are ever to stop the destruction. I don't think we'll win over the locals in a big way, there isn't *time* to win over their hearts and minds, but the reality of the situation will click in for some people the way the concept of old growth clicked in for the mush brained masses after EF!ers shouted the words for several years.

As an example of the people who were brought to Redwood Summer, I look to the group of people I was in jail with after our blockade in Murrelet Grove—among them a 19-year-old woman from Massachusetts doing her first C.D., a woman from Minnesota who came to Redwood Summer because she heard about the bombing, and Dakota from Louisiana who told a reporter, "I just started crying, seeing these old trees just laying there dead . . . the loggers were yelling at us, pushing stuff at us and we're yelling back and saying don't cut this tree. I'm pretty much of a nonconfrontational person but I just hugged that tree and it was so big I couldn't see the people around the bend . . ." The logger put down his chain saw.

Are Dakota and the others empowered enough to go out and do their own action in defense of a Louisiana swamp or a Minnesota hardwood forest, or against a toxic waste dump in Massachusetts? Some are, some aren't, but I think the percentages are pretty good and the point is we escalated the battle, we got in the way of the destruction of the ecosystem constantly and however we could. To a large degree that's the only way we can gauge "success"—are we still out there fighting? You bet your ass we are.

CHAPTER 8

Ecofeminist Activism

Introduction to the Selections

Ecofeminists sometimes argue that environmentalist tactics should not be directed only at the obvious situations where humans are destroying nature but should also focus on behavior that oppresses women in society. This approach would expand the scope of environmental protest to include many acts which are usually described as "feminist" rather than "ecofeminist," as I indicated in the Introduction to this anthology. Nevertheless I have arbitrarily included in this chapter only actions focused in some way directly on environmental issues, to give the reader a sense of what ecofeminist environmental protest is like. The fact is that radical ecofeminists have not mounted separate ecofeminist environmental actions to the degree that some other radical environmental groups have, and they have usually participated in environmental protests along with or as parts of such groups. One ecofeminist takes this movement to task for misdescribing some cases of activism by women as ecofeminist when they weren't motivated by ecofeminist ideas but by other causes.[1] Still, some of the actions of women clearly have ecofeminist reasoning behind them and are conducted by women to further the goals of environmentalism.

One of the most famous environmental "actions" by women in the history of feminism anywhere in the world has been the Chipko movement in India. While these actions took place some time ago on a different continent, the efforts of poor women there to save trees by hugging them has long been an inspiration for ecofeminists and other environmentalists in North America and is briefly described in the first selection by Pamela Philipose, an Indian journalist and feminist.

Some acts of antimilitary protest have been organized exclusively by women from various feminist and ecofeminist groups in the western world throughout the 1980s and have been justified on ecofeminist grounds. The second selection presents the "Unity Statement" of the Women's Pentagon Action group which was prepared by a coalition of women's groups in 1980 for actions at the Pentagon in November 1980 and 1981.[2] This coalition was planning to protest military violence and

213

sexual and economic violence in the everyday lives of women. Recall that Ynestra King argued in Chapter 2 that antimilitarism is an important focus of ecofeminist praxis, and thus these actions and others like them are good examples of radical ecofeminist tactics. Notice also that the Unity Statement identifies various forms of dominance and oppression by men over women in society and calls for the elimination of all forms of abuse. Moreover the philosophical justifications for this are explicitly ecofeminist and based on "ecological" ideas such as the belief that all life is connected on the earth.

The third selection is by Cynthia Hamilton, a grass-roots organizer and college professor in Los Angeles, and it presents her analysis of the actions of an ad-hoc group called "Concerned Citizens of South Central Los Angeles" in 1986 to oppose a solid waste incinerator slated for their community, a poor, Black and Hispanic, residential area. This group consisted of a majority of women who, in the process of organizing, discovered the threat that this facility posed to their homes and children. Women in the area responded in defense of their community and were joined by women from other parts of Los Angeles. The citizens group adopted a form of organization and response which is more distinctive of women than men, she argues, using group equality and democracy and various nonviolent forms of response to the incinerator issue. In the end their collective action succeeded in stopping the siting of this facility in their neighborhood, despite the power of the experts who thought better.

Finally, in the last selection, Chaia Heller, an ecofeminist from the Burlington Ecofeminist Network in Vermont, rallies ecofeminists and others for the 1990 Earth Day Wall Street Action. This day-long action took place on April 21, 1990, and brought together activists from many radical political groups to protest the complicity of the American capitalist corporate elite in wars against women and the earth. Heller makes very clear the stake which radical ecofeminism has in disrupting business as usual on Wall Street. She thus connects radical ecofeminism with the critique of American capitalism, a connection that political radicals of many stripes have been pushing for years outside of the environmental movement.

Notes

1. Janet Biehl, "Arrogant Ecofeminists," *The Nation* (November 18, 1991), p. 610.
2. Ynestra King describes the origins of the Pentagon actions in "The Ecofeminist Imperative." See the book edited by Leonie Caldecott and Stephanie Leland, *Reclaim the Earth*, listed in the Selected Bibliography, Part I.

WOMEN ACT: WOMEN AND ENVIRONMENTAL PROTECTION IN INDIA
Pamela Philipose

. . . The Chipko movement clearly demonstrated, as no other movement did before it, that women have a deep commitment to preserving their environment, since it is directly connected to their household needs. It also shows how nonviolent methods can sometimes "move mountains."

The first incident that heralded this new movement took place at Gopeshwar village, in the Chamoli district of U.P. Three hundred ash trees in the region had been allotted to a sports goods manufacturer by forest officials.

In March 1973, the agents of the company arrived at Gopeshwar to oversee the felling of the trees. Meanwhile, the villagers met and decided together that they would not allow a single tree to be cut down by the company.

With the support of Sarvodaya activists (Sarvodaya workers believe in the nonviolent ideology of Gandhi), they walked in a procession, beating drums and singing traditional songs. They had decided to hug the trees that the laborers, hired by the company, were to axe. The agents of the sports company had to retreat in the face of this unexpected onslaught.

The Gopeshwar incident was only the first of a long line of similar actions, but already the enthusiastic participation of the women was very evident.

Actually, flooding had helped to dramatize the issue, when the Alaknanda River, which runs through the region, breached its banks in 1970. Hundreds of homes were swept away. Sarvodaya workers, notably a young man called C. P. Bhatt (who has since won one of Asia's most prestigious awards—the Magsaysay) succeeded in explaining the links between the flooding and the consistent tree-felling by lumber companies, which had resulted in tremendous soil erosion. In 1973, when the floods occurred again, the villagers were quite conscious of the deforestation problem.

A year had gone by since Gopeshwar village had managed to retain its trees. The Forest Department announced an auction of almost 2,500 trees in the Reni forest, overlooking the Alaknanda River. This time it was the women who acted.

It so happened that the men of the village were away collecting compensation for some land taken from them when the employees of the lumber company appeared on the scene. One little girl spotted them and ran to inform Gaura Devi about it. Gaura Devi, a widow in her fifties, was a natural leader, and organized a group of about thirty women and children who went to talk to the contractor's men.

Gaura Devi is said to have pushed her way forward and stood before a gun carried by one of the laborers. She defied him to shoot her first, before touching the trees. "Brother, this forest is our *maika* (mother's home). Do not axe it. Landslides will ruin our homes and fields." She and her companions were successful in forcing the angry contractor and his men to return without their logs. That night, the women of the village stood guard over their beloved trees.

Soon after this incident the U.P. government set up an official committee to inquire into the validity of the Chipko activists' demands. After two years, the committee reported that the Reni forest belt was a sensitive area and that no trees should be felled there. The government banned tree-felling in the area for ten years.

News of the Reni victory soon spread. The real importance of the Chipko movement was that it did not fizzle out. Its message was taken by committed activists from village to village. A prominent Sarvodaya leader, Sunderlal Bahuguna, participated in a 120-day march on foot, propagating the importance of preserving the forests.

But what was really remarkable was the initiative shown by the women. They agitated in novel ways. In one instance, in November 1977, the women of Advani village in Tehri Garwhal tied sacred threads around trees marked for felling, determined to save the trees, even at the cost of their lives. (According to Hindu custom, tying a sacred thread on somebody establishes the relationship of the protector and the protected.) The forest officer who had visited the village on that occasion to persuade the women to relent finally lost his temper and shouted, "You foolish women. Do you know what the forests bear? Resin, timber, foreign exchange." One woman responded in the same tone, "Yes, we know what forests bear. Soil, water and pure air."

Then, in August 1980 a curious thing happened, at another village in Dangori Pantoli. The all-male village council had made an agreement with the Horticultural Department under which a nearby oak forest was to be felled in exchange for a cemented road, a higher secondary school, a hospital, and electricity for the village.

On hearing about this deal, the Sarvodaya activists working there tried to persuade the council to change its stand. The men did not agree, but the women in the village decided they would protect the oak forest at any cost. The men were so incensed by this that they warned the women they would be killed if they defied the council's decision. Undeterred, a large number of women went ahead, held a Chipko demonstration, and saved the forest. The government soon banned tree-felling in this region as well.

The incident showed just how far the women had progressed. They had new confidence. They now demanded to be members of village councils; they formed *Mahila Mandals* (women's committees) to ensure the protection of forests; they appointed watch-women who received regular wages to supervise the extraction of forest products; they planted saplings.

Today, there is a woman leader in the Gopeshwar (local government) that was unheard of earlier. Little wonder, then, that the image the Chipko movement brings to mind is that of a group of toil-worn women hugging a tree to save it.

Similar movements are taking place in other regions of India too—like the Appiko Movement in the western Ghatts region of Karnataka; the Girnar Movement in Gujarat and Goa. The bad news is that, according to the latest satellite data, India is losing 1.3 million hectares of forest per year. The Indian government's ambitious social forestry programmes seem to cater more to the needs of paper and other wood-based industries than to the fuel and fodder requirements of the people who are being robbed of their forests. So unless more and more Chipko-type movements take place, the harvest will be a bitter one. . . .

UNITY STATEMENT OF THE WOMEN'S PENTAGON ACTION, 1980

We are gathering at the Pentagon on November 16 because we fear for our lives. We fear for the life of this planet, our Earth, and the life of our children who are our human future.

We are mostly women from the north-eastern region of our United States. We are city women who know the wreckage and fear of our city streets, we are country women who grieve the loss of the small farm and have lived on the poisoned earth. We are young and older, we are married, single, lesbian. We live in different kinds of households: in groups, families, alone, some are single parents.

We work at a variety of jobs. We are students, teachers, factory workers, office workers, lawyers, farmers, doctors, builders, waitresses, weavers, poets, engineers, homeworkers, electricians, artists, blacksmiths. We are all daughters and sisters.

We have come here to mourn and rage and defy the Pentagon because it is the workplace of the imperial power which threatens us all. Every day while we work, study, love, the colonels and generals who are planning our annihilation walk calmly in and out of doors of its five sides. They have accumulated over 30,000 bombs at the rate of three to six bombs every day.

They are determined to produce the billion-dollar MX missile. They are creating a technology called Stealth—the invisible, unperceivable arsenal. They have revived the cruel old killer, nerve gas. They have proclaimed Directive 59 which asks for "small nuclear wars, prolonged but limited." The Soviet Union works hard to keep up with United States initiatives. We can destroy each other's cities, towns, schools, and children many times over. The United States has sent "advisors," money and arms to El Salvador and Guatemala to enable those junta to massacre their own people.

The very same men, the same legislative committees that offer trillions of dollars to the Pentagon have brutally cut day care, children's lunches, battered women's shelters. The same men have concocted the Family Protection Act which will mandate the strictly patriarchal family and thrust federal authority into our home life. They are preventing the passage of ERA's simple statement and supporting the Human Life Amendment which will deprive all women of choice and many women of life itself.

We are in the hands of men whose power and wealth have separated them from the reality of daily life and from imagination. We are right to be afraid.

At the same time our cities are in ruins, bankrupt; they suffer the devastation of war. Hospitals are closed—our schools deprived of books and teachers. Our Black and Latino youth are without decent work. They will be forced, drafted to become the cannon fodder for the very power that oppresses them. Whatever help the poor receive is cut or withdrawn to feed the Pentagon which needs about $500,000,000 a day for its murderous health. It extracted $157 billion dollars last year from our own tax money; $1,800 from a family of four.

With this wealth our scientists are corrupted; over 40% work in government and corporate laboratories that refine the methods for destroying or deforming life. The lands of the Native American people have been turned to radioactive rubble in order to enlarge the nuclear warehouse. The uranium of South Africa, necessary to the nuclear enterprise, enriches the white minority and encourages the vicious system of racist oppression and war.

The President has just decided to build the neutron bomb, which kills people but leaves property (buildings like this one) intact. There is fear among the people, and that fear, created by the industrial militarists, is used as an excuse to accelerate the arms race. "We will protect you . . ." they say, but we have never been so endangered, so close to the end of human time.

We woman are gathering because life on this precipice is intolerable. We want to know what anger in these men, what fear, which can only be satisfied by destruction, what coldness of heart and ambition drives their days. We want to know because we do not want that dominance which is so exploitative and murderous in international relations, and so dangerous to women and children at home—we do not want that sickness transferred by the violent society through the fathers to the sons.

What is it that we women need for our ordinary lives, that we want for ourselves and also for our sisters in new nations and old colonies who suffer the white man's exploitation and too often the oppression of their own countrymen?

We want enough good food, decent housing, communities with clear air and water, good care for our children while we work. We want work that is useful to a sensible society. There is a modest technology to minimize drudgery and restore joy to labor. We are determined to use skills and knowledge from which we have been excluded—like plumbing or engineering or physics or composing. We intend to form women's groups or unions that will demand safe workplaces, free of sexual harassment, equal pay for work of comparable value. We respect the work women have done in caring for the young, their own and others, in maintaining a physical and spiritual shelter against the greedy and militaristic society. In our old age we expect our skills, our experience, to be honored and used.

We want health care which respects and understands our bodies. Physically challenged sisters must have access to gatherings, actions, happy events, work. For this, ramps must be added to stairs and we must become readers, signers, supporting arms. So close, so many, why have we allowed ourselves not to know them?

We want an education for children which tells the true story of our women's lives, which describes the earth as our home to be cherished, to be fed as well as harvested.

We want to be free from violence in our streets and in houses. One in every three of us will be raped in her lifetime. The pervasive social power of the masculine ideal and the greed of the pornographer have come together to steal our freedom, so that whole neighborhoods and the life of the evening and night have been taken from us. For too many women the dark country road and the city alley have concealed the rapist. We want the night returned: the light of the moon, special in the cycle of our female lives, the stars and the gaiety of *city streets*.

We want the right to have or not have children—we do not want gangs of politicians and medical men to say we must be sterilized for the country's good. We know that this technique is the racist's method for controlling populations. Nor do we want to be prevented from having an abortion when we need one. We think this freedom should be available to poor women as it always has been to rich. We want to be free to love whomever we choose. We will live with women or with men or we will live alone. We will not allow the oppression of lesbians. One sex or sexual preference must not dominate another.

We do not want to be drafted into the army. We do not want our young brothers drafted. We want them equal with us.

We want to see the pathology of racism ended in our time. It has been the imperial arrogance of white male power that has separated us from the wisdom and suffering of our sisters in Asia, Africa, South America and in our own country. Many North American women look down on the minority nearest them: the Black, the Hispanic, the Jew, the Native American, the Asian, the immigrant. Racism has offered them privilege and convenience; they often fail to see that they themselves have been bent to the unnatural authority and violence of men in government, at work, at home. Privilege does not increase knowledge or spirit or understanding. There can be no peace when one race dominates another, one people, one nation, one sex, despises another.

We must not forget the tens of thousands of American women who live much of their lives in cages, away from family, loves, all the growing-up years of their children. Most of them were born at the intersection of oppressions: people of color, female, poor. Women on the outside have been to taught to fear those sisters. We need each other's knowledge and anger in our common struggle against the builders of jails and bombs.

We want the uranium left in the earth and the earth given back to the people who tilled it. We want a system of energy which is renewable, which does not take resources out of the earth without returning them. We want those systems to belong to the people and their communities, not to the giant corporations which invariably turn knowledge into weaponry. We want the sham of Atoms for Peace ended, all nuclear plants decommissioned and the construction of new plants stopped. That is another war against the people and the child to be born in fifty years.

We want an end to the arms race. No more bombs. No more amazing inventions for death.

We understand all is connectedness. We know the life and work of animals and plants in seeding, reseeding and in fact simply inhabiting this planet. Their exploitation and the organized destruction of never to be seen again species threatens and sorrows us. The earth nourishes us as we with our bodies will eventually feed it. Through us our mothers connected the human past to the human future.

With that sense, the ecological right, we oppose the financial connections between the Pentagon and the banks and multinational corporations that the Pentagon serves. Those connections are made of gold and oil. We are made of blood and bone, we are made of the sweet and finite resource, water. We will not allow these violent games to continue. If we are here in our stubborn thousands today, we will certainly return in the hundreds of thousands in the months and years to come.

We know that there is a healthy and sensible loving way to live and we intend to live that way in our neighborhoods and farms in these United States, and among our sisters and brothers in all the countries of the world.

WOMEN, HOME, AND COMMUNITY: THE STRUGGLE IN AN URBAN ENVIRONMENT
Cynthia Hamilton

In 1956, WOMEN IN SOUTH AFRICA began an organized protest against the pass laws. As they stood in front of the office of the prime minister, they began a new freedom song with the refrain "now you have touched the women, you have struck a rock." This refrain provides a description of the personal commitment and intensity women bring to social change. Women's actions have been characterized as "spontaneous and dramatic," women in action portrayed as "intractable and uncompromising."[1] Society has summarily dismissed these as negative attributes. When in 1986 the City Council of Los Angeles decided that a 13-acre incinerator called LANCER (for Los Angeles City Energy Recovery Project), burning 2,000 tons a day of municipal waste, should be built in a poor residential, Black, and Hispanic community, the women there said "No." Officials had indeed dislodged a boulder of opposition. According to Charlotte Bullock, one of the protestors, "I noticed when we first started fighting the issue how the men would laugh at the women . . . they would say, 'Don't pay no attention to them, that's only one or two women . . . they won't make a difference.' But now since we've been fighting for about a year the smiles have gone."[2]

Minority communities shoulder a disproportionately high share of the by-products of industrial development: waste, abandoned factories and warehouses, leftover chemicals and debris. These communities are also asked to house the waste and pollution no longer acceptable in White communities, such as hazardous landfills or dump sites. In 1987, the Commission of Racial Justice of the United Church of Christ published *Toxic Wastes and Race*. The commission concluded that race is a major factor related to the presence of hazardous wastes in residential communities throughout the United States. Three out of every five Black and Hispanic Americans lives in communities with uncontrolled toxic sites; 75 percent of the residents in rural areas in the Southwest, mainly Hispanics, are drinking pesticide-contaminated water; more than 2 million tons of uranium tailings are dumped on Native American reservations each year, resulting in Navajo teenagers having seventeen times the national average of organ cancers; more than 700,000 inner city children, 50 percent of them Black, are said to be suffering from lead poisoning, resulting in learning disorders. Working-class minority women are therefore motivated to organize around very pragmatic environmental issues, rather than those associated with more middle-class organizations. According to Charlotte Bullock, "I did not come to the fight against environmental problems as an intellectual but rather as a concerned mother. . . . People say, 'But you're not a scientist, how do you know it's not safe?' I have common sense. I know if dioxin and mercury are going to come out of an incinerator stack, somebody's going to be affected."

When Concerned Citizens of South Central Los Angeles came togther in 1986 to oppose the solid waste incinerator planned for the community, no one thought much about environmentalism or feminism. These were just words in a community with a 78 percent unemployment rate, an average income ($8,158) less than half that of the general Los Angeles population, and a residential density more than twice that of the whole city. In the first stages of organization, what motivated and directed individual actions was the need to protect home and children; for the group this individual orientation emerged as a community-centered battle. What was left in this deteriorating district on the periphery of the central business and commercial district had to be defended—a "garbage dump" was the final insult after years of neglect, watching downtown flourish while residents were prevented from borrowing enough to even build a new roof.

The organization was never gender restricted but it became apparent after a while that women were the majority. The particular kind of organization the group assumed, the actions engaged in, even the content of what was said, were all a product not only of the issue itself, the waste incinerator, but also a function of the particular nature of women's oppression and what happens as the process of consciousness begins.

Women often play a primary part in community action because it is about things they know best. Minority women in several urban areas have found themselves part of a new radical core as the new wave of environmental action, precipitated by the irrationalities of capital-intensive growth, has catapulted them forward. These individuals are responding not to "nature" in the abstract but to the threat to their homes and to the health of their children. Robin Cannon, another activist in the fight against the Los Angeles incinerator, says, "I have asthma, my children have asthma, my brothers and sisters have asthma, there are a lot of health problems that people living around an incinerator might be subjected to and I said, 'They can't do this to me and my family.' "

Women are more likely than men to take on these issues precisely because the home has been defined and prescribed as a woman's domain. According to British sociologist Cynthia Cockburn, "In a housing situation that is a health hazard, the woman is more likely to act than the man because she lives there all day and because she is impelled by fear for her children. Community action of this kind is a significant phase of class struggle, but it is also an element of women's liberation.[3]

This phenomenon was most apparent in the battle over the Los Angeles incinerator. Women who had no history of orgainizing responded as protectors of their children. Many were single parents, others were older women who had raised families. While the experts were convinced that their smug dismissal of the validity of the health concerns these women raised would send them away, their smugness only reenforced the women's determination. According to Charlotte Bullock:

> People's jobs were threatened, ministers were threatened . . . but I said, "I'm not going to be intimidated." My child's health comes first, . . . that's more important than my job.
>
> In the 1950s the city banned small incinerators in the yard and yet they want to build a big incinerator . . . the Council is going to build something in my community which might kill my child. . . . I don't need a scientist to tell me that's wrong.

None of the officials were prepared for the intensity of concern or the consistency of agitation. In fact, the consultants they hired had concluded that these women did not fit the prototype of opposition. The consultants had concluded:

> Certain types of people are likely to participate in politics, either by virtue of their issue awareness or their financial resources, or both. Members of middle or higher socioeconomic strata (a composite index of level of education, occupational prestige, and income) are more likely to organize into effective groups to express their political interests and views. All socioeconomic groupings tend to resent the nearby siting of major facilities, but the middle and upper socioeconomic strata possess better resources to effectuate their opposition. Middle and higher socioeconomic strata neighborhoods should not fall at least within the one mile and five mile radii of the proposed site.
>
> . . . although environmental concerns cut across all subgroups, people with a college education, young or middle aged, and liberal in philosophy are most likely to organize opposition to the siting of a major facility. Older people, with a high school education or less, and those who adhere to a free market orientation are least likely to oppose a facility.[4]

The organizers against the incinerator in South Central Los Angeles are the antithesis of the prototype: they are high school educated or less, above middle age and young, nonprofessionals and unemployed and low-income, without previous political experience. The consultants and politicians thus found it easy to believe that opposition from this group could not be serious.

The intransigence of the City Council intensified the agitation, and the women became less willing to compromise as time passed. Each passing month gave them greater strength, knowledge, and perseverance. The council and its consultants had a more formidable enemy than they had expected, and in the end they have had to compromise. The politicians have backed away from their previous embrace of incineration as a solution to the trash crisis, and they have backed away from this particular site in a poor, Black and Hispanic, residential area. While the issues are far from resolved, it is important that the willingness to compromise has become the official position of the city as a result of the determination of "a few women."

The women in South Central Los Angeles were not alone in their battle. They were joined by women from across the city, White, middle-class, and professional women. As Robin Cannon puts it, "I didn't know we all had so many things in common . . . millions of people in the city had something in common with us—the environment." These two groups of women, together, have created something previously unknown in Los Angeles—unity of purpose across neighborhood and racial lines. According to Charlotte Bullock, "We are making a difference . . . when we come together as a whole and stick with it, we can win because we are right."

This unity has been accomplished by informality, respect, tolerance of spontaneity, and decentralization. All of the activities that we have been told destroy organizations have instead worked to sustain this movement. For example, for a year and a half the group functioned without a formal leadership structure. The unconscious acceptance of equality and democratic process resulted practically in rotating the chair's position at meetings. Newspeople were disoriented when they asked for the spokesperson and the group responded that everyone could speak for the neighborhood.

It may be the case that women, unlike men, are less conditioned to see the value of small advances.[4] These women were all guided by their vision of the possible: that it *was* possible to completely stop the construction of the incinerator, that it is possible in a city like Los Angeles to have reasonable growth, that it is possible to humanize community structures and services. As Robin Cannon says, "My neighbors said, 'You can't fight City Hall . . . and besides, you work there.' I told them I would fight anyway."

None of these women was convinced by the consultants and their traditional justifications for capital-intensive growth: that it increases property values by intensifying land use, that it draws new businesses and inventment to the area, that it removes blight and deterioration—and the key argument used to persuade the working class—that growth creates jobs. Again, to quote Robin Cannon, "They're not bringing real development to our community. . . . They're going to bring this incinerator to us, and then say 'We're going to *give* you fifty jobs when you get this plant.' Meanwhile they're going to shut down another factory [in Riverside] and eliminate two hundred jobs to buy more pollution rights. . . . They may close more shops."

Ironically, the consultants' advice backfired. They had suggested that emphasizing employment and a gift to the community (of $2 million for a community development fund for park improvement) would persuade the opponents. But promises of heated swimming pools, air-conditioned basketball courts and fifty jobs at the facility were more insulting than encouraging. Similarly, at a public hearing, an expert witness' assurance that health risks associated with dioxin exposure were less than those associated with "eating peanut butter" unleashed a flurry of derision.

The experts' insistence on referring to congenital deformities and cancers as "acceptable risks" cut to the hearts of women who rose to speak of a child's asthma, or a parent's influenza, or the high rate of cancer, heart disease, and pneumonia in this poverty-stricken community. The callous disregard of human concerns brought the women closer together. They came to rely on each other as they were subjected to the sarcastic rebuffs of men who referred to their concerns as "irrational, uninformed, and disruptive." The contempt of the male experts was directed at professionals and the unemployed, at Whites and Blacks—all the women were castigated as irrational and uncompromising. As a result, new levels of consciousness were sparked in these women.

The reactions of the men backing the incinerator provided a very serious learning experience for the women, both professionals and non-professionals, who came to the movement without a critique of patriarchy. They developed their critique in practice. In confronting the need for equality, these women forced the men to a new level of recognition—that working-class women's concerns cannot be simply dismissed.

Individual transformations accompanied the group process. As the struggle against the incinerator proceeded to take on some elements of class struggle, individual consciousness matured and developed. Women began to recognize something of their own oppression as women. This led to new forms of action not only against institutions but to the transformation of social relations in the home as well. As Robin Cannon explains:

> My husband didn't take me seriously at first either. . . . He just saw a whole lot of women meeting and assumed we wouldn't get anything done. . . . I had to split my time . . . I'm the one who usually comes home from work, cooks, helps the kids with their homework, then I watch a little TV and go to bed to get ready for the next morning. Now I would rush home, cook, read my materials on LANCER . . . now the kids were on their own . . . I had my own homework. . . . My husband still wasn't taking me seriously. . . . After about 6 months everyone finally took me seriously. My husband had to learn to allocate more time for baby sitting. Now on Saturdays, if they went to the show or to the park, I couldn't attend . . . in the evening there were hearings . . . I was using my vacation time to go to hearings during the workday.

As parents, particularly single parents, time in the home was strained for these women. Children and husbands complained that meetings and public hearings had taken priority over the family and relations in the home. According to Charlotte Bullock, "My children understand, but then they don't want to understand. . . . They say, 'You're not spending time with me.' " Ironically, it was the concern for family, their love of their families, that had catapulted these women into action to begin with. But, in a pragmatic sense, the home did have to come second in order for health and safety to be preserved. These were hard learning experiences. But meetings in individual homes ultimately involved children and spouses alike—everyone worked and everyone listened. The transformation of relations continued as women spoke up at hearings and demonstrations and husbands transported children, made signs, and looked on with pride and support at public forums.

The critical perspective of women in the battle against LANCER went far beyond what the women themselves had intended. For these women, the political issues were personal and in that sense they became feminist issues. These women, in the end, were fighting for what they felt was "right" rather than what men argued might be reasonable. The coincidence of the principles of feminism and ecology that Carolyn Merchant explains in *The Death of Nature* (San Francisco: Harper & Row, 1981) found expression and developed in the consciousness of these women: the concern for Earth as a home, the recognition that all parts of a system have equal value, the acknowledgment of process, and, finally, that capitalist growth has social costs. As Robin Cannon says, "This fight has really turned me around, things are intertwined in ways I hadn't realized. . . . All these social issues as well as political and economic issues are really intertwined. Before, I was concerned only about health and then I began to get into the politics, decision making, and so many things."

In 2 years, what started as the outrage of a small group of mothers has transformed the political climate of a major metropolitan area. What these women have aimed for is a greater level of democracy, a greater level of involvement, not only in their organization but in the development process of the city generally. They have demanded accountability regarding land use and ownership, very subversive concerns in a capitalist society. In their organizing, the group process, collectivism, was of primary importance. It allowed the women to see their own power and potential and therefore allowed them to consolidate effective opposition. The movement underscored the role of principles. In fact, we citizens have lived so long with an unquestioning acceptance of profit and expediency that sometimes we forget that our objective is to do "what's right." Women are beginning to raise moral concerns in a very forthright manner, emphasizing that experts have left us no other choice but to follow our own moral convictions rather than accept neutrality and capitulate in the face of crisis.

The environmental crisis will escalate in this decade and women are sure to play pivotal roles in the struggle to save our planet. If women are able to sustain for longer periods some of the qualities and behavioral forms they have displayed in crisis situations (such as direct participatory democracy and the critique of patriarchal bureaucracy), they may be able to reintroduce equality and democracy into progressive action. They may also reintroduce the value of being moved by principle and morality. Pragmatism has come to dominate all forms of political behavior and the results have often been disastrous. If women resist the "normal" organizational thrust to barter, bargain, and fragment ideas and issues, they may help set new standards for action in the new environmental movement.

Notes

1. See Cynthia Cockburn, "When Women Get Involved in Community Action," in Marjorie Mayo (ed.), *Women in the Community* (London: Routledge & Kegan Paul, 1977).
2. All of the quotes from Charlotte Bullock and Robin Cannon are personal communications, 1986.
3. Cockburn, "When Women," p. 62.
4. Cerrell Associates, *Political Difficulties Facing Waste to Energy Conversion Plant Siting* (Los Angeles: California Waste Management Board, 1984), pp. 42–43.
5. See Cockburn, "When Women," p. 63.

TAKE BACK THE EARTH
Chaia Heller

For thousands of years the patriarchy has waged a war against women; a war in which it controls and violates our bodies with rape, battering, forced motherhood, and conditioned self-hatred. As well as assigning women the exclusive sexual functions of reproduction and providing men pleasure, the patriarchy reduces women to instruments of labour: Currently women do two-thirds of the world's agricultural and industrial work while owning less than 91% of the world's land and property.

There is another war on the planet; a war against nature. Industrial capitalism, in both its state and corporate forms, has emerged as an economic system which reduces human labor and all of nature into lifeless objects, cashing them in for the profit of a few elite, white men.

Western industrial society treats nature with the same condescending and paternalistic attitude historically reserved for women. Patriarchal thought defines women as irrational, passive and in need of men's control. According to this view, men's protection of women is "traded" generously for complete access to women's bodies and labour. In the same way, nature is also defined as a passive, irrational "thing" to be protected and plundered according to men's needs. The justification for the domination of nature flows smoothly out of the justification for the domination of women. Within Western society, all forms of human and natural life are defined as a mere "resource" to be controlled and squandered for the enhancement of "civilization."

Ecofeminism is a movement of women who understand the connection between the war against women and the war against nature. It is women working together to fight all forms of social and ecological exploitation in order to increase our chance of survival. Ecofeminists see the oppression of women, people of color, children, lesbians and gays and the destruction of nature as linked and mutually reinforcing in a system of domination which is legitimized and perpetuated by various institutions such as the state, the military, religion, the patriarchal family and industrial capitalism. We fight for the freedom and self-determination of all oppressed peoples as well as for a harmonious relationship with nature: We realize that until we are all free from social and ecological exploitation, no one is free.

Women feel directly the destruction of the planet: In so called "developing countries," lands are confiscated and poisoned, making it impossible for women to feed their children. All over the world women are subject to forced sterilization, literally worked to death in factories, and poisoned by toxic chemicals. Everywhere, the toxics that are dumped into water, dumped into backyards, impair women's reproductive systems, poisoning their breast-milk, their food and their children.

Inheriting thousands of years of compulsory motherhood and caretaking activities, women have been socialized to care only for others, never for themselves. Understandably then, some feminists fear that ecofeminism could be yet another setup for women, compelling them, in the name of ecology, to take on the house-cleaning chores of the world. However, ecofeminists need not fall into the trap of janitorial martyrdom: Fighting oppressive and ecologically destructive institutions saves *women's* lives. We choose to fight for our *own* survival, as well as for the survival of others. Fighting for our own liberation as women is inextricably linked to the survival of the planet.

In addition, ecofeminism demands more than ecological survival. We fight so that we may flourish. We will be free from the shackles of the state and the church who want to deny women the choice to parent when and *if* we choose and to love *whomever* we choose. We demand to be free from constant threats and acts of violence: We will be free from rape and battering in our homes, in the streets, and harrassment on the job. We will fight for our passions, our pleasures, creating democratic communities in which work, art and ethics are both mutually and ecologically enhancing.

Already, women all over the world are striking out against the devastation of women and nature. In the Chipko movement in India, women are saving entire forests through direct action. Women in the South Pacific are speaking out against the poisoning of their bodies and their land from the nuclear testings of the 1950s. In Israel, Jewish and Palestinian women are speaking out for the right to peaceful cooperation between their peoples and for an end to violence, poverty and oppression perpetuated by the Israeli, Arab and American governments. The ecofeminist movement in the U.S. is lagging way behind in the ecological and land reform movements of women all over the world. We must respond.

It is time to take it to Wall Street. Last time we were there was in 1984 for the "Not In Our Name" action; the demonstration in which over 1000 women took to the streets of New York City. We were there to inform the world that the U.S. corporations could no longer wage war against people all over the world in the name of American women. In that action, we swarmed the headquarters of the corporations and banks that manufacture and finance everything from nuclear weapons to apartheid in South Africa.

This year, in 1990, we will return to Wall Street with others in the ecology, labour, peace and human liberation movements to shut down the headquarters of the perpetrators of the war against women and nature; the perpetrators of the war against the planet itself.

We will disrupt the lethal flow of the day-to-day activity of the corporate elite who whimsically murder the wills and bodies of women all over the world, stripping the earth of its creativity and diversity.

The patriarchy has determined the fates of women's bodies. Now capitalism seeks to determine the fate of the earth. We will not have our fate determined by a few corporate and governmental elite whose only aspirations are to increase their own personal power and wealth. Women from all over the country will gather at Wall Street to throw a wrench into the gears of their deadly machine, saying "No More. We will take back our lives! We will take back the Earth!"

CHAPTER 9

Bioregionalist Activism

Introduction to the Selections

Bioregionalism is a very practically oriented ecophilosophy, as I suggested in Chapter 3. It proposes a positive plan of political and social action to heal the earth by reinhabiting local places and creating new forms of small-scale community, alternative economic systems, and participatory political structures, all of which are in harmony with the spirit of bioregions. Bioregional resistance amounts to "ecology with a vengeance," Jim Dodge says earlier in this anthology. This means refusing to destroy nature as the dominant society does, but also preventing others from doing so by any nonviolent means possible. Bioregionalists thus provide a unique form of activism while joining other radical environmental and social groups in their efforts to defend the earth.

Peter Berg is one of the founders of bioregionalism and has given a great deal of thought to how to put it into practice. His view is that bioregionalism is more than just saving what's left in the wild, as some environmentalists would have it. Instead, bioregionalists believe that there will have to be specific bioregional programs for our non-wilderness areas as well, including programs for our cities, suburbs, and rural areas. Berg has thus proposed a "green city program" for the San Francisco Bay area which incorporates bioregional strategies.

In this selection, Berg presents his views about how a person can grow a "life-place politics" in a place. He suggests that you begin by analyzing the local conditions which exist where you live, then grow outward from there toward your watershed neighbors and beyond to the whole bioregion. This means inventing new political organizations that reflect the social and ecological relations in your bioregion, and joining together with political groups in other bioregions of the continent to cooperate in large bioregional congresses. As one bioregionalist puts it, one must develop strategies for an alternative nation within the existing, surrounding nation, and this will require a large dose of hard work, creativeness, and organization.[1]

Notes

1. Bill Millison, "Strategies for an Alternative Nation," in Andruss et al., eds., *Home! A Bioregional Reader,* p. 149; Selected Bibliography, Part I.

GROWING A LIFE-PLACE POLITICS
Peter Berg

The most obvious conclusions sometimes disguise the most mysterious situations. Ask city dwellers where their water comes from, for instance. Most will answer with something like "The faucet, of course. Want water? Turn the tap handle." But the faucet is only the last place water was, not where it came from. Before that it was in the plumbing, and before that in the mains. It got there from a reservoir, and from an aqueduct connected to a storage lake. "So tell me the name of the lake and I'll know where the water really comes from." Finding out the name and, even better, walking on the shore of that lake is definitely a start toward acquiring a sense of care and gratitude. But even that lake is just another place where water was. It got there as runoff from rain or snow that fell from clouds. Where do clouds come from? Evaporated ocean water? Two weather systems meeting? Whatever forces are involved in making any particular cloud, the source of every particle of water in it remains a deep mystery. If anything can be said about the ultimate state of water, it is probably that it doesn't begin or end anywhere but is constantly cycled through one form and location to another.

Here's another easy observation: We all live in some geographic place. And here's the accompanying mysterious and very critical situation: the places where we live are alive. They are *bio*regions, unique life-places with their own soils and land forms, watersheds and climates, native plants and animals, and many other distinct natural characteristics. Each characteristic affects the others and is affected by them as in any other living system or body. And bioregions are all different from each other. Not just "mountains," but Appalachian Mountains or Rockies. Not just "river valley," but Hudson or Sacramento.

People are also an integral part of life-places. What we do affects them and we are in turn affected by them. The lives of bioregions ultimately support our own lives, and the way we live is becoming crucial to their ability to continue to do so.

Knowing that water is always cycling has a lot of practical value (regardless of how frail our sense of every station in the cycle may be). It means, for example, that simply dumping water that is dirty with sewage or chemicals won't really get rid of those pollutants. They'll just be carried along to the next station wherever it happens to be, to the water intake of a town downstream, perhaps, or through the ground to later seep into a well. Since water that we've used has a good chance of quickly becoming someone else's, limiting what goes into it and treating it before sending it along becomes a realm of social responsibility and reciprocity. That's the basis of what could be termed "water cycle politics," and it's serious business. Most town, city and country governments have official departments to oversee water supplies and sewage, and questions of water quality and use can arouse some of the most serious public debates.

What's the practical response to knowing that we share in the lives of bioregions? If what we do degrades them, how does that fit with our concepts of social responsibility and reciprocity? What is a life-place politics?

Rootstock

It's probably best to begin by looking at the actual conditions that exist where some people live. Doing this may run the risk of over-particulariz-ing, but at least it won't deliver the kind of over-generalization and abstraction that can turn political thinking sour with ideology.

Right now I'm in a clearly defined sixty-mile-long watershed that empties into the Pacific Ocean on a fairly remote stretch of the northern California coast. I've been teaching Shakespeare's Sonnets ("When I consider everything that grows . . .") at the small high school my daughter attends here, work-learning about fruit trees from a local master pruner, and helping with some community projects. A borrowed cabin provides heat by woodstove and light by kerosene lamps. Water comes from the same creek that later flows through salmon-rearing tanks tended by self-taught homesteaders who are trying to bring native fish back up to their historical levels of population in the river.

Living here has never been especially prosperous. Fifth-generation families still cut and haul firewood, maintain excellent gardens and home-can everything from cherries to salmon. So do many of the new settlers. Much of the work that requires more than one person's labor is carried out on an informal exchange or volunteer basis that is held together with good-willed neighborliness. (People's skills and the services they can make available are wide-ranging and sometimes astonishing.) A volunteer fire department garage is the most visible municipal institution in the nearest town, a small post office is the only sign of a distant national government. If police are ever called, they will come from the county sheriff's office two mountain ridges and an hour and a half away. "Folk anarchism" wouldn't be a bad term for the social ethos that guides generally respectful relations between this valley's residents. Most of them are here because they like it that way.

"You make it sound too idyllic," remarks my pruner friend. "I live here but I'd move *there,* the way you're describing this place. You've left out the mentality about doing anything you want to on your own land even if it means destroying it. How about bickering over water rights or the other personal grudges that can go on for years?"

There's all that, but a visitor who has any interest in reversing the degradation of life-places couldn't help but be struck by seeing the rootstock for sustainable inhabitation in the future that exists here.

Plentiful local renewable wood for heating fuel, good water from springs and creeks, natural building materials, varying but workable soil, and some natural provision of food from fish are native resources. Human resources include broad skills, a spirit of informal mutualism, serious work on natural preservation and fishery enhancement projects, and a growing ecologically-centered culture.

Actually achieving a workable harmony with natural systems in this valley is another matter, however, and much more difficult than it would appear to be to a casual visitor. For one thing, it would require acceptance of a political perspective that is different from anything that most people here (or elsewhere) have known.

Let's start with the place itself, which hasn't been treated very well over the last century since settlers arrived and native inhabitants suffered extermination or removal. Cattle and sheep overgrazing (with forest-burning to create larger pastures) and brutal logging have scarred most of the hills. Subsequent erosion carried away vast amounts of soil, caused huge landslides and filled the formerly pristine river with gravel bars. A sustainable future would first of all have to be based on a local commitment to restore and maintain the river, soil, forests, and wildlife that ultimately support inhabitation here.

Next would come developing means for meeting human needs in ways that are both sustainable and self-reliant. Current food production, although more evident than in some other places, is really only minimal. Even hay for animals often comes from outside the valley. Energy needs, now partially met with local wood, could be completely filled by using alternative techniques and other renewable sources such as solar and micro-hydro power. Gasoline is presently one-fifth more expensive here than it is just outside the valley. Nearly all manufactured goods are carried or shipped in from outside. There are a few health practitioners, but complicated cases (or even ones requiring eyeglasses or dentistry) have to travel outside the watershed limits for care. And public transportation is non-existent.

Finally, there is the problem of earning a living in a place where there is little regular employment. Income from the present boom in marijuana cultivation (which also exists in many other deeply rural areas) is in perpetual jeopardy from law enforcement zealots. Even if marijuana became legalized, the most effective long-term economic solution would be to build on other existing activities that are more boom-and-bust proof and compatible with restoring, rather than further depleting, natural systems—natural enhancement projects, education (especially in sustainable fishing, forestry, grazing, and farming practices), visitor services, and local crafts and culture. The internal need for cash can simultaneously be reduced through community undertakings that "make money by not using money"—some large commonly-held farms, tool and machinery sharing co-ops, labor exchanges for new improvements like refitting homes for energy efficiency, a local currency or system of credits for trading goods and services, a transportation sharing system, and other formal ways to heighten social interdependence.

Restore natural systems, satisfy basic human needs, and develop support for individuals: those are the most fundamental requirements for sustainability and should be the goals of watershed-scaled bioregional politics in the valley. Achieving these is already a concern among some of the people, and their numbers could easily grow in the future. Even so, those who have been involved the longest feel they won't see full fruition in their lifetimes. How many generations might it take to restore the valley? (For that matter, has it really ever happened anywhere else before?) How self-reliant in regard to food, energy, manufacturing, education, and health can this place ever become? How much continuing outside support is needed, and under what terms should extra-watershed support be secured? As for increasing social interdependence, what political means can enable all the individualistic and differing personal beliefs that exist here to coalesce in formal co-operation without losing the free-souled spirit that the valley nurtures now?

Closer to hand, there are plenty of issues that need immediate attention. There should be a moratorium on logging the few stands of first-growth trees that still remain. A full recycling program should replace hauling away unsorted garbage from the local dump. A valley-wide alternative energy plan should be mapped out and put into action. Watershed education, although featured at the small high school, should be a concern of the larger elementary and junior high schools and should be offered to adults as well. There's a lot to keep everyone busy before politics can be largely framed by the principles of restoring natural systems, filling human needs and developing support for individuals.

EVOLVING WATERSHED-SCALED GOVERNMENTS

Growing the politics for a life-place has to be based on the reality of living there, and it's necessary to remind ourselves that no facts are established without evidence. Someone has to do something that is consistent with the vision of fitting into ongoing natural processes before any reasonable person will support the vision.

No outside agency proclaimed that salmon enhancement should begin in the valley, for instance. A desire to see past numbers of salmon running the river again led a few people to investigate how this might be accomplished and inspired them to commit time-consuming labor (with frustratingly numerous false starts and mistakes) that eventually led to some small success. They communicated their vision to other people, involved them in the project, and consequently increased their chances for success. Now that more neighbors are involved, the threats to restoring salmon—such as loss of fish habitat through further logging, over-grazing, over-fishing, and stream destruction—are becoming more widely exposed and understood issues. If it becomes a generally shared ethic, "Don't do anything that could hurt the spawning cycle" could lead to profound changes here.

Bioregional politics originate with individuals who identify with real places and find ways to interact positively with the life-web around them. Involving close-by watershed neighbors creates a "socialshed." This seed group is and will remain the most important unit of bioregional political interaction.

Several socialsheds of neighbors working on a wide variety of different projects (co-ops, community gardens, renewable energy, bioregional education, recycling, and many others) can easily join together to form an organization for the broader local community. In effect, it would be a watershed council, rightfully claiming representation for the closely shared place itself. A watershed council is the appropriate forum for directly addressing present inhabitory issues and also for stating new objectives that are based on the principles of restoring natural systems, meeting human needs and supporting individuals. It can effectively contend with the closest institutions of government (town, city and county) to secure positions. These established governments may be arbitrary units in bioregional terms, with unnatural straight-lined borders or control over a patchwork of different natural geographies, but their policies hold for parts of real life-places and must be dealt with while the council presses for eventual self-determination in the watershed.

Whole bioregions are usually larger than one watershed and are overlaid with equally arbitrary and even more powerful governments— several counties, state(s), national departments and agencies—too many in fact to serve as practical institutions for resolving bioregion-wide problems. Rather than seeking to influence anything higher than local governments, watershed councils must band together to form an independent body in order to represent their entire bioregion. A council from the valley, for instance, while holding positions on town and council issues, would also join with similar northern California (Shasta bioregion) groups in a federation or congress.

Watershed councils and bioregional congresses have, in fact, sprung up in parts of North America reaching from Cascadia in the Pacific Northwest to the Lower Hudson estuary in New York. One might ask (as even the environmentalist establishment does) whether these new groups are really necessary. Couldn't the goals of sustainability be reached through existing forms, and wouldn't it be better if those forms were made to work rather than cranking up something that is probably going to be seen as unacceptably radical anyway? And how about places other than remote valleys—areas that are more populated or nearer to metropolitan centers?

It goes without saying that creating a new political framework is difficult and that it will inevitably be seen at first as too radical (with some justification, considering the snaggy, frustrated and boilingly ambitious types it may attract). The only reason to bother is to gain something that is absolutely necessary but can't be achieved through existing means. The question becomes: Is there any other way to preserve life-places? Aside from immediately local ones, governments and dominant political parties aren't open to accepting sustainability as a serious goal. They seem barely able to hear outcries against obvious large-scale destruction of the planetary biosphere from merely reform-minded environmentalists now, and aren't likely to take bioregionalists seriously until the District of Columbia itself becomes totally uninhabitable. Government has forfeited defense of life-places to the people who live in them. Watershed councils and bioregional groups are necessary to secure inhabitory rights.

Is sustainability really necessary? Rather than reviewing all of the colonialist, resource-depleting and environmental horror stories of the twentieth century that continue in the present and which without opposition will definitely extend in a compounded form into the next century, let's simply look at who we want to be. Do we want to degrade ourselves by participating in the degradation of humanity and the planet? And don't both of these processes begin where we live? *Un*sustainability simply isn't a lifesome alternative. Struggling for sustainability is necessary if we want to achieve it, like freedom.

As for abstracting from the situation in a northern California valley to other places, won't that be committing the same error that earlier was said to turn political thinking sour with ideology? Frankly, yes. No two life-places are the same, for one thing, and the differences between backcountry, rural, suburban, and city environs are enormous. Are there any similarities? Yes to that, too. Every site of human inhabitation is part of some watershed or other and exists within a distinct bioregion. The goals of restoring natural systems, meeting human needs and supporting individuals that are appropriate in the valley apply wherever else people are living. The problem lies in searching out how human activities in any life-place are ultimately rooted in natural processes and discovering how to fit into them.

A more populated rural area, for instance, may share the same watershed as a nearby urban center. This is the case for most of the agricultural country near cities on the Atlantic seaboard stretching from Boston to Atlanta, although the population-dense coastal edge is commonly seen as one long megalopolis and the connection between each city (usually sited on a river or at the mouth) and its watershed of support is virtually ignored. This natural continuity must be restored to our consciousness, and recognizing the differences between whole bioregions that lie within the territory separating the Atlantic Coast and Appalachian Mountains is an important initial step toward developing sustainability in that part of the continent.

In the Great Plains, however, cities are much smaller and often already identify with the country surrounding them. The problem there is that agricultural use of the land has supplanted native features nearly completely. Mammoth farming operations exhaustively mine soil and water and export it in the form of grain and meat to places as far away as the Soviet Union. The Great Plains (like the great valleys of California) is a resources colony for global monoculture and is rapidly being stripped of the basic components of sustainability. Watershed councils and bioregional groups in this increasingly endangered part of the continent advocate restoring the native prairies, non-abusive farming methods and greater diversification to relieve dependency on mono-crop agriculture.

There's tremendous diversity among bioregions, from the Sonoran Desert to the Gulf of Maine, from the Great Lakes to the Ozarks, but the schema for growing native life-place politics starting with socialsheds of neighbors, joining these in watershed councils, and proceeding to the creation of bioregional federations or congresses can fit them all.

Green Cities

Cities don't hover on space platforms. They are all within bioregions and can be surprisingly dependent on fairly close sources for food and water, at least. All of them can become more responsible for sustainability by lessening their strain on the bioregions where they are situated. Urban life-place politics can be expressed through Green City programs for whatever aspects of restoring natural places, meeting human needs and supporting individuals are realistically possible. And there are more ways to do this than a typical city-dweller might think.

Processing urban sewage into fertilizer that can be returned to farm land would reciprocate directly with provision of food, for example. Establishing neighborhood common gardens and orchards would partially relieve the outlying countryside while helping to make a city more self-reliant. Energy demands could be sharply reduced by public projects to retrofit buildings and homes for alternative sources and heat efficiency. City governments can help facilitate starting new neighborhood food cooperatives, and establish centers for lending tools and equipment. (Public libraries for books are an impressive precedent.) Neighborhood-scaled recycling programs could be established. Cities can sponsor urban-rural exchanges to trade labor for agricultural produce. They can create wild-corridor parks so that native creeks, vegetation, birds and other animals can pass through and provide a natural presence. Bioregional arts programs and city-wide celebrations of total life-forms are projects easily begun.

Some of the points in a Green City program may seem similar to current environmentalist proposals but there is a fundamental difference between them. From a bioregionalist perspective, people are *part* of a life-place, as dependent on natural systems as native plants and animals. Green City proposals aren't based on simply cleaning up the environment but rather on securing reciprocity between the urban way of life and the natural life-web that supports it.

On the surface there seem to be few ways to demonstrate bioregional connectedness to city people. They don't see the actual sources for their food, for example, and often don't know where they are. But that doesn't make the life-place link any less real; it just confirms the need to expose it. Since cities are educational, cultural and media centers, the means for exposure are already there. Green City programs can emphasize natural underpinnings by proposing curricula and art that communicate with everyone from school children to theater audiences. They can promote appearances by speakers and cultural groups from outside the city to bring a sense of bioregional partnership. Green City "bioregion reports" could readily become an aspect of daily news. When these and all the other urban informational possibilities are considered, developing life-place consciousness in cities may not be so difficult after all.

North American Bioregional Congresses

What makes sense after the watershed council and bioregional group (now including a Green City program) levels of life-place politics? Representation of these at larger naturally-scaled assemblies seems to follow, and just as there are currently dozens of watershed-bioregion groups, there was in May, 1984, the first North American Bioregional Congress. But the air becomes thinner at this level, and it's good to take a deep breath before climbing up.

The intent of such an assembly should be to extend whatever links have been previously made between groups, make new ones, prepare mutually-felt statements on continent-wide concerns, and decide on an effective course of action that all of the different groups can taken in common. Some of this was accomplished at the first Congress. Representatives met each other, information was exchanged, there were statements on some positions, and a few working committees were established.

The continental air is thin because it's difficult enough to understand one's own watershed and then fit it into a larger bioregion, but much more so to "think like a continent." For one reason or other, many attendees at NABC I were basically unfamiliar with bioregional ideas and activities. Some had come to learn what these are. Some others came to represent their own different movements. North America as a living entity in the planetary biosphere was eventually understood and celebrated, but how bioregions interact with each other, what neighboring relationships might be, how groups can assist with real projects in different places, and other matters that presumably should be covered were hardly touched on.

To overcome the thin air, future continental congresses will have to be more definite about their identity and intent. Crucial discussions and decisions should be framed in terms of their usefulness to active representatives of life-places, and there should be more addresses by those who can assist in "thinking like a continent," an array extending from geographers and water basin specialists to story-tellers and poets. A North American Bioregional Congress is an important new political forum, and there is much needed work that it can do. National and state governments persistently maintain destructive policies toward the continent's life-places. A Congress that authentically represents North America can claim authority to initiate beneficial ones. It can confront the problem of arbitrary (and multiple) government power over bioregions. It can select priority issues to bring attention to situations in particular life-places (such as ruinous diversion of rivers in desert Sunbelt areas) and organize exchanges of expertise, work parties and cultural events to support member groups. It can eventually stand as the main voice for a large continent-wide movement.

We've come a long distance from a remote northern California valley to the North American Bioregional Congress, and have picked up new long-term struggles at every level along the way. Restoring the valley will take several generations—the Shasta bioregion several more. How many for the continent? Meeting basic human needs of all its people? Creating means of support for them? They're hugely challenging goals, but undoubtedly worthwhile since they are ways to retrieve the future and offer a definite vision for what is vaguely termed "post-industrial society." Achieving them is the work, the *do,* of bioregionalism.

A Basis For Alliances

There are opportunities for life-place political alliances at all the levels from a local watershed to North America (and eventually with other continents' assemblies). Only a fanatical mind-set would dictate that the basis for these should be to convert everyone else into a bioregionalist, and that would make a travesty of the terms for coalitions. Let's go back to the work of fitting into real natural processes to find more legitimate terms.

Active bioregionalists don't merely raise their hands to vote on issues but also find ways to interact positively with the life-web around them. They work with neighbors to carry out projects and build a bioregional culture together. Put another way, they are the working practitioners of what academics and others term "a paradigm shift." There is a very wide range of ways to express life-place consciousness and no need to exclude anyone's creativity in doing so, but bioregionalists do share a common interest in actually applying their convictions to local situations (in addition to having opinions about more distant ones). Their political activity is an extension of the work they do. They have a hands-on identity that is compatible with the goals of restoring natural systems, meeting basic human needs and creating support for individuals.

Some other groups have a natural affinity for these same goals. Native Americans are an obvious example. Renewable energy, alternative technology and permaculture (sustainable agriculture) proponents can easily share support on many issues. Earth-spirit women's groups, radical conservationists, natural living advocates, and deep ecology adherents envision a similar bio-centric future. It wouldn't even be too difficult for many current environmentalists to fit their causes into a longer-range bioregional perspective.

Less apparent, perhaps, is the basis for alliances with progressive movements that are aimed at affecting policies of existing large government structures and political parties. Disarmament, non-intervention, anti-nuclear, and other movements with a more distant focus than on the immediately local level leave little room for sharing direct support. Bioregionalists don't want nuclear arms or power facilities where they live, of course, and would certainly join with specifically anti-nuclear groups to make those places nuclear-free. Whether or not a watershed council or North American Bioregional Congress should endorse positions of every group or movement that each representative at those assemblies finds deserving is another matter. Some positions will be found in common, but the bioregional movement has its own character and own concerns. Without these it wouldn't be worth much as an ally anyway.

There has been some confusion about the relationship between life-place concerns and "green politics" ever since the first North American Bioregional Congress. A few participants at that event have even stated since that there is no difference between the two. The distinctions are very clear, however, and should be understood so that genuine bioregional goals can be realized.

First of all, green politics attempts to cover a more extensive range of areas, but where there are similarities, bioregional directions are much more definite and specific. This is obvious in a statement of definition from the initial Green Organizing Planning Meeting:

Green politics interweaves ecological wisdom, decentralization of economic and political power whenever practical, personal and social responsibility, global security, and community self-determination within the context of respect for diversity of heritage and religion. It advocates nonviolent action, cooperative world order, and self-reliance.

Some of the words are the same, but the sense of them is very different. Bioregionalists have a specific direction for "ecological wisdom:" they want to restore and maintain watersheds and bioregions. Those are the places to which they want to decentralize and where they wish to practice self-determination. Their "personal and social responsibility" is to meet basic human needs and create ways to support individuals in life-places. As for extending their goals to "global security . . . co-operative world order," bioregionalists may well choose to ally with groups and movements which develop effective ways to apply that sentiment, but their own primary effort is to solve problems where they live. (And that may be the best locale for rooting a planetary perspective, after all.)

The first North American Bioregional Congress recognized this distinction by declaring, "If the emerging Green political organization does indeed reflect these bioregional concerns, we urge support from bioregional groups and individuals from around the continent." *If* it does, and at this point no unified acceptance of bioregional goals by "greens" has been stated.

Another distinction is evident in the way "green politics" is developing structurally. At the Green Organizing Planning Meeting in August, 1984, committees were formed to represent mega-regions based on the compass points in the United States: Northeast, South, Midwest, West, and Northwest. Isn't this the old centralized way of describing territory? All of these areas have several bioregions within them. People have been identifying and seeking to fit into these unique life-places for some time. Do they really need another arbitrarily-defined political district? The "green" structure seems to be oriented from the top down. Bioregional movement groups originate on the watershed level and move up to join in naturally-scaled continental assemblies.

The most critical difference between the movements may lie with their actual ecological orientation. How much "ecological wisdom" are they really prepared to accept? Bioregionalists answer, "All we can get!" They see their lives as intertwined with ongoing natural processes, part of the life of a place. From their biocentric viewpoint, human society is ultimately based on interdependence with other forms of life. They follow that conviction to make choices about which kinds of work to undertake and to oppose Late Industrial depredations.

It is not established that followers of green politics are similarly committed, and questionable as to whether they will become so. Theirs is a multiplicity of concerns (Ecological Wisdom is only one of ten key values listed), and among many Greens, ecological awareness is limited to an older environmentalist perspective, attempting to reform industrialism instead of aiming to replace it. Some bioregionalists who are also active in green politics feel that they can reach members of that movement and change its direction. No doubt some will be persuaded, but wishful evangelism isn't a good foundation for building coalitions. Truly relevant life-place politics will originate from watershed councils, bioregional groups and the North American Bioregional Congress. When support for the positions of these naturally-scaled groups is sought, Greens may yet prove to be very strong allies regardless of their different emphasis and direction.

Leaving No One Out

Is it realistic to assume that anyone, the next person you meet, for instance, will be able to understand and sympathize with bioregional goals? Would most people be able to suspend conventional political ideas long enough, or be able to see past labels like "environment," "natural resources," and so on?

Admittedly, many people are likely to have only slight awareness of day-to-day contact with non-human forms of life and to view natural systems as something to be insulated from. The best ground for introducing life-place consciousness may lie further forward in their minds and involve feelings about the course of present society. Try asking if society hasn't lost its ethical basis by subjecting human and natural life to continuous threats and damage. Most people feel that a disaster can occur before they are actually told that one was even possible, that it happens more and more frequently, and that the next one will be more horrendous than the last. Usually they'll agree that industrial society has been and continues to be irresponsible about endangering both Nature and people.

How about the promise of the future? Can present society ever right the balance of its demands on Nature? It may come as a surprise, but many people are reluctant to discuss the future. They may even fear it, and when they don't, unguarded optimism is rarely offered.

On the positive side, encourage remembering that we really are part of all life, that we are born as mammalian creatures and continue to survive, sense the seasons and experience weather as mammals—that life is always looping through us: food, water, energy, and materials sustain us before moving on as wastes and refuse. Point out that although our skillful mobility permits changing locations more quickly than we can become familiar with a new place, we always end up in some bioregion or other and are part of it no matter how briefly. Suggest that Nature isn't a remotely distant entity but actually exists everywhere and can be experienced by simply recognizing the unique characteristics of the places where we live. Invite imagining how deeply we could feel and in how many ways we could celebrate, restore, defend, and identify with those places.

The Mystery Remains and We No Longer Deny It

There were no unsolvable physical mysteries during the industrial era, and Nature was thought to be merely physical. Physics, chemistry and engineering could unravel any puzzle for what was thought to be the inevitable betterment of humankind: produce anything imaginable, restructure any environment, remove any amount of a wanted resource, and exterminate or discard anything unwanted. If it came to the point that doing these things created new problems (considered a doubtful outcome for the greatest part of the period), there were still ways that were believed capable of restoring an upper human hand: (a) just be thankful for what progress has been made and accept living with whatever negative consequences come with it: (b) stop doing something that is known to be disastrous and start doing some new thing whose effects are completely unknown; and (c) apply more industrial techniques to solve problems brought though industrialism in the first place. The result of all this self-deception? We live with poisons up to the waist in a junkyard of breaking machines.

More environmental agencies won't ultimately relieve our situation. They would only be further appendages of a political core that is welded to industrialism itself. We need a core based on the design of Nature instead, from watershed to bioregion and continent to planetary biosphere. Is it self-defeating to avoid established governments other than immediately local ones? Not if we want to anticipate a society whose direction already lies outside those institutions. We need to uncover and follow a natural design that lies beneath industrial asphalt.

What about world spheres of influence, global economies and other international considerations? The whole planet is undergoing the severe strains of the Late Industrial period now: chemical plagues, wholesale mechanical removal of landscapes, disruption of the most major river courses, accelerated destruction of ecosystems, and overnight disappearance of habitats. Couldn't we tame that suicidal appetite by adopting sustainability as a goal? If we become bioregionally self-reliant won't that be a large step toward taking the strain off the rest of the planet's life-places?

On a farm in the country or in a city apartment, we're all completely enmeshed in the web of life. We can't know all of the details of all the connections. Bioregional politics doesn't try to overcome the mystery, it is aimed toward making a social transition so that we can live with that mystery. Can we stop tearing the web apart and consciously build a role as partners in all life? We'd better, and we can, by beginning where we live.

PART III

Critical Response
to Ecotage

CHAPTER *10*

Responses

Introduction to the Selections

Ecotage has come in for its share of criticism over the past fifteen years, and some of this has been internal to the radical environmental movement itself. One focus of this criticism has been the use of violence against machines. Thus Dave Foreman, as early as 1982, was moved to personally defend the use of such violence, though he stated that Earth First! as a whole did not advocate violence or monkeywrenching and that this was an individual choice.[1] In a subsequent discussion of this issue Foreman argued that he was impressed with the philosophy and power of nonviolence and also with other tools for preserving wilderness such as monkeywrenching. Neither civil disobedience nor monkeywrenching, however, was for everyone, and the latter could sometimes muddy the waters and make things dangerous if it was done at the same time that other environmentalists were engaging in acts of civil disobedience. Still, Foreman claimed that both were tools which could fit certain situations and certain individuals. In effect he argued that this was a situational and personal matter which could not be decided by any general rule.[2]

Some voices in Earth First! supported Foreman. Thus Howie Wolke, another leader in Earth First! activism, argued that there was a difference between tactical and philosophical nonviolence. To him, "a philosophical commitment to total nonviolence, under all circumstances, would . . . be both unrealistic and unnatural. The most basic human animal instinct is to fight back when under attack or when members of your tribe are under attack."[3] If nonviolence worked in stopping the destruction of a Forest Service wilderness area by road-building, then that was the bottom line. If it was ineffective in a given situation, Earth First!ers would have to reassess their tactics. This practical approach to violence was not endorsed by all Earth First!ers, however, one of whom warned that the conflict between violent and nonviolent attitudes was an Earth First! "powderkeg with a short fuse."[4]

Eugene Hargrove, the editor of the influential philosophical journal *Environmental Ethics*, has also expressed his reservations about the monkeywrenching tactics of Earth First!, and these are presented in the first selection in Chapter 10. Hargrove argues that if Abbey's fictional gang confined itself to civil disobedience, there would probably be no cause for alarm, but the activities touted in *The Monkey Wrench Gang* are criminal and imitations of the gang's actions could not be described as civil disobedience. Instead the gang's operations are closer to terrorism and are one step away from harming humans.

The next two selections give the responses of Abbey and Foreman to Hargrove's criticism. Abbey protests that there is a difference between terrorism and sabotage, the first being a form of deadly violence directed against people and other living beings, the second the use of force against inanimate property. In any event, ecotage is justified as a last resort when all other means of wilderness defense have failed and one has to protect one's life, family, home, and nature from violent assault. Foreman replied that there was a wide variety of opinion about monkeywrenching in Earth First!, and he did not advocate it as an editor of the *Earth First! Journal*. In Hargrove's response to Abbey and Foreman, he remains unconvinced that Earth First! does not seek to inspire others to carry out acts of monkeywrenching. And he recommends that other available legal and moral alternatives be used to accomplish environmental goals.

Hargrove's reaction to monkeywrenching is not unique; other representatives of the establishment also responded in similar ways. Thus Michael Kerrick, Forest Supervisor of the Willamette National Forest in Eugene, Oregon, argued in 1985 that there were legitimate avenues and established procedures to address the concerns of monkeywrenchers in our system, including public agency land management processes, the federal courts, and Congress. Environmentalists should use such channels to address their concerns about the logging of old growth forests. Others in the environmental movement, such as Ed Marston, the editor of *High Country News* in Colorado, a well-known environmental newspaper, also expressed reservations about ecotage. Marston commented that "we cannot save the natural world unless we can reform ourselves, our communities, our society." Ecotage was a form of destructive behavior that would remain a "cop show" only, would further corrupt and brutalize our society, and would delay the day when people in the western United States would begin restoring the land that they had degraded.[5]

In 1990 *Environmental Ethics* published a more careful evaluation of the justification of monkeywrenching, and this is excerpted in the final selection in Chapter 10. In the selection, Michael Martin, a philosopher at Boston University, focuses on both higher law justifications of ecotage and utilitarian or consequentialist justifications. He finds the higher law arguments to be unconvincing and thus, by implication, rejects Paul Watson's defense of ecotage through appeal to ecological laws, laws which Watson takes to supercede all of the human laws of nations. Martin argues that Dave Foreman, on the other hand, does provide something like a consequentialist argument for ecotage and that this kind of argument could work if the right premises were provided to back it up. However Martin concludes that ecosaboteurs like Foreman have yet to show that "public nonviolent acts of conscientious wrongdoing cannot work *and* that acts of ecosabotage can," and, until they do, their case for ecotage will not be convincing.

A Final Observation

Where does this criticism leave ecotage?

Clearly orthodox philosophical traditions in our political system do not condone the use of violence in our society, for good reason. Our democratic political philosophy is not always clear on this point, but it generally implies that the closer environmental tactics are to conventional, peaceful political tactics, such as the use of political lobbying, administrative appeals, and lawsuits, the more responsible they are ethically. On the other hand, the closer they are to lawbreaking and ultimately to criminality, especially to the use of force, coercion, and even violence against property, the harder they are to justify ethically and the less credibility they have politically. The burden then is on radical environmentalists to defend the use of ecotage, no matter how personal they believe that ethics and politics are.

There is a certain common sense in this continuum of ethical judgment in our system, this way of looking at public and at secret political behavior. For it reveals deep principles about the grounds for obedience to our political and legal system and deeply held convictions about how individuals should achieve their political goals, including the goals of environmentalism. Our system still rightly asks that radical protesters show that they have exhausted the personal, legal, and institutional means that are available to cope with environmental destruction, before they proceed with more vigorous tactics. It favors the techniques of peaceful change and nonviolent resistance over any more extreme methods to save the wilderness. In my judgment, then, the case has yet to be made by supporters of ecotage, and Martin is correct. Until they can show that peaceful acts of protest and conscientious environmental civil disobedience cannot work and ecotage is necessary, others have a right to be skeptical about their methods.

Notes

1. "Violence and Earth First!", *Earth First! Newsletter* 2 (March 20, 1982), p. 4.
2. See "Earth First! and Non-Violence, A Discussion," *Earth First!* 3 (September 12, 1983), p. 11.
3. "On Violence," *Earth First!* 3 (September 23, 1983), p. 12.
4. Peter Swanson, *ibid.*, p. 12.
5. "Ecotage Isn't a Solution, It's Part of the Problem," *High Country News* (June 19, 1989), p. 15.

ECOLOGICAL SABOTAGE: PRANKS OR TERRORISM?

Eugene Hargrove

In 1975 Edward Abbey wrote a novel called *The Monkey Wrench Gang* which recounts the adventures of three men and one woman filled with "healthy hatred" who decide to sabotage construction projects which they find environmentally distasteful. Meeting accidentally near the Glen Canyon Dam, casual conversation about the possibility of blowing up the dam turns to serious plans for ecological sabotage on a smaller scale. Passing reference is made to the Luddite movement of the nineteenth century and *sabotage* is defined as the destruction of machinery using wooden shoes. No underlying philosophy, set of principles, or ideology is developed, however, then or at any time later in the book:

> "Do we know what we are doing and why?"
> "No."
> "Do we care?"
> "We'll work it out as we go along. Let our practice form our doctrine, thus assuring precise theoretical coherence."

The group agrees to stop short of murdering people—planning to murder machines instead—but such niceties fall by the wayside as the police close in after an abortive attempt to blow up a bridge. Two surrender. One is captured without a fight. The fourth, the Vietnam veteran, chooses to fight it out to the end, an end in which his "riddled body hung on the rimrock for a final moment before the impact of the hail of steel, like hammer blows, literally pushed it over the edge," and it "fell like a sack of garbage into the foaming gulf of the canyon, vanishing forever from men's eyes."

Now, seven years later, this book is the inspiration for a new environmental group, Earth First! which, according to *Newsweek* (19 July 1982, pp. 26-27), is "pledged to 'ecological sabotage' and other forms of civil disobedience," and is endorsed by Abbey himself who is quoted as telling the organization: "Oppose, resist and if necessary subvert. Of course, I never advocate illegal action at any time. Except at night. . . ."

Perhaps if the group is really able to engage in civil disobedience (pranks, according to *Newsweek*), there will be no cause for alarm—but the activities in Abbey's book, as acknowledged by the characters themselves, are criminal, not civil, in nature, and it is hard to imagine a group of people enthusiastically inspired by Abbey's book foregoing the acts described in it indefinitely. Indeed, it seems hard to imagine the ecological sabotage of the book having anything to do with civil disobedience at all. Persons who engage in civil disobedience normally participate in some legally unacceptable activity in order to get arrested and thereby publicize their cause. The book, however, is filled with paramilitary operations for the purpose of destroying equipment and bridges. The participants try to keep their identities a secret and avoid capture. These activities seem closer to terrorism than civil disobedience, and seem to differ from them only in the preference for killing machines, rather than humans, a preference abandoned easily by the most militant member of the gang once the police arrive.

Although presumably the organization, like the book, has no clear philosophy, there does seem to be something there implicitly and it is more radical than any position put forward in the field of environmental ethics to date. In the past, environmental ethicists have talked about *extending* moral considerability in some way to include nature (Leopold and his followers, for example), but here nature, rather than being included, is given priority. This nature chauvinism is a nonhumanistic, indeed an antihumanistic, position, and probably has much to do with Abbey's earlier attitudes in *Desert Solitaire:* "I'm a humanist; I'd rather kill a *man* than a snake."

I would doubt that many members of Earth First! would be ready at this time to put Abbey's sentiments into action; however, as their practice forms their doctrine, who knows where their theory will lead them? We live in a society socially and politically dedicated to the protection of property (including construction equipment and bridges). As Locke put it long ago, a man who destroys property declares a state of war with society and in that state, society has the right to destroy the offender "as a *Lyon* or a *Tyger,* one with whom Men can have no Society nor Security." This right was invoked when the Vietnam veteran took his stand in the book, and it is what will inevitably happen in real life if authentic ecological sabotage begins. From there, it should be a small step for the surviving and uncaptured saboteurs to begin protecting the snake by killing the man.

In the twentieth century, terrorism (the use of force as a political weapon to demoralize, intimidate, and subjugate) has been the last resort when normal political action was frustrated and improvement through peaceful means was absolutely impossible. The environmental movement, however, with its beginnings in the nineteenth century with Yosemite and Yellowstone and culminating in the 1960s and 1970s with the wilderness, endangered species, and clean air and water acts, to name a few, has been an immensely successful political movement. In this context, what could be the practical, ethical, or political justification for acts which could easily create a terrible backlash undoing all the good that has been done and preventing future accomplishments?

EARTH FIRST! AND THE MONKEY WRENCH GANG
Edward Abbey

Thank you for inviting me to respond to your editorial regarding Earth First! and *The Monkey Wrench Gang* [see *Environmental Ethics* 4 (1982): 291].

So far as I know, Earth First! as an organization—though it's more a spontaneous grouping than an organization, having neither officers nor bylaws—is not "pledged to ecological sabotage." If *Newsweek* said that, *Newsweek* is hallucinating (again). We *are* considering acts of civil disobedience, in the usual sense of that term, when and where they might be useful. For example, if the Getty Oil Co. attempts to invade Gros Ventre wilderness (Wyoming) with bulldozers, we intend to peaceably assemble and block the invasion with guitars, American flags, live human bodies, and maybe an opposing D-9 tractor. If arrested, we shall go to jail, pay the fines, and try again. We invite your readers to join us. A good time will be had by all.

As for the book, please note that *The Monkey Wrench Gang* is a novel, a work of fiction, and—I like to think—a work of art. It would be naïve to read it as a tract, a program for action, or a manifesto. The book is a comedy, with a happy ending. It was written to entertain, to inspire tears and laughter, to amuse my friends and to aggravate our enemies. (Aggravate their ulcers.) So far about a million readers seem to have found that approach appealing.

The book does not condone terrorism in any form. Let's have some precision in language here: terrorism means deadly violence—for a political and/or economic purpose—carried out against people and other living things, and is usually conducted by governments against their own citizens (as at Kent State, or in Vietnam, or in Poland, or in most of Latin America right now) or by corporate entities such as J. Paul Getty, Exxon, Mobil Oil, etc., etc., against the land and all creatures that depend upon the land for life and livelihood. A bulldozer ripping up a hillside to strip-mine for coal is committing terrorism; the damnation of a flowing river followed by the drowning of Cherokee graves, of forest and farmland, is an act of terrorism.

Sabotage, on the other hand, means the application of force against inanimate property, such as machinery, which is being used, for example, to deprive human beings of their rightful work, as in the case of Ned Ludd and his mates; sabotage—for whatever purpose—has never meant and has never implied the use of violence against living creatures. The characters in *Monkey Wrench* engage in industrial sabotage in order to defend a land they love against industrial terrorism. They do this only when it appears that in certain cases and places all other means of defense of land and life have failed and that force—the final resort—becomes morally justified. Not only justified but a moral obligation, as in the defense of one's own life, one's own family, one's own home, one's own *nature*, against a violent assault.

Such is the basis of my characters' rationale in *The Monkey Wrench Gang*. How the reader chooses to interpret all this is the reader's business. And if the reader is impelled to act out in real life the exploits of Doc, Bonnie, Slim, & Hayduke, that too is a matter for decision by the individual conscience. But first and last it should be remembered that the book is a fiction, make-believe, a story, and no more than a story.

As for my own views on environmental ethics, I refer to state them in the essay form: see *The Journey Home* (1977), *Abbey's Road* (1979), and *Down the River* (1982).

MORE ON EARTH FIRST! AND THE MONKEY WRENCH GANG
Dave Foreman

I certainly agree that the question of monkeywrenching is an important one and deserves discussion. I am currently preparing an essay justifying such action which I'll send to you for later consideration in *Environmental Ethics*.

I am sorry that you wrote your editorial [*Environmental Ethics* 4 (1983): 291] based on such sketchy knowledge of Earth First! I'm enclosing some additional information. The *Newsweek* article was rather sensationalistic and simplistic.

It is important to point out that Earth First! is a movement and not a formally organized group. There is a wide variety of opinion within EF! over monkeywrenching. As editor of the *Earth First! Journal*, I do not advocate it nor do I *not* advocate it. It is a personal decision.

I would like to touch on two points in your editorial. You charge that there is no underlying philosophy in *The Monkey Wrench Gang* and therefore none in Earth First! I have written, "Let our actions set the finer points of our philosophy." Too often, philosophers are rendered impotent by their ability to act without analyzing everything to an absurd detail. To act, to trust your instincts, to go with the flow of natural forces, *is* an underlying philosophy. Talk is cheap. Action is dear.

You say the environmental movement has been immensely successful. Only on the surface, I think. It appears to be successful because it asks for so little and actually threatens the corporate state to such a minor extent. The great ecologist Paul Sears suggested preserving twenty-five percent of our land in a wilderness condition. We've protected only one and one-half percent. The Sierra Club has asked for only three percent. That's success? The California condor faces imminent extinction. The grizzly may soon be eliminated from the lower forty-eight states. That's success? Thousands die each year because of toxic substances in our air, our water, our soil, our food, our mother's milk—that's success?

EDITOR'S RESPONSE
Eugene Hargrove

Although I now have a deeper understanding of Earth First! thanks to the two letters above and the material supplied by Dave Foreman, my concern over the ethical or moral implications of the nonorganization remains unchanged. In an article called "Earth First!" (published in *The Progressive*, 1981, and reprinted in the February 1982 issue of *Earth First!*), Foreman writes that one of the original purposes of Earth First! was "to inspire others to carry out activities straight from the pages of *The Monkey Wrench Gang* even though EARTH FIRST!, we agreed, would itself be ostensibly law-abiding." A sample of this approach seems to be the following statement by Foreman from the August 1982 issue of *Earth First!* "While we don't advocate illegal acts in defense of Mother Earth, we admire those who have the guts to fight." The group's admiration of monkeywrenching seems to be a legal euphemism intended to encourage ("inspire") others to commit acts of sabotage while evading legal responsibility for those acts. Even if this tactic is successful, it is hard to imagine how the group can avoid moral responsibility for acts which are both criminal and morally reprehensible by normal moral or ethical standards. While I can understand the frustration of the nonleaders of the nonorganization that so little was accomplished by environmentalist administrators during the Carter Administration (the reason Earth First! was started), there are still legal and moral alternatives which could be pursued. An environmentalist political party like the Green Party in Germany, for instance, might provide the support that environmentalist administrators need to accomplish their goals—without the legal and moral difficulties Earth First!ers may face in the near future. I am amused by Foreman's characterization of philosophy as cheap talk, since the nonphilosophy of the nonorganization, in order for the group to avoid criminal prosecution, also has to be all talk and no action.

ECOSABOTAGE AND CIVIL DISOBEDIENCE
Michael Martin

Introduction

The recent arrest by the FBI of Dave Foreman, founder of the radical environmental group Earth First!, for conspiracy to sabotage two nuclear power plants and a facility that manufactures triggers for nuclear bombs[1] raises anew the issue of the morality of breaking the law for ethical purposes. In this paper I explore a number of analytic and moral questions connected with what has been called ecosabotage: sabotage for the purpose of ecological protection. What is ecosabotage? Is it a form of civil disobedience? Can it be morally justified? Have advocates of ecosabotage such as Foreman in fact provided an ethically acceptable justification for what they sometimes advocate? Although ecosabotage has received wide coverage in popular magazines[2] and other periodicals,[3] these important and difficult questions have been in large part neglected by environmental ethicists.[4] . . .

Can Ecosabotage Be Given a Consequentialist Justification?

. . . As I have just shown, without an expanded analysis of civil disobedience, ecosabotage cannot be viewed as a form of civil disobedience. Nevertheless, the civil disobedience literature can still provide insight into ecosabotage's possible justification. Most theorists of civil disobedience maintain that because acts of civil disobedience break the law and conflict with accepted modes of social conduct, they require some special justification to overcome what seems to be their prima facie wrongness. The same could be said about acts of ecosabotage.

If one follows this line of argument, the burden of justification is clearly on the civil disobedient person or the ecosaboteur. This burden is thought to be especially difficult to meet in a democracy because when laws are made by the people's representatives, they seem to have a legitimate claim to the obedience of all citizens. Yet this claim is never absolute. Democratic processes do not work perfectly: unjust and evil laws can be enacted; shortsighted and destructive policies can be pursued; it can either be impossible or can take too much time to change laws by lawful means. Thus, concerned citizens may sometimes legitimately entertain illegal means of changing the status quo and educating and arousing their fellow citizens. Before they become civil disobedients or ecosaboteurs, however, they need to have a clear rational justification for their actions.[5]

Carl Cohen, in his comprehensive study of civil disobedience, reports that historically there have been two basic ways to justify civil disobedience: the appeal to higher law and the appeal to teleological or consequentialist considerations.[6] Although both approaches are relevant to the justification of ecosabotage, I focus on the consequentialist justification in detail in this essay.[7] This emphasis is in no way intended to suggest, however, that there are no limits to consequentialist justification.[8]

As Cohen maintains, a consequentialist justification need not be restricted to a specific calculus of goods or evils:

> It simply indicates that the justification will rely upon some intelligent weighing of consequences of the disobedient act. The protester here argues, in effect, that his particular disobedience of a particular law, at a particular time, under given circumstances, . . . is likely to lead in the long run to a better or more just society than would his compliance, under those circumstances, with the law in question.[9]

According to Cohen, the disobedient person appeals to two sorts of factors to justify his or her actions: moral principles that specify the goal of the disobedient act and factual considerations that specify the means to achieving this goal. The goals of the disobedient act, Cohen argues, are usually not in question but are shared by the vast majority of the citizens of the community. In the rare cases that they are not in harmony with the community, their justification "is almost certain to fail."[10] On the other hand, the means of achieving the goals are controversial and their justification involves a delicate and often inconclusive balancing of conflicting considerations. The person who is contemplating a disobedient act must consider the *background* of the case at hand and ask questions such as: "How serious is the injustice whose remedy is the aim of disobedient protest? How pressing is the need for that remedy? . . . Have extraordinary but lawful means—assemblies of protests, letter-writing campaigns, etc.—been given full trial?"[11] The potentially disobedient person must also consider the *negative* effects of the disobedience and ask questions such as:

How great is the expense incurred by the community as a consequence of the disobedience? . . . Is any violence entailed or threatened by the disobedient act? And if so, to property or to persons? . . . Has a bad example been set, a spirit of defiance or hooliganism been encouraged? Has respect for law been decreased in the community, or the fundamental order to society disturbed?[12]

Finally, the potential disobedient must estimate the *positive* results from the contemplated action and ask questions such as: How much influence will the disobedient act have in accomplishing change? Will it bring significant pressure to bear on legislatures that can bring about change? Can it attract public attention to some wrong or evil? Will the public put pressure on lawmakers? Or will the action of the disobedient be misunderstood and cause resentment? Will there be a backlash against the protesters?

These considerations are surely relevant to any consequentialist justification of acts of ecosabotage. Further, there seems to be no reason why a successful justification could not be given for at least some such acts. . . .

Have Advocates of Ecosabotage Successfully Justified Ecosabotage?

One might reasonably conclude from the above that although ecosabotage can be morally justified on consequentialist grounds in some contexts and although there are no general arguments standing in the way of such justification, the case for particular acts of ecosabotage has yet to be made. Although it is beyond the scope of this paper to provide such a justification, I consider critically how in fact advocates of ecosabotage such as Foreman have attempted to justify ecosabotage. In some cases where there is a gap in the justification, I fill in what I believe is a reasonable extrapolation or reconstruction of what a rational ecosaboteur might say. I show that the rationales given by advocates of ecosabotage follow in outline the sort of argument that, according to Cohen, a consequentialist justification of civil disobedience should take.

In a consequentialist justification, the moral goals of the civil disobedient are usually shared by the community. When they are not, they are likely to fail to persuade the community and not succeed politically. I have argued above that the general goals of ecosabotage are probably shared by most members of the community and that even the particular ones may be. However, Foreman explicitly interprets these goals in a nonanthropocentric way. Advocating the environmental philosophy of deep ecology, he argues:

> Deep ecology says that *every* living thing in the ecosystem has intrinsic worth and a nature-given right to be there. The grizzly bear, for example,

has a right to exist for its *own* sake—not just for material or entertainment value to human beings. Wilderness has a right to exist for its *own* sake, and for the sake of the diversity of life-forms it shelters; we shouldn't have to justify the existence of the wilderness area by saying, "Well, it protects the watershed, and it's a nice place to backpack and hunt, and it's pretty. . . . Furthermore, deep ecology goes beyond the individual and says that it's the *species* that's important. And more important yet is the *community of species* that makes up a given biosystem. And ultimately, our concern should be with the community of *communities*—the ecosystem.[13]

Whether Foreman's biocentrism and holism is philosophically justified, we cannot decide here.[14] But what does seem likely is that these points of view are not widely shared by the vast majority of the moral community and would be considered by the majority of the community to be rather eccentric. Given his biocentric and holistic interpretation of the goals of Earth First!, therefore, the means as well as the goals of the organization become controversial. As Cohen points out: "Even if the community is wrong [about the goals], and the eccentrics right, deliberate disobedient pursuit of their special objectives, as long as they are in the moral minority, is not likely to advance the protesters' goals and not likely to be defensible on utilitarian grounds."[15] However, the ecosaboteur need not pursue what the moral community will perceive as eccentric goals. There are good anthropocentric reasons why natural diversity should be preserved,[16] why tropical forest should be safeguarded,[17] why whales should be saved,[18] and so on.

According to Cohen, a civil disobedient must consider the background of the case at hand and evaluate both the importance of the goals and whether legal means have been given a fair trial. Foreman's statement certainly suggests that he advocates deliberating on the background of acts of ecosabotage very carefully and has considered the importance of the goals of ecosabotage and legal alternatives to it. Thus, he maintains:

Species are going under everyday. Old-growth forests are disappearing. Overgrazing continues to ruin our western public lands. Off-road vehicles are cutting up the countryside everywhere. Poisons are continually and increasingly being injected into the environment. Rain forests are being clear-cut. In short, the environment is *losing* . . . everywhere. And to try to fight such an essential battle with less than every weapon we have available to us is foolish and, in the long run, suicidal.[19]

One need not just take Foreman's word for this bleak picture of environmental devastation. Many environmentalists have painted a similar picture, albeit in more scholarly and less colorful tones.[20]

But are there not legal means of stopping the destruction? Foreman at one time certainly thought there were. At the beginning of his environmental career he was a Washington lobbyist for the conventional environmental group, the Wilderness Society. However, personal experience quickly led to his disillusionment with the effectiveness of such groups in bringing about change and stopping the devastation.[21] Now as a member of Earth First! he has had personal experience of illegal actions being effective. He cites one example in which the legal action of the Sierra Club, a conventional environmental organization, failed to stop the destruction of a wilderness while Earth First!'s blockage of road construction by civil disobedience provided enough public awareness to be successful.[22]

One wonders, of course, if Foreman's experience is typical and if he has reported the facts accurately. Are there cases not mentioned by Foreman where legal means have succeeded and where illegal ones have not? To give a more adequate justification, one would have to consider in a systematic way a wider range of cases than Foreman considers in which legal and illegal methods have been tried in order to see their relative effectiveness. His anecdotal evidence at most makes a prima facie case that illegal means are sometimes more effective than legal means for affording environmental protection.[23]

Cohen also suggests that in any utilitarian justification of civil disobedience it is important to consider the possible negative consequences of one's action. Foreman gives evidence of having done this. When asked whether monkey wrenching—his term for ecosabotage—is counterproductive to the environmental cause and serves only to make environmentalists look bad, Foreman had this to say:

> On the surface, this argument seems worth considering. But the fact is, there's *already* an awful lot of monkey wrenching going on, and such a backlash hasn't come about. The Forest Service tries to keep it quiet, industry tries to keep it quiet, and I think that there has even been an effort in the media to downplay the extent and effectiveness of monkey wrenching in America today. . . . It's easy to be cowed into compromising and being overly moderate by the charge that you are going to cause a negative reaction, going to tarnish the whole environmental movement. But in my opinion, the *argument itself* is a more fearsome anti-environmental weapon than any actual backlash could ever hope to be, because it keeps many of us from using all the tools we have available to slow down the destruction.[24]

Again independent evidence for a negative reaction should be sought. For example, do Greenspeace's door-to-door canvassers find it harder than a few years ago to obtain contributions because of the negative publicity occasioned by Earth First!? Do polls show that the public is becoming less sympathetic to environmental causes than it was before news of ecosabotage? Until evidence such as this is obtained we will not know if ecosabotage is having a negative impact. But Foreman is certainly justified in remaining skeptical about the purported negative impact until such evidence is produced.

Another possible negative consequence of ecosabotage is the unintentional injury to human beings. This problem is considered to be especially worrisome in the case of tree spiking. The main danger is that a saw blade can break and cause injury to the saw operator or to other people involved in the milling process. Ecosaboteurs respond to this problem in at least three different ways. Some tree spikers mark the trees they have spiked. For example, it is reported that after Mike Roselle, a member of Earth First!, spiked trees in Cathedral Forest, he painted a large *S* on them.[25] Thus, the recommended procedure is the notification of all parties who would be involved in cutting and milling trees. Consequently, only those who defied the warning were in jeopardy.[26] Other spikers, however, try to keep their spikes from being detected,[27] arguing that automation places most mill operators in control booths out of danger.[28] Although this might be true, it would not protect the sawyers cutting down the tree. The chain on the sawyer's chain saw can break upon hitting a spike, whip back into the sawyer and cause serious injuries. Moreover, some ecosaboteurs may argue that although they should take care not to injure people, "nothing is more dangerous to the long-term health of the people of this planet than the largescale destruction of the environment, and we have to stop that."[29] Consequently, any potential danger to the mill workers must be weighed against the greater danger to the world's population through environmental damage. Whether these answers are completely adequate is a difficult issue that we cannot pursue here.[30]

Cohen also maintains that a potential civil disobedient must estimate the positive results from the contemplated action. Does ecosabotage have positive results? For example, does it accomplish the goal of slowing or stopping the destruction of the environment? Foreman says:

> I'm convinced that monkey wrenching can be one of the most effective ways of protecting our few remaining wild places. If a sufficient number of sincere individuals and small groups around the country were to launch a serious campaign of strategic monkey wrenching—a totally defensive effort to halt the continued destruction of wilderness—it would in fact cause the retreat of industrial civilization from millions of acres of wildlands.
>
> For example, if a logging company knows that the trees are going to be consistently spiked with large nails—which plays hell with expensive saw blades at the mills—or that roads will be repeatedly blocked by having rocks dumped onto them, it quickly becomes impractical to try to maintain a profitable operation . . . so industrialization will retreat, leaving more land for the grizzly bear, for elk, for old-growth forests. . . .
>
> For these reasons, along with the fact that conventional efforts to save the environment *are not working*, I believe that monkey wrenching is probably the single most effective thing that can be done to save natural diversity.[31]

It is important to notice that in this quotation Foreman argues only that ecosabotage *could* work, not that it *has* worked or *will* work. However, Foreman does cite actual cases in which conventional civil disobedience methods, for example, blockage of a road by human beings, have been successful in getting public sympathy and attention. An ecosaboteur might argue by analogy: because conventional methods of civil disobedience have worked, it is likely that methods of ecosabotage will work as well. However, this analogy is far from perfect. Human beings blocking a road may make good press and create favorable publicity whereas tree spiking and rock dumping may not. Foreman's argument, in any case, is not based on the favorable publicity that monkey wrenching will cause. He maintains that ecosabotage will make it economically unfeasible for industry to continue to destroy the wilderness. In principle, this may be true. But does the use of ecosabotage in fact work in this way? Until evidence is cited of industrialization *actually* retreating, "leaving more land for the grizzly bear, for elk, for old-growth forest" as a result of tree spiking and other acts of ecosabotage, one should leave as an open question whether ecosabotage is justified in terms of Cohen's utilitarian model of justification.

It is also important to note that in the passage just cited Foreman argues that ecosabotage can be effective if "a sufficient number" of individuals and groups engage in it. If it is not successful now, Foreman might argue, it is because not enough people are trained and devoted ecosaboteurs. This may or may not be true, but a similar argument could be invoked by environmentalists who are opposed to ecosabotage. After all, it might be argued, if enough people marched on Washington, wrote letters to their government representatives, and performed public acts of conscientious wrongdoing, that is, engaged in conventional civil disobedience, it would "cause the retreat of industrial civilization from millions of acres of wildlands." The number of people needed is unclear. But it is plausible to suppose that public outrage would have to be extensive—as, for example, it ultimately was in relation to the Vietnam War—to have the sort of impact that Foreman desires.

Foreman argues simultaneously that ecosabotage is already widespread, but that its presence is being covered up by government, industry, and the media, that the environment is losing, and that a sufficient number of ecosaboteurs would save the environment. Although there is no inconsistency in these remarks, they do raise the question of just how much more ecosabotage would have to occur to prevent the environment from losing and to save the environment from destruction. In response, it might be argued that the number of ecosaboteurs that would be necessary for making a significant impact on environmental protection is several orders of magnitude less than the number of legal protesters, letter writers, public acts of civil disobedience, and so on that would produce the same impact. For this reason at least, it may be said, ecosabotage is to be recommended over conventional strategies. On the other hand, the training and dedication that is involved in leading the life of an ecosaboteur would surely limit the number of potential candidates. Indeed, it is not clear that there are enough potential ecosaboteurs to make the difference that Foreman wants. Furthermore, in view of probable arrests it would seem that their ranks would have to be constantly replenished. There are then indirect considerations suggesting that ecosabotage is not likely in practice to have the impact that Foreman anticipates in theory.

Although Foreman does not cite evidence that ecosabotage actually works, a very recent article by C. M. does.[32] C. M. maintains that monkey wrenching is probably costing the government and industry about 20 to 25 million dollars per year in terms of damaged equipment, lost time, and legislative and law enforcement expenses. "This represents money industry is not able to use to deforest public lands, sink oil wells in the backcountry, invest in more destructive equipment, influence politicians with campaign contributions. . . ."[33] Even if corporations pass on these costs to their customers, according to C.M., monkey wrenching will cause the price of wood products to increase and thus indirectly decrease their consumption.

C.M. supplements this theoretical argument by citing actual cases in which ecosabotage has worked. For example, C.M. claims that there have been two cases in which the Forest Service withdrew timber sales after learning that trees were spiked. Moreover, C.M. argues that the firebombing of a $250,000 wood chipper in Hawaii, which "was grinding rainforest into fuel for sugar mills (without a permit and in violation of a court order)," left the company bankrupt. Finally, he or she argues that the controversial nature of ecosabotage has publicity value by taking "seemingly obscure environmental issues out the dark of scientific calculations into the limelight of individual passion and commitment."[34]

C.M.'s arguments for ecosabotage, nevertheless, are not enough to justify its use on utilitarian grounds. For this, C.M. would also have to show that typical acts of civil disobedience, that is, public acts of conscientious wrongdoing, were ineffective, for surely these are more desirable otherwise on utilitarian grounds than acts of ecosabotage if only because they are less likely to be interpreted as showing contempt for the law. In general, nonpublic acts of conscientious wrongdoing can be justified only when public nonviolent acts of conscientious wrongdoing cannot be utilized. Presumably there was no public way to help runaway slaves.[35] In the case of ecosabotage, however, public illegal means seem to be available. Road construction can be halted, for example, by lying down in front of the equipment, as well as by monkey wrenching the engines that run the equipment; trees can be protected by climbing them as well as by spiking. These nonviolent acts of conscientious wrongdoing also cost the government and industry a large amount of money, and have publicity value. In order to make their case, ecosaboteurs must show that public nonviolent acts of conscientious wrongdoing cannot work *and* that acts of ecosabotage can. To my knowledge they have not done so.[36]

Notes

1. Jim Robbins, "For Environmentalist, Illegal Acts Are Acts of Love," *Boston Globe*, 2 June 1989, p. 3.

2. See for example, John J. Berger, "Tree Shakers," *Omni* 9 (1987): 20–22; Jamie Malanowski, "Monkey-Wrenching Around," *The Nation*, 2 May 1987, pp. 568–70; Joe Kane, "Mother Nature's Army," *Esquire*, February 1987, pp. 98–106.

3. J. A. Savage, "Radical Environmentalists: Sabotage in the Name of Ecology," *Business and Society Review* 56–59 (Summer 1986): 35–37; David Peterson, "The Plowboy Interview: Dave Foreman: No Compromise in Defense of Mother Earth," *Mother Earth News*, January–February 1985, pp. 16–22.

4. Two notable exceptions are Eugene C. Hargrove, "Ecological Sabotage: Pranks or Terrorism?" *Environmental Ethics* 4 (1982): 291–92, and Roderick Nash, *The Rights of Nature: A History of Environmental Ethics* (Madison: University of Wisconsin Press, 1989), pp. 189–98.

5. In order to apply this argument to ecosabotage in the United States, certain assumptions must be made that might well be challenged. For example, it must be assumed that the laws that facilitate environmental destruction are democratically established and that it is prima facie wrong to disobey a democratically established law.

6. Carl Cohen, *Civil Disobedience: Conscience, Tactics and the Law* (New York: Columbia University Press, 1971), chapter 5.

7. According to Cohen, civil disobedients have often attempted to justify their conduct by appeals to a law higher than human law. This higher law justification has taken two major forms: an appeal to commands of God that are revealed to human beings in the Bible or other allegedly divinely inspired works or an appeal to nontheological higher laws that are discerned by the light of natural reason. There are three serious problems with both types of justifications. First, there seems to be no objective way to decide what these higher laws are. Second, principles of higher law are usually stated vaguely and abstractly. Consequently, it seems impossible to reach any objective decision on how they apply to concrete cases. Third, such justification would at best justify *direct* civil disobedience, that is, the breaking of a law that is itself morally objectionable in terms of higher law principles. But many acts of civil disobedience are indirect—that is, the civil disobedient disobeys some law that he or she has no objection to because the disobedience is a means to eliminate some serious injustice in a related area. It could be argued that these same problems are found in any attempt to justify ecosabotage by appeal to higher law principles. However, Cohen is mistaken in limiting nonconsequentialist justifications of civil disobedience to the higher law tradition. A complete account of nonconsequentialist justifications of civil

disobedience would also have to take into account deontological theories of justification ranging from Kant to Rawls.

8. For a review of some recent literature see Hugo Bedau, "The Limits of Utilitarianism and Beyond," *Ethics* 95 (1985): 333–41. For a standard criticism of utilitarianism see William Frankena, *Ethics*, 2d ed. (Englewood Cliffs: Prentice-Hall, 1973), chap. 3. See also G. E. Moore, *Principia Ethica* (Cambridge: Cambridge University Press, 1903), chap. 5, secs. 91–93.

9. Cohen, *Civil Disobedience*, p. 120. If Cohen means that the goal must be shared by the vast majority to be *morally* justified, he is mistaken. I do not interpret him in this way, however. It is correct, nevertheless, that unless the goal is shared by the majority, the civil disobedient will not be practically successful—that is, the disobedient will have failed to justify his or her action to the community, and thus the disobedient will not be politically effective.

10. *Ibid.*, p. 123.

11. *Ibid.*, p. 125.

12. *Ibid.*, pp. 125–26.

13. Peterson, "The Plowboy Interview," p. 18.

14. For a recent critique of these points of view see Bryan G. Norton, *Why Preserve Natural Variety?* (Princeton: Princeton University Press, 1989), chaps. 8 and 9.

15. Cohen, *Civil Disobedience*, p. 123.

16. See Norton, *Why Preserve Natural Variety?* chap. 11.

17. Norman Myers, *The Primary Source: Tropical Forests and Our Future* (New York: W. W. Norton & Company, 1985), chaps. 10–15.

18. Peter M. Dora, "Cataceans: A Litany of Cain," *People, Penguins, and Plastic Trees*, ed. Donald VanDeVeer and Christine Pierce (Belmont, Calif.: Wadsworth Publishing Co. , 1986), pp. 127–34.

19. Peterson, "The Plowboy Interview," p. 22; see also Foreman, "Strategic Monkeywrenching," *Ecodefense*, pp. 10–14.

20. See, for example, Lester R. Brown, Christopher Flavin, and Sandra Postel, "A World at Risk," *The State of the World: 1989*, ed. L. Brown et al. (New York: W. W. Norton & Company, 1989), pp. 3–20; Myers, *The Primary Source*, chaps. 5–9; Norman Myers, "The Sinking Ark," *People, Penguins, and Plastic Trees*, pp. 111–119.

21. Kane, "Mother Nature's Army," p. 100.

22. Peterson, "The Plowboy Interview," p. 19. It should be noted that this was not an act of ecosabotage.

23. However, the independent evidence provided by the effectiveness of the illegal actions of Greenpeace in protecting whales and seals confirms Foreman's contention. See Jan Kippers Black, "Greenpeace: The Ecological Warriors," *USA Today*, (Nov. 1986), pp. 26–29.

24. Peterson, "The Plowboy Interview," pp. 21–22.

25. Kane, "Mother Nature's Army," p. 98.

26. Savage, "Radical Environmentalists," p. 35.

27. See Foreman and Haywood, *Ecodefense*, pp. 24–51.

28. Malanowski, "Monkey-Wrenching Around," p. 569. But whether all employees of the mills, for example, the head rig offbearers who guide the logs, are safe is another question.

29. *Ibid.*

30. It should be noted that according to defenders of ecosabotage there has never been a documented case of anyone being seriously injured from its practice. See C. M., "An Appraisal of Monkeywrenching," *Earth First!* 2 February 1990.
31. Peterson, "The Plowboy Interview," p. 21.
32. See C.M., "An Appraisal of Monkeywrenching." According to *Earth First!* C.M. "is a widely published writer and scholar whose career dictates anonymity."
33. *Ibid.*
34. *Ibid.*
35. See Lester Rhodes, "Carrying on a Venerable Tradition," *Earth First!,* 2 February 1990. Rhodes compares ecosaboteurs to those who ran the underground railroad.
36. To be sure, Foreman has argued that monkey wrenching should not be used when there is a nonviolent civil disobedience action such as blockages taking place. But what must be shown is that blockages and the like cannot bring about the same results as ecosabotage. See Foreman, "Strategic Monkeywrenching." *Ecodefense,* p. 15.

Selected Bibliography

Note: This brief bibliography is designed to help the reader find additional reading materials on radical environmentalism and ecophilosophy, and is a supplement to the sources already used in the text. It is not designed to be comprehensive but to provide a sampling of books, journals, and articles.

Part I: Radical Ecophilosophy

Deep Ecology

Devall, Bill. "The Deep Ecology Movement." *Natural Resources Journal* 20 (April 1980), 299–322.

Devall, Bill. "Deep Ecology and Radical Environmentalism." *Society and Natural Resources* 4 (1991), 247–58.

Devall, Bill. *Simple in Means, Rich in Ends, Practicing Deep Ecology* (Salt Lake City: Peregrine Smith Books, 1988).

Devall, Bill, and George Sessions. *Deep Ecology, Living as if Nature Mattered* (Salt Lake City: Peregrine Smith Books, 1985).

Drengson, Alan R. *Beyond Environmental Crisis: From Technocratic to Planetary Person* (New York: Peter Lang, 1989).

Drengson, Alan R. "Shifting Paradigms: From the Technocratic to the Person-Planetary." *Environmental Ethics* 2 (Fall 1980), 221–40.

Evernden, Neil. *The Natural Alien* (Toronto: University of Toronto Press, 1985).

Fox, Warwick. "The Deep Ecology-Ecofeminism Debate and Its Parallels." *Environmental Ethics* 11 (1989), 5–25.

Fox, Warwick. *Approaching Deep Ecology: A Response to Richard Sylvan's Critique of Deep Ecology*. Environmental Studies Occasional Paper No. 20 (Hobart, Australia: University of Tasmania, 1986).

Fox, Warwick. *Toward a Transpersonal Ecology: Developing New Foundations for Environmentalism* (Boston: Shambhala, 1990).

Guha, Ramachandra. "Radical American Environmentalism and Wilderness Preservation: A Third World Critique." *Environmental Ethics* 11 (Spring 1989), 71–83.

Johns, David M. "The Relevance of Deep Ecology to the Third World: Some Preliminary Comments." *Environmental Ethics* 12 (Fall 1990), 233–52.

LaChapelle, Dolores. *Earth Wisdom* (Silverton, Co.: Way of the Mountain Center, 1978).

LaChapelle, Dolores. "Systemic Thinking and Deep Ecology." In *Ecological Consciousness: Essays from the Earthday X Colloquium*, edited by Robert C. Shultz and J. Donald Hughes (Washington, D.C.: University Press of America, 1981).

Naess, Arne. *Ecology, Community and Lifestyle* (Cambridge: Cambridge University Press, 1989).

Naess, Arne. "The Deep Ecological Movement: Some Philosophical Aspects." *Philosophical Inquiry* 8 (1986), 10–31.

Seed, John, Joanna Macy, Pat Fleming, and Arne Naess. *Thinking Like a Mountain, Towards a Council of All Beings* (Philadelphia: New Society Publishers, 1988).

Sessions, George. "Shallow and Deep Ecology: A Review of the Philosophical Literature." In *Ecological Consciousness: Essays from the Earthday X Coloquium*, edited by Robert C. Schultz and J. Donald Hughes (Washington, D.C.: University Press of America, 1981).

Sessions, George. "Spinoza and Jeffers on Man in Nature." *Inquiry* 20 (1977), 481–528.

Snyder, Gary. *The Old Ways* (San Francisco: City Lights Books, 1977).

Snyder, Gary. *Turtle Island* (New York: New Directions Books, 1974).

Sylvan, Richard. "A Critique of Deep Ecology." *Radical Philosophy* 40 (1984), 2–12; and "A Critique of Deep Ecology, Part II." *Radical Philosophy* 41 (1985), 10–22.

Tobias, Michael, ed. *Deep Ecology* (San Diego: Avant Books, 1985).

The Trumpeter. LightStar: P.O. Box 5853. Victoria, B.C. Canada V8R-6S8.

Zimmerman, Michael E. "Feminism, Deep Ecology, and Environmental Ethics." *Environmental Ethics* 9 (1987), 21–44.

Zimmerman, Michael E. "Toward a Heideggerean 'Ethos' for Radical Environmentalism." *Environmental Ethics* 5 (1983), 99–131.

Ecofeminism

Biehl, Janet. *Rethinking Ecofeminist Politics* (Boston: South End Press, 1991).

Caldecott, Leonie, and Stephanie Leland, eds. *Reclaim the Earth: Women Speak Out for Life on Earth* (London: The Women's Press, 1983).

Cheney, Jim. "The Neo-Stoicism of Radical Environmentalism." *Environmental Ethics* 11 (Winter 1989), 293–325.

Cheney, Jim. "Eco-Feminism and Deep Ecology." *Environmental Ethics* (1987), 115–45.

Daly, Mary. *Gyn/Ecology: The Metaphysics of Radical Feminism* (Boston: Beacon Press, 1978).

Diamond, Irene, and Gloria Feman Orenstein, eds. *Reweaving the World, The Emergence of Ecofeminism* (San Francisco: Sierra Club Books, 1990).

Gray, Elizabeth Dodson. *Green Paradise Lost* (Wellesley, Mass.: Roundtable Press, 1979).

Griffin, Susan. *Women and Nature: The Roaring Inside Her* (New York: Harper and Row Publishers, Inc., 1978).

Heresies #13: Feminism and Ecology 4 (1981).

Hypatia. Special Issue on Ecological Feminism 6 (Spring 1991).

Kolodny, Annette. *The Lay of the Land: Metaphor as Experience and History in American Life and Letters* (Chapel Hill: University of North Carolina Press, 1975).

Merchant, Carolyn. *The Death of Nature: Women, Ecology, and the Scientific Revolution* (New York: Harper and Row Publishers, Inc., 1983).

Ortner, Sherry B. "Is Female to Male as Nature is to Culture?" In *Women, Culture and Society.* Edited by Michelle Rosaldo and Louise Lamphere (Stanford, Ca.: Stanford University Press, 1974).

Reuther, Rosemary Radford. *New Woman, New Earth: Sexist Ideologies and Human Liberation* (New York: The Seabury Press, 1975).

Salleh, Ariel Kay. "Deeper than Deep Ecology: The Eco-Feminist Connection." *Environmental Ethics* 6 (Winter 1984), 339–45.

Spretnak, Charlene. "Ecofeminism: Our Roots and Flowering." In Diamond and Orenstein, eds. *Reweaving the World,* 3–14.

Studies in the Humanities 15, no. 2 (1988). Special Issue on Feminism, Ecology, and the Future of the Humanities. Edited by Patrick Murphy.

Warren, Karen J. "Feminism and Ecology: Making Connections." *Environmental Ethics* 9 (1987), 3–20.

Warren, Karen J., and Jim Cheney. "Ecological Feminism and Ecosystem Ecology." *Hypatia* 6 (Spring 1991), 179–97.

Social Ecology and Bioregionalism

Andruss, Van, Christopher Plant, Judith Plant, and Stephanie Mills, eds. *Home! A Bioregional Reader* (Philadelphia: New Society Publishers, 1990).

Berg, Peter. "More than Just Saving What is Left." *Raise the Stakes* 8 (Fall 1983).

Berg, Peter. "What Is Bioregionalism?" *The Trumpeter* 8 (Winter 1991), 6–8.

Berg, Peter, and Raymond F. Dasmann. "Reinhabiting California." In *Rehabiting a Separate Country, A Bioregional Anthology of Northern California* (San Francisco: Planet Drum Foundation, 1978).

Bookchin, Murray. *The Ecology of Freedom: The Emergence and Dissolution of Hierarchy* (Palo Alto: Cheshire Books, 1982).

Bookchin, Murray. *The Philosophy of Social Ecology: Essays on Dialectical Naturalism* (Toronto: Black Rose Books, 1990).

Bookchin, Murray. *Post-Scarcity Anarchism* (San Francisco: Ramparts Press, 1971).

Bookchin, Murray. *Remaking Society: Pathways to a Green Future* (Boston: South End Press, 1990).

Bookchin, Murray. "Social Ecology versus 'Deep Ecology': A Challenge for the Ecology Movement." *Green Perspectives*, Newsletter of the Green Program Project, Burlington, Vt. Nos. 4 & 5 (Summer 1987), 1–23.

Bookchin, Murray. *Toward an Ecological Society* (Montreal: Black Rose Books, 1980).

Bookchin, Murray. "Toward a Philosophy of Nature—The Bases for an Ecological Ethic." In *Deep Ecology*, edited by Michael Tobias (San Diego: Avant Books, 1985).

Bradford, George. *How Deep Is Deep Ecology? A Challenge to Radical Environmentalism* (Ojai, Ca.: Times Change Press, 1989).

Clark, John, ed. *Renewing the Earth: The Promise of Social Ecology* (London: Green Print, 1990).

Clark, John. *The Anarchist Moment: Reflections on Culture, Nature, and Power* (Toronto: Black Rose Books, 1984).

Eckersley, Robyn. "Divining Evolution: The Ecological Ethics of Murray Bookchin." *Environmental Ethics* 11 (Summer 1989), 99–116.

Harbinger: The Journal of Social Ecology. P.O. Box 89. Plainfield, Vt. 05667.

Herber, Lewis (Murray Bookchin). *Our Synthetic Environment* (New York: Alfred A. Knopf, 1962).

House, Freeman. "To Learn the Things We Need to Know: Engaging the Particulars of the Planet's Recovery." *Whole Earth Review* 66 (Spring 1990), 36–46.

The New Catalyst Quarterly.

Raise the Stakes. Planet Drum Foundation. P.O. Box 31251. San Francisco, Ca. 94131.

Sale, Kirkpatrick. *Dwellers in the Land, The Bioregional Vision* (San Francisco: Sierra Club Books, 1985).

Spretnak, Charlene and Fritjof Capra. *Green Politics*, rev. ed. (Sante Fe: Bear and Company, 1986).

Part II: Radical Ecoactivism and Ecotactics

Arnold, Ron. *Ecology Wars, Environmentalism As If People Mattered* (Bellevue, Wa.: The Free Enterprise Press, 1987).

Abbey, Edward. *Abbey's Road* (New York: E. P. Dutton, 1979).

Abbey, Edward. *Hayduke Lives!* (Boston: Little, Brown and Company, 1990).

Abbey, Edward. *The Monkey Wrench Gang* (New York: Avon Books, 1976).

Abbey, Edward. *One Life at a Time, Please* (New York: Henry Holt and Company, 1988).

Bandow, Doug. "Ecoterrorism: The Dangerous Fringe of the Environmental Movement." *Backgrounder* 764, *The Heritage Foundation* (April 12, 1990).

Brown, Michael, and John May. *The Greenpeace Story* (New York: Dorling Kindersley, Inc., 1991).

Chase, Steve, ed. *Defending the Earth, A Dialogue Between Murray Bookchin and Dave Foreman* (Boston: South End Press, 1991).

Davis, John, and Dave Foreman, eds. *The Earth First! Reader, Ten Years of Radical Environmentalism* (Salt Lake City: Peregrine Smith, 1991).

Day, David. *The Whale War* (San Francisco: Sierra Club Books, 1987).

Day, David. *The Environmental Wars* (New York: St. Martin's Press, 1989).

Earth First! The Radical Environmental Journal. P.O. Box 5176, Missoula, Montana 59806.

Editors of *Ramparts*. *Eco-Catastrophe* (San Franciso: Canfield Press, 1970).

Foreman, Dave. *Confessions of an Eco-Warrior* (New York: Harmony Books, 1991).

Foreman, Dave, and Howie Wolke. *The Big Outside: A Descriptive Inventory of the Big Wilderness Areas of the U.S.* (Tucson: Ned Ludd Books, 1989).

Franklin, Karen E., and Janet Sowell. "The Timber Terrorists." *American Forests* 93 (March/April 1987), 41–42.

Guha, Ramachandra. *The Unquiet Woods: Ecological Change and Peasant Resistance in the Himalaya* (Berkeley: University of California Press, 1990).

Hepworth, James, and Gregory McNamee, eds. *Resist Much, Obey Little, Some Notes on Edward Abbey* (Salt Lake City: Dream Garden Press, 1985).

Hunter, Robert. *Warriors of the Rainbow, A Chronicle of the Greenpeace Movement* (New York: Holt, Rinehart and Winston, 1979).

Hunter, Robert, and Watson, Paul. *Cry Wolf!* (Vancouver, Canada: Shepherds of the Earth, 1985).

Kerrick, Michael. *Ecotage from Our Perspective, An Explanation of the Willamette National Forest's Policy on Environmental Sabotage Known as 'Ecotage'*. A Report for Civic Leaders (Eugene, Or.: Willamette National Forest, September 1985).

Love, Sam, ed. *Earth Tool Kit, A Field Manual for Citizen Activists* (New York: Pocket Books, 1971).

Love, Sam, and David Obst, eds. *Ecotage!* (New York: Pocket Books, 1972).

Manes, Christopher. *Green Rage* (Boston: Little, Brown and Company, 1990).

Manes, Christopher. "Philosophy and the Environmental Task." *Environmental Ethics* 4 (1982), 255–60.

Marston, Ed. "Ecotage Isn't a Solution, It's Part of the Problem." *High Country News* (June 19, 1989), 15.

Matthiessen, Peter. *Wildlife in America*. Rev. ed. (New York: Elisabeth Sifton Books, Viking, 1987).

Mitchell, John G., with Constance L. Stallings. *Ecotactics: The Sierra Club Handbook for Environment Activists* (New York: Pocket Books, 1970).

Mowat, Farley. *Sea of Slaughter* (New York: Atlantic Monthly Press, 1984).

Nash, Roderick. *The Rights of Nature, A History of Environmental Ethics* (Madison: U. of Wisconsin Press, 1989).

Nash, Roderick. "Rounding Out the American Revolution: Ethical Extension and the New Environmentalism." In *Deep Ecology*. Edited by Michael Tobias (San Diego: Avant Books, 1985).

Parfit, Michael. "Earth First!ers Wield a Mean Monkey Wrench." *Smithsonian* 21 (April 1990), 184–204.

Paehlke, Robert. *Environmentalism and the Future of Progressive Politics* (New Haven, Conn.: Yale University Press, 1989).

Palmer, Tim. *Stanislaus: The Struggle for a River* (Berkeley: University of California Press, 1982).

Russell, Dick. "The Monkeywrenchers." In *Crossroads, Environmental Priorities for the Future,* edited by Peter Borrelli (Washington, D.C.: Island Press, 1988).

Sea Shepherd Log. Newsletter of the Sea Shepherd Conservation Society. 1314 2nd St., Santa Monica, Ca. 90401.

Scarce, Rik. *Eco-Warriors, Understanding the Radical Environmental Movement* (Chicago: The Noble Press, Inc., 1990).

Steinhart, Peter. "Respecting the Law: There Must Be Limits to Environmental Protest." *Audubon* 89:6 (November 1987), 10–13.

Tokar, Brian. "Exploring the New Ecologies, Social Ecology, Deep Ecology and the Future of Green Political Thought." *Alternatives* 15, No. 4 (1988), 31–43.

Tokar, Brian. *The Green Alternative, Creating an Ecological Future* (San Pedro: R. & E. Miles, 1987).

Watson, Paul, and Warren Rogers. *Sea Shepherd: My Fight for Whales and Seals* (New York: W. W. Norton, 1982).

Watson, Paul. Session on "Environmental Advocacy and Civil Disobedience." Public Interest Law Conference, University of Oregon Law School, Eugene, Oregon, March 1990.

Wild Earth. P.O. Box 492, Canton, New York 13617.

World Rainforest Report. Rainforest Information Centre. P.O. Box 368, Lismore, 2480, Australia.

Acknowledgments

p. 19, Arne Naess, "The Shallow and the Deep, Long-Range Ecology Movements: A Summary," *Inquiry* 16, Spring 1973, pp. 95–100. Reprinted by permission of the publisher.

p. 24, Arne Naess, "Identification as a Source of Deep Ecological Attitudes," in Michael Tobias, ed., *Deep Ecology*, San Diego: Avant Books, 1985, pp. 256–270. Reprinted by permission of the author and Avant Books.

p. 38, Bill Devall and George Sessions, "Deep Ecology," in *Deep Ecology: Living as if Nature Mattered*, Salt Lake City: Peregrine Smith Books, 1985, pp. 65–73. Reprinted by permission of the publisher.

p. 49, Carolyn Merchant, "Ecofeminism and Feminist Theory," in Irene Diamond and Gloria Feman Orenstein, eds., *Reweaving the World: The Emergence of Ecofeminism*, San Francisco: Sierra Club Books, 1990. Reprinted by permission of Irene Diamond.

p. 55, Elizabeth Dodson Gray, "We Must Re-Myth Genesis," in Elizabeth Dodson Gray, *Green Paradise Lost*, Wellesley, Mass.: Roundtable Press, 1979, p. 144–158, 165. Reprinted by permission of Roundtable Press.

pp. 58–59, 68–69, "Sunday Psalm" and "In Praise of Diversity," from *The Loveletters of Phyllis McGinley* by Phyllis McGinley. Copyright 1951, 1952, 1953, 1954 by Phyllis McGinley. Copyright renewed © 1979, 1980, 1981, 1982 by Phyllis Hayden Blake. Used by permission of Viking Penguin, a division of Penguin Books USA, Inc.

pp. 65–67, reprinted from *Plant Dreaming Deep* by May Sarton, by permission of W. W. Norton & Company, Inc. Copyright © 1968 by May Sarton.

p. 70, reprinted by permission of the publisher from Rothschild, Joan, ed., *Machina Ex Dea: Feminist Perspectives on Technology.* (New York: Pergamon Press, © 1983 by Joan Rothschild. All rights reserved.), King chapter, pp. 118–128.

p. 81, excerpted from Karen J. Warren, "The Power and the Promise of Ecological Feminism," *Environmental Ethics* 12, Summer 1990, pp. 125–126, 138–145. Reprinted by permission of the author and the publisher.

p. 93, reprinted from *The Modern Crisis* by Murray Bookchin, Philadelphia: New Society Publishing, 1986, pp. 49–76. Reprinted by permission of the publisher.

p. 108, Jim Dodge, "Living by Life: Some Bioregional Theory and Practice," *The CoEvolution Quarterly,* Winter 1981, No. 32, pp. 6–12. Reprinted by permission of The Whole Earth Review.

p. 117, Kirkpatrick Sale, "Dwellers in the Land," in *Dwellers in the Land: the Bio-Regional Vision,* San Francisco: Sierra Club Books, 1985, pp. 41–51. Reprinted by permission of the author.

p. 124, Judith Plant, from *The New Catalyst* (January/February 1986), p. 12. Reprinted by permission of the author.

p. 134, "Greenpeace Declaration of Interdependence," from *Greenpeace Chronicles, Second Edition,* Vol. 2, No. 2, Spring/Summer 1976, p. 2. Reprinted by permission of Greenpeace.

p. 136, Bob Hunter, "Taking on the Goliaths of Doom," from *Greenpeace Chronicles, First Edition,* Vol. 1, No. 1, Autumn 1975, pp. 4–5. Reprinted by permission of Greenpeace.

p. 142, Paul Watson, "Shepherds of the Labrador Front: Taking on the Goliaths of Doom," from *Greenpeace Chronicles, Second Edition,* Vol. 2, No. 2, Spring/Summer 1976, pp. 6–7. Reprinted by permission of Greenpeace.

p. 150, "Shadows from the Big Woods," from *The Journey Home* by Edward Abbey. Copyright © 1977 by Edward Abbey. Used by permission of the publisher, Dutton, an imprint of New American Library, a division of Penguin Books USA, Inc.

p. 152, reprinted from *The Monkey Wrench Gang* by Edward Abbey, New York: Avon Books, 1976, pp. 71–89. Reprinted by permission of Don Congden Associates, Inc.

p. 169, reprinted from *Sea Shepherd: My Fight for Whales and Seals,* by Paul Watson, as told to Warren Rogers, edited by Joseph Newman, by permission of W. W. Norton & Company, Inc. Copyright © 1982 by Paul Watson, Warren Rogers, and Joseph Newman.

p. 172, from *Earth First!* VII (December 21, 1986), pp. 1, 6. Reprinted by permission of the publisher.

p. 177, from *Earth First!* XI (November 1, 1990), pp. 1, 7. Reprinted by permission of the publisher.

p. 187, from *The Progressive* 45 (October 1981), pp. 40–42. Reprinted by permission from The Progressive, 409 E. Main St., Madison, WI 53703.

p. 192, from Dave Foreman and Bill Haywood, *Ecodefense: A Field Guide to Monkeywrenching,* Second Edition, Tucson: Ned Ludd Books, 1985. Reprinted by permission of Ned Ludd Books.

p. 195, from *Earth First!* IV (June 20, 1984), pp. 1, 5. Reprinted by permission of the publisher.

p. 198, from *Earth First!* IV (June 20, 1984), p. 4. Reprinted by permission of the publisher.

p. 200, from *Earth First!* IV (June 20, 1984), p. 4. Reprinted by permission of the publisher.

p. 201, from *Earth First!* X (August 1, 1990), p. 7. Reprinted by permission of the publisher.

p. 202, from *Earth First!* X (August 1, 1990), p. 1. Reprinted by permission of the publisher.

p. 203, from *Earth First!* XI (November 1, 1990), pp. 9, 10. Reprinted by permission of the publisher.

p. 207, from *Earth First!* XI (November 1, 1990), pp. 8, 9. Reprinted by permission of the publisher.

p. 215, excerpted from Judith Plant, ed., *Healing the Wounds: The Promise of Ecofeminism,* Philadelphia: New Society Publishers, 1989, pp. 68–70. Reprinted by permission of the publisher.

p. 217, from *Reclaim the Earth: Women Speak Out for Life on Earth,* edited by Leonie Caldecott and Stephanie Leland, first published by The Women's Press Ltd., 1983, 34 Great Sutton St., London. Reprinted by permission of Stephanie Leland.

p. 221, from *Reweaving the World: The Emergence of Ecofeminism,* edited by Irene Diamond and Gloria Feman Orenstein, San Francisco: Sierra Club Books, 1990, pp. 215–222. Reprinted by permission of Irene Diamond.

p. 227, from the *Earth Day Wall Street Action Handbook,* New York, 1990. Reprinted by permission of Chaia Heller.

p. 231, from *Raise the Stakes,* The Planet Drum Review, No. 8, (Fall 1983). Reprinted by permission of Planet Drum, P.O. Box 31251, San Francisco, CA 94131.

p. 250, from Eugene Hargrove, "From the Editor, 'Ecological Sabotage: Pranks or Terrorism?'," *Environmental Ethics* 4 (Winter 1982), pp. 291–292. Reprinted by permission of the author and publisher.

p. 252, from Edward Abbey, "Earth First! and the Monkey Wrench Gang," *Environmental Ethics* 5 (Spring 1983), pp. 94–95. Reprinted by permission of Don Congdon Associates, Inc. © 1975 by Edward Abbey.

p. 253, from Dave Foreman, "More on Earth First! and the Monkey Wrench Gang," *Environmental Ethics* 5 (Spring 1983), pp. 95–96. Reprinted by permission of the author and publisher.

p. 254, from Eugene Hargrove, "Editor's Response," from *Environmental Ethics* 5 (Spring 1983), p. 96. Reprinted by permission of the author and publisher.

p. 255, excerpted from Michael Martin, "Ecosabotage and Civil Disobedience," *Environmental Ethics* 12 (Winter 1990), pp. 291–292, 298–300, 303–309. Reprinted by permission of the author and publisher.